Java Fundamentals

A fast-paced and pragmatic introduction to one of the world's most popular programming languages

Gazihan Alankus, Rogério Theodoro de Brito,
Basheer Ahamed Fazal, Vinicius Isola and Miles Obare

Java Fundamentals

Authors: Gazihan Alankus, Rogério Theodoro de Brito, Basheer Ahamed Fazal, Vinicius Isola, and Miles Obare

Reviewer: Vishnu Kulkarni

Managing Editor: Rutuja Yerunkar

Acquisitions Editor: Koushik Sen

Production Editor: Nitesh Thakur

Editorial Board: David Barnes, Ewan Buckingham, Shivangi Chatterji, Simon Cox, Manasa Kumar, Alex Mazonowicz, Douglas Paterson, Dominic Pereira, Shiny Poojary, Saman Siddiqui, Erol Staveley, Ankita Thakur and Mohita Vyas.

First Published: March 2019

Production Reference: 1080319

ISBN: 978-1-78980-173-6

Published by Packt Publishing Ltd.

Livery Place, 35 Livery Street

Birmingham B3 2PB, UK

Table of Contents

Preface

About

This section briefly introduces the author, the coverage of this book, the technical skills you'll need to get started, and the hardware and software requirements required to complete all of the included activities and exercises.

About the Book

Since its inception, Java has stormed the programming world. Its features and functionalities provide developers with the tools needed to write robust cross-platform applications. *Java Fundamentals* introduces you to these tools and functionalities that will enable you to create Java programs. The book begins with an introduction to the language, its philosophy, and evolution over time, up until the latest release. You'll learn how the **javac/java** tools work and what Java packages are, as well as the way in which a Java program is usually organized. Once you are comfortable with this, you'll be introduced to advanced concepts of the language, such as control flow keywords. You'll explore object-oriented programming and the part it plays in making Java what it is. In the concluding lessons, you'll get to grips with classes, typecasting, and interfaces, and gain an understanding of the uses of data structures, arrays, and strings; handling exceptions; and creating generics.

By the end of this book, you will have learned how to write programs, automate tasks, and follow advanced books on algorithms and data structures, or explore more advanced Java books.

About the Authors

Gazihan Alankus is an assistant professor at Izmir University of Economics, where he teaches books related to mobile applications, games, and IoT. He received his PhD from Washington University in St. Louis and worked as an intern at Google. In 2019, he became a Google Developer Expert in the Dart programming language. He enjoys working on a variety of research and development projects.

Rogério Theodoro de Brito has a bachelor's degree in computer science and a master's degree in computational biology, both from the University of São Paulo, Brazil. Academically, he is a free/open source software (FOSS) enthusiast and teaches various subjects in computer science and IT at the Mackenzie Presbyterian University in São Paulo, Brazil. He was the technical reviewer of Packt's *edX E-Learning Course Marketing*.

After completing his master's degree, he started his role as an academic instructor and has been working with many languages, such as C, C++, Java, C, Perl, and Python.

Basheer Ahamed Fazal works as a technical architect at a renowned Software as a Service-based product company in India. He had advanced his career with technology organizations such as Cognizant, Symantec, HID Global, and Ooyala. He has seasoned his programming and algorithmic abilities by solving complex problems around agile product development, including those to do with microservices, Amazon Web Services, Google Cloud-based architectures, application security, and big data- and AI- driven initiatives.

Vinicius Isola has a diverse background with a bachelors' degree in physics from the University of Campinas. He started learning how to program ActionScript, when Macromedia Flash was taking over the internet. While taking a 10-month course on Visual Basic, he used it to build a simulation of life using Cellular Automata combined with Genetic Algorithms for his scientific initiation program at university.

Nowadays, he works as a full-time software engineer at Everbridge and spends his spare time learning new programming languages, such as Go, and building tools to help developers implement powerful continuous integration and continuous deployment of automated pipelines.

Miles Obare leads the data engineering team at Betika, a Nairobi-based sports betting firm. He works on building real-time, scalable backend systems. Formerly, he worked as a data engineer for a fintech start-up, where his role involved developing and deploying data pipelines and machine learning models to production. He holds a degree in electrical and computer engineering and often writes about distributed systems.

Objectives

- Create and run Java programs
- Use data types, data structures, and control flow in your code
- Implement best practices when creating objects
- Work with constructors and inheritance
- Understand advanced data structures to organize and store data
- Employ generics for stronger check-types during compilation
- Learn to handle exceptions in your code

4. Choose the preferred installation options and click **Next**:

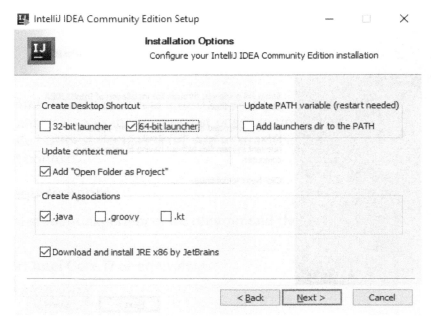

Figure 0.3: Wizard to choose the installation options

5. Choose the start menu folder and click on **Install**:

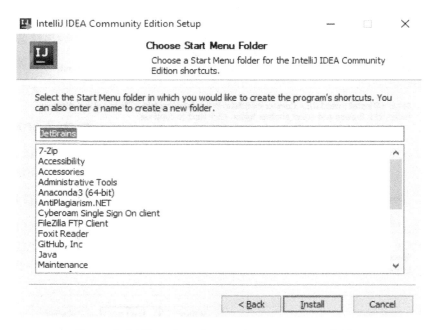

Figure 0.4: Wizard to choose the start menu folder

6. Click on **Finish** once the download is complete:

Figure 0.5: Wizard to finish the installation

Reboot your system once IntelliJ is installed.

Install Java 8 JDK

Java Development Kit (JDK) is a development environment for building applications using the Java programming language:

1. To install the JDK, go to https://www.oracle.com/technetwork/java/javase/downloads/jdk8-downloads-2133151.html.

2. Go to **Java SE Development Kit 8u201** and select the **Accept License Agreement** option.

3. Download the JDK specific to your operating system.

4. Run the installer once the file is downloaded.

Introduction to Java

Learning Objectives

By the end of this lesson, you'll be able to:

- Describe the working of the Java ecosystem
- Write simple Java programs
- Read input from the users
- Utilize classes in the java.util package

Introduction

In this first lesson, we are embarking on our study of Java. If you are coming to Java from a background of working with another programming language, you probably know that Java is a language for programming computers. But Java goes beyond just that. It's more than a very popular and successful language that is virtually present everywhere, it is a collection of technologies. Besides the language, it encompasses a very rich ecosystem and it has a vibrant community working on many facets to make the ecosystem as dynamic as it can be.

The Java Ecosystem

The three most basic parts of the Java ecosystem are the **Java Virtual Machine (JVM)**, the **Java Runtime Environment (JRE)**, and the **Java Development Kit (JDK)**, which are *stock* parts that are supplied by Java implementations.

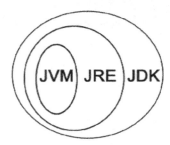

Figure 1.1: A representation of the Java ecosystem

Every Java program runs under the control of a **JVM**. Every time you run a Java program, an instance of JVM is created. It provides security and isolation for the Java program that is running. It prevents the running of the code from clashing with other programs within the system. It works like a non-strict sandbox, making it safe to serve resources, even in hostile environments such as the internet, but allowing interoperability with the computer on which it runs. In simpler terms, JVM acts as a *computer inside a computer*, which is meant specifically for running Java programs.

> **Note**
>
> It is common for servers to have many JVMs in execution simultaneously.

Up in the hierarchy of stock Java technologies is the **JRE**. The JRE is a collection of programs that contains the JVM and also many libraries/class files that are needed for the execution of programs on the JVM (via the **java** command). It includes all the base Java classes (the runtime) as well as the libraries for interaction with the host system (such as font management, communication with the graphical system, the ability to play sounds, and plugins for the execution of Java applets in the browser) and utilities (such as the Nashorn JavaScript interpreter and the keytool cryptographic manipulation tool). As stated before, the JRE includes the JVM.

At the top layer of stock Java technologies is the **JDK**. The JDK contains all the programs that are needed to develop Java programs, and it's most important part is the Java Compiler (**javac**). The JDK also includes many auxiliary tools such as a Java disassembler (**javap**), a utility to create packages of Java applications (**jar**), system to generate documentation from source code (**javadoc**), among many other utilities. The JDK is a superset of the JRE, meaning that if you have the JDK, then you also have the JRE (and the JVM).

But those three parts are not the entirety of Java. The ecosystem of Java includes a very large participation of the community, which is one of the reasons for the popularity of the platform.

> **Note**
>
> Research into the most popular Java libraries that are used by the top Java projects on GitHub (according to research that has been repeated in 2016 and 2017) showed that JUnit, Mockito, Google's Guava, logging libraries (log4j, sl4j), and all of Apache Commons (Commons IO, Commons Lang, Commons Math, and so on), marked their presence, together with libraries to connect to databases, libraries for data analysis and machine learning, distributed computing, and almost anything else that you can imagine. In other words, for almost any use that you want to write programs to, there are high chances of an existing library of tools to help you with your task.

Besides the numerous libraries that extend the functionality of the stock distributions of Java, there is a myriad of tools to automate builds (for example, Apache Ant, Apache Maven, and Gradle), automate tests, distribution and continuous integration/delivery programs (for example, Jenkins and Apache Continuum), and much, much more.

Our First Java Application

As we briefly hinted before, programs in Java are written in source code (which are plain text, human-readable files) that is processed by a compiler (in the case of Java, **javac**) to produce the Java bytecode in class files. The class files containing Java bytecode are, then, fed to a program called java, which contains the Java interpreter/JVM that executes the program that we wrote:

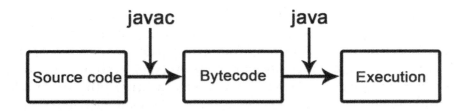

Figure 1.2: The process of compilation in Java

Syntax of a Simple Java Program

Like all programming languages, the source code in Java must follow particular syntaxes. Only then, will the program compile and provide accurate results. Since Java is an object-oriented programming language, everything in Java is enclosed within classes. A simple Java program looks similar to this:

```
public class Test { //line 1
    public static void main(String[] args) { //line 2
        System.out.println("Test"); //line 3
    } //line 4
} //line 5
```

Every java program file should have the same name as that of the class that contains **main ()**. It is the entry point into the Java program.

Therefore the preceding program will compile and run without any errors only when these instructions are stored in a file called **Test.java**.

Another key feature of Java is that it is case-sensitive. This implies that **System.out. Println** will throw an error as it is not capitalized correctly. The correct instruction should be **System.out.println**.

`main()` should always be declared as shown in the sample. This is because, if `main()` is not a `public` method, it will not be accessed by the compiler, and the java program will not run. The reason `main()` is static is because we do not call it using any object, like you would for all other regular methods in Java.

> **Note**
>
> We will discuss these the public and static keywords later in this book, in greater depth.

Comments are used to provide some additional information. The Java compiler ignores these comments.

Single line comments are denoted by **//** and multiline comments are denoted by **/* */**.

Exercise 1: A Simple Hello World Program

1. Right-click the **src** folder and select **New | Class**.

2. Enter **HelloWorld** as the class name, and then click **OK**.

3. Enter the following code within the class:

```
public class HelloWorld{
public static void main(String[] args) {  // line 2
        System.out.println("Hello, world!");  // line 3
    }
}
```

4. Run the program by clicking on **Run | Run 'Main'**.

   The output of the program should be as follows:

```
Hello World!
```

Exercise 2: A Simple Program for Performing Simple Mathematic Operations

1. Right-click the **src** folder and select **New | Class**.

2. Enter **ArithmeticOperations** as the class name, and then click **OK**.

3. Replace the code inside this folder with the following code:

```
public class ArithmeticOperations {
    public static void main(String[] args) {
            System.out.println(4 + 5);
            System.out.println(4 * 5);
            System.out.println(4 / 5);
            System.out.println(9 / 2);
    }
}
```

4. Run the main program.

   The output should be as follows:

```
9
20
0
4
```

In Java, when you divide an integer (such as 4) by another integer (such as 5), the result is always an integer (unless you instruct the program otherwise). In the preceding case, do not be alarmed to see that 4 / 5 gives 0 as a result, since that's the quotient of 4 when divided by 5 (you can get the remainder of the division by using a % instead of the division bar).

To get the result of 0.8, you would have to instruct the division to be a floating-point division instead of an integer division. You can do that with the following line:

```
System.out.println(4.0 / 5);
```

Yes, this does mean, like most programming languages, there is more than one type of number in Java.

Exercise 3: Displaying Non-ASCII Characters

1. Right-click the **src** folder and select **New | Class**.

2. Enter **ArithmeticOperations** as the class name, and then click **OK**.

3. Replace the code in this folder with the following code:

```
public class HelloNonASCIIWorld {
    public static void main(String[] args) {
            System.out.println("Non-ASCII characters: ☺");
            System.out.println("∀x ∈ R: ⌈x⌉ = −⌊−x⌋");
            System.out.println("π ≅ " + 3.1415926535); // + is used to
concatenate
        }
}
```

4. Run the main program.

    The output for the program should be as follows:

```
Non-ASCII characters: ☺
∀x ∈ R: ⌈x⌉ = −⌊−x⌋
π ≅ 3.1415926535
```

Activity 1: Printing the Results of Simple Arithmetic Operations

To write a java program that prints the sum and the product of any two values, perform the following steps:

1. Create a new class.

2. Within **main()**, print a sentence describing the operation on the values you will be performing along with the result.

3. Run the main program. Your output should be similar to the following:

```
The sum of 3 + 4 is 7
The product of 3 + 4 is 12
```

Note

The solution for this activity can be found on page 304.

Getting Input from the User

We previously studied a program that created output. Now, we are, going to study a complementary program: a program that gets input from the user so that the program can work based on what the user gives the program:

```java
import java.io.IOException; // line 1


public class ReadInput { // line 2
    public static void main(String[] args) throws IOException { // line 3
        System.out.println("Enter your first byte");
        int inByte = System.in.read(); // line 4
        System.out.println("The first byte that you typed: " + (char)
inByte); // line 5
        System.out.printf("%s: %c.%n", "The first byte that you typed",
inByte); // line 6
    } // line 7
} // line 8
```

Now, we must dissect the structure of our new program, the one with the public class **ReadInput**. You might notice that it has more lines and that it is apparently more complex, but fret not: every single detail will be revealed (in all its full, glorious depth) when the time is right. But, for now, a simpler explanation will do, since we don't want to lose our focus on the principal, which is taking input from the user.

First, on line 1, we use the **import** keyword, which we have not seen yet. All Java code is organized in a hierarchical fashion, with many packages (we will discuss packages in more detail later, including how to make your own).

Here, hierarchy means "organized like a tree", similar to a family tree. In line 1 of the program, the word **import** simply means that we will use methods or classes that are organized in the **java.io.Exception** package.

On line 2, we, as before, create a new public class called **ReadInput**, without any surprises. As expected, the source code of this program will have to be inside a source file called **ReadInput.java**.

On line 3, we start the definition of our **main** method, but, this time, add a few words after the closing parentheses. The new words are **throws IOException**. Why is this needed?

The short explanation is: "Because, otherwise, the program will not compile." A longer version of the explanation is "Because when we read the input from the user, there may be an error and the Java language forces us to tell the compiler about some errors that our program may encounter during execution."

Also, line 3 is the line that's responsible for the need of the **import** in line 1: the **IOException** is a special class that is under the **java.io.Exception** hierarchy.

Line 5 is where the real action begins: we define a variable called **inByte** (short for "byte that will be input"), which will contain the results of the **System.in.read** method.

The **System.in.read** method, when executed, will take the first byte (and only one) from the standard input (usually, the keyboard, as we already discussed) and give it back as the answer to those who executed it (in this case, we, in line 5). We store this result in the **inByte** variable and continue the execution of the program.

With line 6, we print (to the standard output) a message saying what byte we read, using the standard way of calling the **System.out.println** method.

Notice that, for the sake of printing the byte (and not the internal number that represents the character for the computer), we had to use a construct of the following form:

- An open parenthesis
- The word **char**
- A closing parenthesis

We use this before the variable named **inByte**. This construct is called a type cast and will be explained in much more detail in the lessons that follow.

On line 7, we use a different way to print the same message to the standard output. This is meant to show you how many tasks may be accomplished in more than one way and that there is "no single correct" way. Here, we use the **System.out.println** function.

The remaining lines simply close the braces of the **main** method definition and that of the **ReadInput** class.

Some of the main format strings for **System.out.printf** are listed in the following table:

Format	Meaning
%d	Integer output in base 10 (decimal).
%x	Integer output in base 16 (hexadecimal).
%o	Integer output in base 8 (octal).
%f	Floating-point number.
%n	Appropriate line break for the operating system at runtime.
%s	String.
%c	Character
%%	The percent sign itself

Table 1.1: Format strings and their meaning

There are many other formatting strings and many variables, and you can find the full specification on Oracle's website.

We will see some other common (modified) formatted strings, such as %.2f (which instructs the function to print a floating-point number with exactly two decimal digits after the decimal point, such as 2.57 or -123.45) and %03d (which instructs the function to print an integer with at least three places possibly left filled with 0s, such as 001 or 123 or 27204).

Exercise 4: Reading Values from the User and Performing Operations

To read two numbers from the user and print their product, perform the following steps:

1. Right-click the **src** folder and select **New | Class**.

2. Enter **ProductOfNos** as the class name, and then click **OK**.

3. Import the **java.io.IOException** package:

   ```
   import java.io.IOException;
   ```

4. Enter the following code within the **main()** to read integers:

```
public class ProductOfNos{
public static void main(String[] args){
System.out.println("Enter the first number");
int var1 = Integer.parseInt(System.console().readLine());
System.out.println("Enter the Second number");
int var2 = Integer.parseInt(System.console().readLine());
```

5. Enter the following code to display the product of the two variables:

```
System.out.printf("The product of the two numbers is %d", (var1 * var2));
}
}
```

6. Run the program. You should see an output similar to this:

```
Enter the first number
10
Enter the Second number
20
The product of the two numbers is 200
```

Well done, this is your first Java program.

Packages

Packages are namespaces in Java that can be used to avoid name collisions when you have more than one class with the same name.

For example, we might have more than one class named **Student** being developed by Sam and another class with the same name being developed by David. We need a way to differentiate between the two classes if we need to use them in our code. We use packages to put the two classes in two different namespaces.

For example, we might have the two classes in two packages:

- **sam.Student**
- **david.Student**

The two packages look as follows in File Explorer:

Figure 1.3: Screenshot of the sam.Student and david.Student packages in File Explorer

All the classes that are fundamental to the Java language belong to the **java.lang** package. All the classes that contain utility classes in Java, such as collections, classes for localization, and time utilities, belong to the **java.util** package.

As a programmer, you can create and use your own packages.

Rules to Follow When Using Packages

Here are a few rules to be considered while using packages:

- Packages are written in lowercase

- To avoid name conflicts, the package name should be the reverse domain of the company. For example, if the company domain is **example.com**, then the package name should be **com.example**. So, if we have a **Student** class in that package, the class can be accessed with **com.example.Student.**

- Package names should correspond to folder names. For the preceding example, the folder structure would be as follows:

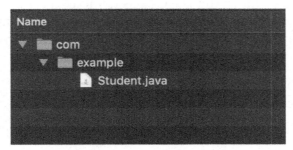

Figure 1.4: Screenshot of the folder structure in File Explorer

To use a class from a package in your code, you need to import the class at the top of your Java file. For example, to use the Student class, you would import it as follows:

```
import com.example.Student;

public class MyClass {


}
```

Scanner is a useful class in the **java.util** package. It is an easy way of inputting types, such as int or strings. As we saw in an earlier exercise, the packages use **nextInt()** to input an integer with the following syntax:

```
sc = new Scanner(System.in);

int x =  sc.nextIn()
```

Activity 2: Reading Values from the User and Performing Operations Using the Scanner Class

To read two numbers from the user and print their sum, perform the following steps:

1. Create a new class and enter **ReadScanner** as the class name

2. Import the **java.util.Scanner** package

3. In the **main()** use **System.out.print** to ask the user to enter two numbers of variables **a** and **b**.

4. Use **System.out.println** to output the sum of the two numbers.

5. Run the main program.

    The output should be similar to this:

    ```
    Enter a number: 12
    Enter 2nd number: 23
    The sum is 35.
    ```

> **Note**
>
> The solution for this activity can be found on page 304.

Activity 3: Calculating the Percent Increase or Decrease of Financial Instruments

Users expect to see the daily percentage of increase or decrease of financial instruments such as stocks and foreign currency. We will ask the user for the stock symbol, the value of the stock on day 1, the value of the same stock on day 2, calculate the percent change and print it in a nicely formatted way. To achieve this, perform the following steps:

1. Create a new class and enter **StockChangeCalculator** as the class name

2. Import the **java.util.Scanner** package:

3. In the **main()** use **System.out.print** to ask the user for the **symbol** of the stock, followed by the **day1** and **day2** values of the stock.

4. Calculate the **percentChange** value.

5. Use **System.out.println** to output the symbol and the percent change with two decimal digits.

6. Run the main program.

    The output should be similar to:

    ```
    Enter the stock symbol: AAPL
    Enter AAPL's day 1 value: 100
    Enter AAPL's day 2 value: 91.5
    AAPL has changed -8.50% in one day.
    ```

    Note

    The solution for this activity can be found on page 305.

Summary

This lesson covered the very basics of Java. We saw some of the basic features of a Java program, and how we can display or print messages to the console. We also saw how we can read values using the input consoles. We also looked at packages that can be used to group classes, and saw an example of **Scanner** in **java.util** package.

In the next lesson, we will cover more about how values are stored, and the different values that we can use in a Java program.

Variables, Data Types, and Operators

Learning Objectives

By the end of this lesson, you will be able to:

- Use primitive data types in Java

- Use reference types in Java

- Implement simple arithmetic operations

- Use type-casting methods

- Input and output various data types

Introduction

In the previous lesson, we were introduced to the Java ecosystem and the tools that are needed to develop Java programs. In this lesson, we will start our journey of the Java language by looking at the fundamental concepts in the language such as variables, data types, and operations.

Variables and Data Types

One of the fundamental concepts in computer programming is memory, used to store information in the computer. Computers use bits as the smallest information that can be stored. A bit is either a 1 or 0. We can group 8 bits to get what is called a **byte**. Because bits are very small, we usually deal with bytes as the smallest unit when programming. When we write programs, what we are essentially doing is fetching some bits from a certain memory location, doing some operations on them, and writing back the result to a memory location.

We need a way to store different kinds of data in the computer's memory and tell the computer what kind of data is stored at what memory location.

Data types are a way for us to specify what kind of data and the size we need to store at a given memory location. An example of a data type is an integer, a character, or a string. Broadly, the data types available in Java can be classified into the following types:

- Primitive data types
- Reference data types

Primitive types are the fundamental types, that is, they cannot be modified. They are indivisible and form the basis for forming complex types. There are eight primitive data types in Java, which we will cover in depth in the subsequent sections:

- byte
- short
- int
- long
- char
- float
- double
- boolean

Reference types are types that refer to data that's stored in a certain memory location. They don't hold the data themselves, but hold the address of the data. Objects, which will be covered later, are examples of reference types:

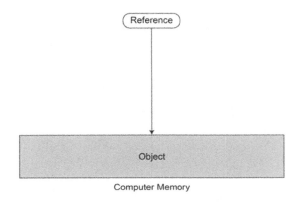

Figure 2.1: Representation of reference types

All data types have the following common properties:

- They are associated with a value.

- They support certain operations on the value they hold.

- They occupy a given number of bits in memory.

For example, an integer can have a value such as 100, support operations such as addition and subtraction, and is represented using 32-bits on the computer's memory.

Variables

Whenever we want to deal with a given data type, we have to create a variable of that data type. For example, to create an integer that holds your age, you would use a line like the following:

```
int age;
```

Here, we are saying the variable is called **age** and is an integer. Integers can only hold values in the range -2,147,483,648 to 2,147,483,647. Trying to hold a value outside the range will result in an error. We can then assign a value to the **age** variable, as follows:

```
age = 30;
```

The **age** variable now holds the value 30. The word **age** is called an **identifier** and is used to refer to the memory location where the value 30 is stored. An identifier is a human-readable word that is used to refer to the memory address of the value.

You can use a word of your choice as an identifier to refer to the same memory address. For example, we could have written this as follows:

```
int myAge ;
myAge = 30;
```

Here is a graphical representation of the preceding code snippet:

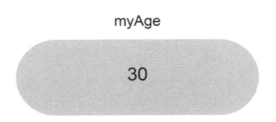

myAge

30

Figure 2.2: Representation of age in memory address

As much as we can use any word as an identifier, Java has some rules on what makes up a valid identifier. The following are some of the rules to adhere to when creating identifier names:

- Identifiers should start with either a letter, _, or $. They cannot start with a number.
- Identifiers can only contain valid unicode characters and numbers.
- Identifiers cannot have spaces in between them.
- Identifiers can be of any length.
- Identifiers cannot be reserved keywords.
- Identifiers cannot have arithmetic symbols such as + or -.
- Identifiers are case-sensitive, for example, age and Age are not the same identifiers.

Reserved Keywords

Java also contains inbuilt words that are reserved and cannot be used as identifiers. These words have special meanings in the language.

Now let's discuss the primitive data types in Java. As we said before, Java has 8 primitive data types, which we will look at in detail.

Integral Data Types

Integral types are types that have integer values. These are int, long, short, byte, and char.

int Data Type

The **int** data type is used to represent integers. Integers are 32-bit numbers in the range of -2,147,483,648 to 2,147,483,647. Example of integers are 0, 1, 300, 500, 389 230, 1,345,543, -500, -324,145, and others in that range. For example, to create an **int** variable to hold a value 5, we write the following:

```
int num = 5;
```

The **num** variable is now an **int** with a value of five. We can also declare more than one variable of the same type in one line:

```
int num1, num2, num3, num4, num5;
```

Here, we have created five variables, all of the **int** type, and initialized to zero. We can also initialize all of the variables to a specific value, as follows:

```
int num1 = 1, num2 = 2, num3 = 3, num4 = 4, num5 = 5;
```

In addition to expressing integers in decimal format, we can also express integers in octal, hexadecimal, and binary format:

- To express in hexadecimal format, we start the **int** with 0x or 0X, that is, a zero followed by x or X. The number has to be at least 2 digits in length. Hexadecimal numbers use 16 digits (0-9 and A-F). For example, to express 30 in hexadecimal, we would use the following code:

  ```
  int hex_num = 0X1E;
  ```

  Printing the number will output 30 as expected. To hold an integer with a value of 501 in hexadecimal, we would write the following:

  ```
  int hex_num1 = 0x1F5;
  ```

- To express in octal format, we start the **int** with a zero and must have at least 2 digits. Octal numbers have 8 digits. For example, to express 15 in octal, we would do the following:

  ```
  int oct_num = 017;
  ```

  Trying to print the preceding variable will output 15. To represent 501 in octal, we would do the following:

  ```
  int oct_num1 = 0765;
  ```

- To express in binary format, we start the **int** with 0b or 0B, that is, a zero followed by b or B. The case doesn't matter. For example, to hold the value 100 in binary, we would do the following:

```
int bin_num = 0b1100100;
```

- To hold the number 999 in binary, we would do the following:

```
int bin_num1 = 0B1111100111;
```

As a summary of the aforementioned four formats of representing integers, all the following variables hold the same value of 117:

```
int num = 117;

int hex_num = 0x75;

int oct_num = 0165;

int bin_num = 0b1110101;
```

long Data Type

long is a 64 bit equivalent of an int. They hold numbers in the range of -9,223,372,036,854,775,808 to 9,223,372,036,854,775,807. Numbers of long type are called long literal and are denoted by an L at the end. For example, to declare a long of value 200, we would do the following:

```
long long_num = 200L;
```

To declare a **long** of value 8, we would do the following:

```
long long_num = 8L;
```

Since integers are 32-bit and hence lie within the range of long, we can convert an **int** into a **long**.

Type Casting

To convert an **int** of value of 23 into a long literal, we would need to do what is called **type casting**:

```
int num_int = 23;

long num_long = (long)num_int;
```

In the second line, we cast the **num_int** of the **int** type to a long literal by using the notation **(long)num_int**. This is referred to as **casting**. Casting is the process of converting one data type into another. Although we can cast a long to an **int**, remember that the number might be outside the **int** range and some numbers will be truncated if they can't fit into the int.

As is with **int**, **long** can also be in octal, hexadecimal, and binary, as shown in the following code:

```
long num = 117L;

long hex_num = 0x75L;

long oct_num = 0165L;

long bin_num = 0b1110101L;
```

Exercise 5: Type Casting

It's often important to change one type to another. In this exercise, we will convert an integer into a floating point:

1. Import **Scanner** and create a public class:

   ```
   import java.util.Scanner;

   public class Main

   {
       static Scanner sc = new Scanner(System.in);
       public static void main(String[] args)
   ```

2. Input a number as an integer:

   ```
   {
       System.out.println("Enter a Number: ");
       int num1 = sc.nextInt();
   ```

3. Print out the integer:

   ```
   System.out.println("Entered value is: " + num1);
   ```

4. Convert the integer into a floating point:

   ```
   float fl1 = num1;
   ```

5. Print out the floating point:

   ```
   System.out.print("Entered value as a floating point variable is: " + fl1);

       }


   }
   ```

byte Data Type

A **byte** is an 8-bit digit that can hold values in the range of -128 to 127. **byte** is the smallest primitive data type in Java, and can be used to hold binary values. To assign a value to a **byte**, it has to be in the range -128 to 127, otherwise the compiler will raise an error:

```
byte num_byte = -32;
byte num_byte1 = 111;
```

You can also cast an **int** to a **byte**, as we did with **long**:

```
int num_int = 23;
byte num_byte = (byte)num_int;
```

In addition to casting, we can assign a **byte** to an **int**:

```
byte num_byte = -32;
int num_int = num_byte;
```

We, however, cannot directly assign an **int** to a **byte** without casting. The following code will raise an error when you try to run it:

```
int num_int = 23;
byte num_byte = num_int;
```

This is because an integer can be outside the byte range (-128 to 127) and hence some precision will be lost. Java doesn't allow you to assign out of range types to lower range types. You have to cast so that the overflow bits will be ignored.

short Data Type

short is a 16-bit data type that can hold numbers in the range of -32,768 to 32,767. To assign a value to a **short** variable, make sure it is in the specified range, otherwise an error will be thrown:

```
short num = 13000;
short num_short = -18979;
```

You can assign a **byte** to a **short** because all the values of a byte fall in the short's range. However, the reverse will throw an error, as explained with **byte** and **int**. To convert an **int** into a **short**, you have to cast to avoid the compile errors. This also applies to converting a **long** into a **short**:

```
short num = 13000;

byte num_byte = 19;

num = num_byte; //OK

int num1 = 10;

short s = num1; //Error

long num_long = 200L;

s = (short)num_long; //OK
```

Boolean Data Type

A **boolean** is a true or false value:

```
boolean finished = true;

boolean hungry = false;
```

> **Note**
>
> Some languages, such as like C and C++, allow Booleans to take a value of 1 for true and 0 for a false. Java doesn't allow you to assign 1 or 0 to Boolean and this will raise a compile-time error.

char Data Type

The **char** data type is used to hold a single character. The character is enclosed in single quotes. Examples of characters are 'a', 'b', 'z', and '5'. Char types are 16 bit and cannot be negative. Char types are essentially integers from 0 to 65,535 to represent Unicode characters. Examples of how to declare chars are as follows:

```
char a = 'a';

char b = 'b';

char c = 'c';

char five = '5';
```

Note that chars are enclosed in single quotes, NOT double quotes. Enclosing a **char** in double quotes changes it to a **string**. A **string** is a collection of one or more chars. An example of a String is "Hello World":

```
String hello = "Hello World";
```

Enclosing a **char** in double quotes will raise an error because the compiler interprets double quotes as a **string**, not a char:

```
char hello = "Hello World"; //ERROR
```

Likewise, enclosing more than one character in single quotes raises a compiler error because chars should be only one character:

```
String hello = 'Hello World'; //ERROR
```

In addition to chars being used to hold single characters, they can also be used to hold escape characters. Escape characters are special characters that have a special use. They consist of a backslash followed by a character and are enclosed in single quotes. There are 8 predefined escape characters, as shown in the following table, along with their uses:

Escape character	Use
'\n'	A newline
'\r'	A carriage return
'\t'	A tab
'\b'	A backspace
'\f'	A form feed
'\\'	A backslash
'\"'	Escapes a double quote
'\''	Escapes a single quote

Table 2.1: Representation of escape characters and their use

Let's say you write a line such as the following:

```
char nl = '\n';
```

The **char** holds a newline and if you try printing it to the console, it skips to the next line.

If you print **'\t'**, a tab is escaped in the output:

```
char tb = '\t';
```

A '\\' will print a backslash in the output.

You can use escape characters to format a string according to your desired output. For example, let's look at the following line:

```
String hello_world = "Hello \n World";
```

Here's the output:

```
Hello
 World
```

This is because the escape character '\n' introduces a new line between **Hello** and **World**.

In addition, chars can also be expressed in Unicode using the Unicode escape character '\u'. Unicode is an international standard of encoding in which a character is assigned a numeric value that can be used on any platform. Unicode aims to support all the available languages in the world, which is in contrast to ASCII.

Floating-Point Data Types

Floating-point data types are numbers that have a fractional part in their representation. Examples include 3.2, 5.681, and 0.9734. Java has two data types to represent types with fractional parts:

- **float**
- **double**

Floating types are represented using a special standard referred to as the IEEE 754 Floating-point standard. This standard was set up by the Institute of Electrical and Electronic Engineers (IEEE) and is meant to make the representation of floating types uniform in the low level parts of the compute. Remember that floating types are usually approximations. When we say 5.01, this number has to be represented in binary format and the representation is usually an approximation to the real number. When working with very high-performance programs where values have to be measured to the order of micro numbers, it becomes imperative that you understand how floating types are represented at the hardware levels to avoid precision loss.

Floating types have two representations: decimal format and scientific notation.

The decimal format is the normal format we usually use, such as 5.4, 0.0004, or 23,423.67.

The scientific notation is the use of the letter e or E to represent a ten raised to a value. For example, 0.0004 in scientific notation is 4E-4 or 4e-4, which is similar to 4×10^{-4}. The number 23,423.67 in scientific notation would be 2.342367E4 or 2.342367e4, which is similar to 2.342367×10^4.

float Data Type

`float` is used to hold 32-bit fractional numbers in the range 1.4 x 10 -45 and as big as 3.4 x 10 38. That is, the smallest number a `float` can hold is 1.4 x 10 -45 and the largest number it can hold is 3.4 x 10 38. Floats are followed by a letter f or F to indicate that they are of `float` type. Examples of floats are shown as follows:

```
float a = 1.0f;
float b = 0.0002445f;
float c = 93647.6335567f;
```

Floats can also be represented in scientific notation, as follows:

```
float a = 1E0f;
float b = 2.445E-4f;
float c = 9.36476335567E+4f;
```

Java also has a class called Float that can encapsulate floats and offers some useful features. For example, to know the largest `float` number and the smallest `float` number available in your environment, you'd call the following:

```
float max = Float.MAX_VALUE;
float min = Float.MIN_VALUE;
```

The Float class also has values to represent positive and negative infinity when a division by zero occurs:

```
float max_inf = Float.POSITIVE_INFINITY;
float min_inf = Float.NEGATIVE_INFINITY;
```

Floats support two types of zeros: -0.0f and +0.0f. As we already said, float types are represented as approximations in the memory, and so even a zero is not an absolute zero. That is why we have two zeros. When a number is divided by positive zero, we get `Float.POSITIVE_INFINITY` and when a number is divided by negative zero, we get `Float.NEGATIVE_INFINITY`.

The Float class also has the constant **NaN** to indicate a number that is not of a **float** type:

```
float nan = Float.NaN;
```

As with the integral types we have discussed, we can assign an **int**, **byte**, **short**, **long**, and char to a float, but cannot do the reverse unless we cast.

> **Note**
>
> Casting an integer to a float and then back to an **int** will not always lead to an original number. Be careful when doing casting between **int** and **float**.

double Data Type

double holds 64-bit numbers with fractional parts. That is, the range 4.9 x 10e -324 to 1.7 x 10e 308. Doubles are used to hold larger numbers than floats. They are represented with a d or D at the end. However, by default, in Java, any number with a fractional part is a **double**, so there is usually no need to append the d or D at the end. Examples of doubles are as follows:

```
double d1  = 4.452345;
double d2 = 3.142;
double d3 = 0.123456;
double d4 = 0.000999;
```

Like floats, doubles can also be represented in scientific notation:

```
double d1  = 4.452345E0;
double d2 = 3.142E0;
double d3 = 1.23456E-1;
double d4 = 9.99E-4;
```

As you might have already guessed it, Java also provides a class called **Double** with some useful constants, as shown in the following code:

```
double max = Double.MAX_VALUE;
double min = Double.MIN_NORMAL;
double max_inf = Double.POSITIVE_INFINITY;
double min_inf = Double.NEGATIVE_INFINITY;
double nan = Double.NaN;
```

Likewise, we can assign the integral types and **float** except the **boolean** type to **double** and not the other way round until we cast. The following are example operations that are allowed and some that are forbidden:

```
int num = 100;
double d1 = num;


float f1 = 0.34f;
double d2 = f1;


double d3 = 'A'; //Assigns 65.0 to d3


int num  = 200;
double d3 = 3.142;


num = d3; //ERROR: We must cast
num = (int)d3; //OK
```

Activity 4: Inputting Student Information and Outputting an ID

Storing and outputting variables in foundational in any developing environment. In this activity you will be creating a program that will ask a student to input their data and then output a simple ID card. The program will use integers and strings along with the scanner class in the **java.util** package.

The following activity uses the string variable and the integer variable to input information about a student and then print it out.

1. Import the scanner package and create a new class.

2. Import the student name as a string.

3. Import the university name as a string.

4. Import the student's age as an integer.

5. Use **System.out.println** to print out the student details.

6. After running the program, the output should be similar to this:

```
Here is your ID
*******************************
Name: John Winston
University: Liverpool University
Age: 19
*******************************
```

> **Note**
>
> The solution for this activity can be found on page 306.

Activity 5: Calculating the Number of Full Fruit Boxes

John is a peach grower. He picks peaches from his trees, puts them into fruit boxes and ships them. He can ship a fruit box if it is full with 20 peaches. If he has less than 20 peaches, he has to pick more peaches so he can fill a fruit box with 20 peaches and ship it.

We would like to help John by calculating the number of fruit boxes that he can ship and the number of peaches left behind, given the number of peaches he was able to pick. To achieve this, perform the following steps:

1. Create a new class and enter **PeachCalculator** as the class name

2. Import the **java.util.Scanner** package:

3. In the **main()** use **System.out.print** to ask the user for the **numberOfPeaches**.

4. Calculate the **numberOfFullBoxes** and **numberOfPeachesLeft** values. Hint: use integer division.

5. Use **System.out.println** to output these two values.

6. Run the main program.

The output should be similar to:

```
Enter the number of peaches picked: 55
We have 2 full boxes and 15 peaches left.
```

> **Note**
>
> The solution for this activity can be found on page 307.

Summary

In this lesson, we learned about the use of primitive and reference data types, along with simple arithmetic operations on data in Java. We learned how to cast data types from one type to another. We then saw how we can work with floating-point data types.

In the next lesson, we will work with conditional statements and looping structures.

3

Control Flow

Learning Objectives

By the end of this lesson, you'll be able to:

- Control the flow of execution using the **if** and **else** statements in Java
- Check through multiple conditions using the switch case statements in Java
- Utilize the looping constructs in Java to write concise code to perform repetitive actions

Introduction

So far, we have looked at programs that consist of a series of statements that the Java compiler executes sequentially. However, in certain cases, we might need to perform actions based on the current state of the program.

Consider the example of the software that's installed in an ATM machine – it performs a set of actions, that is, it allows a transaction to occur when the PIN that's been entered by the user is correct. However, when the PIN that's been entered is incorrect, then the software performs another set of actions, that is, it informs the user that the PIN does not match and asks the user to reenter the PIN. You'll find that such logical constructs that depend upon values or stages are present in almost all real-world programs.

There are also times where a particular task might need to be performed repeatedly, that is, for a particular time duration, for a particular set number of times, or until a condition is met. Continuing from our example of the ATM machine, if the number of times an incorrect password is entered exceeds three, then the card is blocked.

These logical constructs act as building blocks, as we move toward building complex programs in Java. This lesson will dive into these basic constructs, which can be categorized into two general classes, as follows:

- Conditional statements
- Looping statements

Conditional Statements

Conditional statements are used to control the flow of execution of the Java compiler based on certain conditions. This implies that we are making a choice based on a certain value or the state of a program. The conditional statements that are available in Java are as follows:

- The **if** statement
- The **if-else** statement
- The **else-if** statement
- The **switch** statement

The if Statement

The if statement tests a condition, and when the condition is true, the code contained in the if block is executed. If the condition is not true, then the code in the block is skipped and the execution continues from the line after the block.

The syntax for an **if** statement is as follows:

```
if (condition) {
//actions to be performed when the condition is true
}
```

Consider the following example:

```
int a = 9;
if (a < 10){
System.out.println("a is less than 10");
}
```

Since the condition **a<10** is true, the print statement is executed.

We can check for multiple values in the **if** condition as well. Consider the following example:

```
if ((age > 50) && (age <= 70) && (age != 60)) {
System.out.println("age is above 50 but at most 70 excluding 60");
}
```

The preceding code snippet checks whether the value of **age** is above 50, but at most 70, excluding 60.

When the statement in the **if** block is just one line, then we don't need to include the enclosing braces:

```
if (color == 'Maroon' || color == 'Pink')
System.out.println("It is a shade of Red");
```

The else Statement

For some scenarios, we need a different block of code to be executed if the **if** condition fails. For that, we can use the **else** clause. It is optional.

The syntax for the **if else** statement is as follows:

```
if (condition) {
//actions to be performed when the condition is true
}
else {
//actions to be performed when the condition is false
}
```

Exercise 6: Implementing a Simple if-else Statement

In this exercise, we are going to create a program that checks whether bus tickets can be book based on the number of empty seats. Complete the following steps to do so:

1. Right-click the **src** folder and select **New** | **Class**.

2. Enter **Booking** as the class name, and then click **OK**.

3. Set up the **main** method:

```
public class Booking{
public static void main(String[] args){
}
}
```

4. Initialize two variables, one for the number of empty seats and the other for the requested ticket numbers:

```
int seats = 3; // number of empty seats
int req_ticket = 4; // Request for tickets
```

5. Use the **if** condition to check whether the requested ticket numbers are lower than or equal to the empty seats available, and print the appropriate messages:

```
if( (req_ticket == seats) || (req_ticket < seats) ) {
    System.out.print("This booing can be accepted");
    }else
        System.out.print("This booking is rejected");
```

6. Run the program.

   You should get the following output:

   ```
   This booking is rejected
   ```

The else-if Statement

else if statements are used when we wish to compare multiple conditions before the **else** clause is evaluated.

The syntax for the **else if** statement is as follows:

```
if (condition 1) {

//actions to be performed when condition 1 is true

}
else if (Condition 2) {

//actions to be performed when condition 2 is true

}
else if (Condition 3) {

//actions to be performed when condition 3 is true

}

...

...

else if (Condition n) {

//actions to be performed when condition n is true

}
else {

//actions to be performed when the condition is false

}
```

Exercise 7: Implementing the else-if Statements

We are building an e-commerce application that calculates the delivery fee based on the distance between the seller and the buyer. A buyer purchases an item on our website and enters the delivery address. Based on the distance, we calculate the delivery fee and display it to the user. In this exercise, we are given the following table and need to write a program to output the delivery fee to the user:

Distance(KM)	Delivery Fee(USD)
0-5	2
5-15	5
15-25	10
25-50	15
>50	20

Table 3.1: Table showing the distance and its corresponding fee

To do this, perform the following steps:

1. Right-click the **src** folder and select **New** | **Class**.

2. Enter **DeliveryFee** as the class name, and then click **OK**.

3. Open the created class, and then create the main method:

```
public class DeliveryFee{
public static void main(String[] args){


}
}
```

4. Within the **main** method, create two integer variables, one called **distance** and another called **fee**. The two variables will hold the **distance** and delivery fees, respectively. Initialize the **distance** to 10 and the **fee** to zero:

```
int distance = 10;
int fee = 0;
```

5. Create an **if** block to check the first condition in the table:

```java
if (distance > 0 && distance < 5){
    fee = 2;
}
```

This **if** statement checks whether the **distance** is above 0 but below 5 and sets the delivery **fee** to 2 dollars.

6. Add an **else if** statement to check the second condition in the table and set the **fee** to 5 dollars:

```java
else if (distance >= 5 && distance < 15){
    fee = 5;
}
```

7. Add two more **else if** statements to check for the third and fourth conditions in the table, as shown in the following code:

```java
else if (distance >= 15 && distance < 25){
    fee = 10;
}else if (distance >= 25 && distance < 50){
    fee = 15;
}
```

8. Finally, add an **else** statement to match the last condition in the table and set the appropriate delivery **fee**:

```java
else {
    fee = 20;
}
```

9. Print out the value of the fee:

```java
System.out.println("Delivery Fee: " + fee);
```

10. Run the program and observe the output:

```
Delivery Fee: 5
```

Nested if Statements

We can have **if** statements inside other **if** statements. This construct is called a nested **if** statement. We evaluate the outer condition first and if it succeeds, we then evaluate a second inner **if** statement and so on until all the **if** statements have finished:

```java
if (age > 20){


    if (height > 170){


        if (weight > 60){
            System.out.println("Welcome");
        }

    }

}
```

We can nest as many statements as we wish to, and the compiler will evaluate them, starting from the top going downward.

switch case Statements

The **switch case** statements are an easier and more concise way of doing multiple **if else** statements when the same value is being compared for equality. The following is a quick comparison:

A traditional **else if** statement would look like this:

```java
if(age == 10){
    discount = 300;
} else if (age == 20){
    discount = 200;
} else if (age == 30){
    discount = 100;
} else {
    discount = 50;
}
```

However, with the same logic, when implemented using a **switch case** statement, it would look as follows:

```
switch (age){
    case 10:
        discount = 300;
    case 20:
        discount = 200;
    case 30:
        discount = 100;
    default:
        discount = 50;
}
```

Notice how this code is more readable.

To use a **switch** statement, first you need to declare it with the keyword **switch**, followed by a condition in parentheses. The **case** statements are used to check these conditions. They are checked in a sequential order.

The compiler will check the value of **age** against all the cases and if it finds a match, the code in that **case** will execute and so will all the cases following it. For example, if our **age** was equal to 10, the first **case** will be matched and then the second **case**, the third **case**, and the **default case**. The **default case** is executed if all the other cases are not matched. For example, if **age** is not 10, 20, or 30, then the discount would be set to 50. It can be interpreted as the **else** clause in **if-else** statements. The **default case** is optional and can be omitted.

If **age** was equal to 30, then the third **case** would be matched and executed. Since the **default case** is optional, we can leave it out and the execution will end after the third **case**.

Most of the time, what we really wish for is the execution to end at the matched **case**. We want it to be so that if the first **case** is matched, then the code in that **case** is executed and the rest of the cases are ignored. To achieve this, we use a **break** statement to tell the compiler to continue to execute outside the **switch** statement. Here is the same **switch case** with **break** statements:

```
switch (age){
    case 10:
        discount = 300;
        break;
    case 20:
        discount = 200;
        break;
    case 30:
        discount = 100;
        break;
    default:
        discount = 50;
}
```

Because the default is the last **case**, we can safely ignore the **break** statement because the execution will end there anyway.

> **Note:**
>
> It is good design to always add a break statement in case another programmer adds extra cases in the future.

Activity 6: Controlling the Flow of Execution Using Conditionals

A factory pays its workers $10 per hour. The standard working day is 8 hours, but the factory gives extra compensation for additional hours. The policy it follows to calculate the salary is like so:

- If a person works for less than 8 hours – number of hours * $10

- If the person works for more than 8 hours but less than 12 – 20% extra for the additional hours

- More than 12 hours – additional day's salary is credited

Create a program that calculates and displays the salary earned by the worker based on the number of hours worked.

To meet this requirement, perform the following steps:

1. Initialize two variables and the values of the working hours and salary.

2. In the **if** condition, check whether the working hours of the worker is below the required hours. If the condition holds **true**, then the salary should be (working hours * 10).

3. Use the **else if** statement to check if the working hours lies between 8 hours and 12 hours. If that is true, then the salary should be calculated at $10 per hour for the first eight hours and the remaining hours should be calculated at $12 per hour.

4. Use the **else** block for the default of $160 (additional day's salary) per day.

5. Execute the program to observe the output.

> **Note**
>
> The solution for this activity can be found on page 308.

Activity 7: Developing a Temperature System

Write a program in Java that displays simple messages, based on the temperature. The temperature is generalized to the following three sections:

- High: In this case, suggest the user to use a sunblock
- Low: In this case, suggest the user to wear a coat
- Humid: In this case, suggest the user to open the windows

To do this perform the following steps:

1. Declare two strings, **temp** and **weatherWarning**.

2. Initialize **temp** with either **High**, **Low**, or **Humid**.

3. Create a switch statement that checks the different cases of **temp**.

4. Initialize the variable **weatherWarning** to appropriate messages for each case of temp (**High**, **Low**, **Humid**).

5. In the default case, initialize **weatherWarning** to "The weather looks good. Take a walk outside".

6. After you complete the switch construct, print the value of **weatherWarning**.

7. Run the program to see the output, it should be similar to:

```
Its cold outside, do not forget your coat.
```

> **Note**
>
> The solution for this activity can be found on page 309.

Looping Constructs

Looping constructs are used to perform a certain operation a given number of times as long as a condition is being met. They are commonly used to perform a specific operation on the items of a list. An example is when we want to find the summation of all the numbers from 1 to 100. Java supports the following looping constructs:

- **for** loops
- **for each** loops
- **while** loops
- **do while** loops

for Loops

The syntax of the **for** loop is as follows:

```
for( initialization ; condition ; expression) {
    //statements

}
```

The initialization statements are executed when the **for** loop starts executing. It can be more than one expression, all separated by commas. The expressions must all be of the same type:

```
for( int i  = 0, j = 0; i <= 9; i++)
```

The condition section of the **for** loop must evaluate to true or false. If there is no expression, the condition defaults to true.

The expression part is executed after each iteration of the statements, as long as the condition is true. You can have more than one expression separated by a comma.

> **Note**
>
> The expressions must be valid Java expressions, that is, expressions that can be terminated by a semicolon.

Here is how a **for** loop works:

1. First, the initialization is evaluated.

2. Then, the condition is checked. If the condition is true, the statements contained in the **for** block are executed.

3. After the statements are executed, the expression is executed, and then the condition is checked again.

4. If it is still not false, the statements are executed again, then the expression is executed, and the condition is evaluated again.

5. This is repeated until the condition evaluates to false.

6. When the condition evaluates to false, the **for** loop completes and the code sections after the loop are executed.

Exercise 8: Implementing a Simple for Loop

To print all the single digit numbers in increasing and decreasing order, perform the following steps:

1. Right-click the **src** folder and select **New | Class**.

2. Enter **Looping** as the class name, and then click **OK**.

3. Set up the **main** method:

```
public class Looping
{
    public static void main(String[] args) {
    }
}
```

4. Implement a **for** loop that initializes a variable **i** at zero, a condition so that the value remains below 10, and **i** should be incremented by one in each iteration:

```
System.out.println("Increasing order");
for( int i  = 0; i <= 9; i++)
System.out.println(i);
```

5. Implement another **for** loop that initializes a variable **k** at 9, a condition so that the value remains above 0, and **k** should be decremented by one in each iteration:

```
System.out.println("Decreasing order");
for( int k  = 9; k >= 0; k--)
System.out.println(k);
```

Output:

```
Increasing order
0
1
2
3
4
5
6
7
8
9
Decreasing order
9
8
7
6
5
4
3
2
1
0
```

Activity 8: Implementing the for Loop

John, a peach grower, picks peaches from his trees, puts them into fruit boxes and ships them. He can ship a fruit box if it is full with 20 peaches. If he has less than 20 peaches, he has to pick more peaches so he can fill a fruit box with 20 peaches and ship it.

We would like to help John by writing an automation software that initiates the filling and shipping of boxes. We get the number of peaches from John, and we print a message for each group of 20 peaches and say how many peaches have been shipped so far. We print "shipped 60 peaches so far" for the third box, for example. We would like to do this with a **for** loop. We do not need to worry about the peaches leftover. To achieve this, perform the following steps:

1. Create a new class and enter **PeachBoxCounter** as the class name

2. Import the **java.util.Scanner** package:

3. In the **main()** use **System.out.print** to ask the user for the **numberOfPeaches**.

4. Write a for loop that counts the peaches that are shipped so far. This starts from zero, increases 20 by 20 until the peaches left is less than 20.

5. In the **for** loop, print the number of peaches shipped so far.

6. Run the main program.

    The output should be similar to:

    ```
    Enter the number of peaches picked: 42
    shipped 0 peaches so far
    shipped 20 peaches so far
    shipped 40 peaches so far
    ```

    > **Note**
    >
    > The solution for this activity can be found on page 310.

All three sections of the **for** loop are optional. This implies that the line **for(;   ;)** will provide any error. It just provides an invite loop.

This **for** loop doesn't do anything and won't terminate. Variables declared in the for loop declaration are available in the statements of the **for** loop. For example, in our first example, we printed the value of **i** from the statements sections because the variable **i** was declared in the **for** loop. This variable is, however, not available after the **for** loop and can be freely declared. It can't however be declared inside the **for** loop again:

```
for (int i = 0; i <= 9; i++)

    int i = 10;              //Error, i is already declared
```

For loops can also have braces enclosing the statements if we have more than one statement. This is just as we discussed in the **if-else** statements earlier. If we have only one statement, then we don't need to have braces. When the statements are more than one, they need to be enclosed within braces. In the following example, we are printing out the value of **i** and **j**:

```
for (int i = 0, j = 0; i <= 9; i++, j++) {

    System.out.println(i);

    System.out.println(j);

}
```

> **Note**
>
> The expressions must be valid Java expressions, that is, expressions that can be terminated by a semicolon.

A **break** statement can be used to interrupt the **for** loop and break out of the loop. It takes the execution outside the **for** loop.

For example, we might wish to terminate the **for** loop we created earlier if **i** is equal to 5:

```
for (int i = 0; i <= 9; i++){


    if (i == 5)
        break;
    System.out.println(i);

}
```

Output:
```
0
1
2
3
4
```

The preceding **for** loop iterates from 0, 1, 2, and 3 and terminates at 4. This is because after the condition **i**, that is, 5 is met, the break statement is executed, which ends the **for** loop and the statements after it are not executed. Execution continues outside the loop.

The **continue** statement is used to tell the loop to skip all the other statements after it and continue execution to the next iteration:

```
for (int i = 0; i <= 9; i++){


    if (i == 5)
        continue;
    System.out.println(i);

}
```

Output:
```
0
1
2
3
4
6
7
8
9
```

The number 5 is not printed because once the continue statement is encountered, the rest of the statements after it are ignored, and the next iteration is started. The **continue** statements can be useful when there are a few exceptions you wish to skip when processing multiple items.

Nested for Loops

The block of statements within a loop can be another loop was well. Such constructs are known as nested loops:

```java
public class Nested{


    public static void main(String []args){
        for(int i = 1; i <= 3; i++) {
//Nested loop
for(int j = 1; j <= 3; j++) {
    System.out.print(i + "" + j);
    System.out.print("\t");
}
System.out.println();
}


        }
    }
}
```

Output:

11	12	13
21	22	23
31	32	33

For each single loop of **i**, we loop **j** three times. You can think of these **for** loops as follows:

Repeat **i** three times and for each repetition, repeat **j** three times. That way, we have a total of 9 iterations of **j**. For each iteration of **j**, we then print out the value of **i** and **j**.

Exercise 9: Implementing a Nested for Loop

Our goal in this exercise is to print a pyramid of * with seven rows, like so:

```
       *
      ***
     *****
    *******
   *********
  ***********
 *************
***************
```

Figure 3.1: Pyramid of * with seven rows

To achieve this goal, perform the following steps:

1. Right-click the **src** folder and select **New | Class**.

2. Enter **NestedPattern** as the class name, and then click **OK**.

3. In the main method, create a **for** loop that initializes the variable **i** at 1, introduces the condition so that the value of **i** is at most 15, and increments the value of **i** by 2:

```
public class NestedPattern{
public static void main(String[] args) {
for (int i = 1; i <= 15; i += 2) {


}
}
}
}
```

4. Within this loop, create two more **for** loops, one to print the spaces and the other to print the *:

```
for (int k = 0; k < (7 - i / 2); k++) {
    System.out.print(" ");
    }
for (int j = 1; j <= i; j++) {
    System.out.print("*");
    }
```

5. Within the outer **for** loop, add the following code to add the next line:

```
System.out.println();
```

Run the program. You will see the resultant pyramid.

for-each Loops

for each loops are an advanced version of **for** loops that were introduced in Java 5. They are used to perform a given operation on every item in an array or list of items.

Let's take a look at this **for** loop:

```
int[] arr = { 1, 2, 3, 4, 5 , 6, 7, 8, 9,10};
for (int i  = 0; i < 10; i++){
    System.out.println(arr[i]);
}
```

The first line declares an array of integers. An array is a collection of items of the same type. In this case, the variable arr is holding a collection of 10 integers. We then use a **for** loop from **0** to **10**, printing the elements of this array. We are using **i < 10** because the last item is at index **9**, not **10**. This is because the elements of an array start with index 0. The first element is at index **0**, the second at index **1**, the third at **2**, and so on. **arr[0]** will return the first element, **arr[1]** the second, **arr[2]** the third, and so on.

This **for** loop can be replaced with a shorter **for each** loop. The syntax of a **for each** loop is as follows:

```
for( type item : array_or_collection){
      //Code to executed for each item in the array or collection
}
```

For our preceding example, the **for each** loop would be as follows:

```
for(int item : arr){
    System.out.println(item);
}
```

int item is the current element in the array we are at. The **for each** loop will iterate for all the elements in the array. Inside the braces, we print out the item. Note that we didn't have to use **arr[i]** like in the **for** loop earlier. This is because the **for each** loop automatically extracts the value for us. In addition, we didn't have to use an extra **int i** to keep the current index and check if we are below **10 (i < 10)**, like in the **for** loop we used earlier. **for each** loops are shorter and automatically check the range for us.

For example, we can use the **for each** loop to print the squares of all the elements present in the array, **arr**:

```
for(int item : arr){
    int square = item * item;
    System.out.println(square);
}
```

Output:

```
1
4
9
16
25
36
49
64
81
10
```

The while and do while Loops

Sometimes, we wish to execute certain statements repeatedly, that is, as long as a certain Boolean condition is true. Such cases require us to use a **while** loop or a **do while** loop. A **while** loop first checks a Boolean statement and executes a block of code if the Boolean is true, otherwise it skips the **while** block. A **do while** loop first executes a block of code once before it checks the Boolean condition. Use a **do while** loop when you want the code to be executed at least once and a **while** loop when you want the Boolean condition to be checked first before the first execution. The following are the formats of the **while** and **do while** loops:

The syntax for the **while** loop:

```
while(condition) {
//Do something
}
```

The syntax for the **do while** loop:

```
do {
//Do something
}
while(condition);
```

For example, to print all of the numbers from 0 to 10 using a **while** loop, we would use the following code:

```
public class Loops {
    public static void main(String[] args){
        int number = 0;
        while (number <= 10){
            System.out.println(number);
            number++;
        }
    }
}
```

Output:

```
0
1
2
3
4
5
6
7
8
9
10
```

We could also write the preceding code using a **do while** loop:

```java
public class Loops {
    public static void main(String[] args){
        int number = 0;
        do {
            System.out.println(number);
            number++;
        }while (number <= 10);
    }
}
```

With the **do while** loop, the condition is evaluated last, so we are sure that the statements will be executed at least once.

Exercise 10: Implementing the while Loop

To print the first 10 numbers in the Fibonacci series using the **while** loop, perform the following steps:

1. Right-click the **src** folder and select **New | Class**.

2. Enter **FibonacciSeries** as the class name, and then click **OK**.

3. Declare the variables that are required in the **main** method:

    ```
    public class FibonacciSeries {
        public static void main(String[] args) {
            int i = 1, x = 0, y = 1, sum=0;
        }
    }
    ```

    Here, **i** is the counter, **x** and **y** store the first two numbers of the Fibonacci series, and **sum** is a variable that is used to calculate the sum of the variables **x** and **y**.

4. Implement a **while** loop with the condition so that the counter **i** does not go beyond 10:

    ```
    while (i <= 10)
    {
    }
    ```

5. Within the **while** loop, implement the logic to print the value of **x**, and then assign the appropriate values to **x**, **y**, and **sum** so that we are always printing the **sum** of the last and the penultimate number:

    ```
    System.out.print(x + " ");
    sum = x + y;
    x = y;
    y = sum;
    i++;
    ```

Activity 9: Implementing the while Loop

Remember John, who is a peach grower. He picks peaches from his trees, puts them into fruit boxes and ships them. He can ship a fruit box if it is full with 20 peaches. If he has less than 20 peaches, he has to pick more peaches so he can fill a fruit box with 20 peaches and ship it.

We would like to help John by writing an automation software that initiates the filling and shipping of boxes. We get the number of peaches from John, and we print a message for each group of 20 peaches and say how many boxes we have shipped and how many peaches we have left, e.g., "2 boxes shipped, 54 peaches remaining". We would like to do this with a **while** loop. The loop will continue as we have a number of peaches that would fit at least one box. In contrast to the previous activity with **for**, we will also keep track of the remaining peaches. To achieve this, perform the following steps:

1. Create a new class and enter **PeachBoxCounter** as the class name

2. Import the **java.util.Scanner** package:

3. In the **main()** use **System.out.print** to ask the user for the **numberOfPeaches**.

4. Create a **numberOfBoxesShipped** variable.

5. Write a while loop that continues as we have at least 20 peaches.

6. In the loop, remove 20 peaches from **numberOfPeaches** and increment **numberOfBoxesShipped** by 1. Print these values.

7. Run the main program.

   The output should be similar to:

   ```
   Enter the number of peaches picked: 42
   1 boxes shipped, 22 peaches remaining
   2 boxes shipped, 2 peaches remaining
   ```

   Note

   The solution for this activity can be found on page 311.

Activity 10: Implementing Looping Constructs

Our goal is to create a ticketing system so that when the user puts in a request for the tickets, the tickets are approved based on the number of seats remaining in the restaurant.

To create such a program, perform the following steps:

1. Import the packages that are required to read data from the user.

2. Declare the variables to store the total number of seats available, remaining seats, and tickets requested.

3. Within a **while** loop, implement the **if else** loop that checks whether the request is valid, which implies that the number of tickets requested is less than the number of seats remaining.

4. If the logic in the previous step is true, then print a message to denote that the ticket is processed, set the remaining seats to the appropriate value, and ask for the next set of tickets.

5. If the logic in step 3 is false, then print an appropriate message and break out of the loop.

> **Note**
>
> The solution for this activity can be found on page 312.

Activity 11: Continuous Peach Shipment with Nested Loops.

Remember John, who is a peach grower. He picks peaches from his trees, puts them into fruit boxes and ships them. He can ship a fruit box if it is full with 20 peaches. If he has less than 20 peaches, he has to pick more peaches so he can fill a fruit box with 20 peaches and ship it.

We would like to help John by writing an automation software that initiates the filling and shipping of boxes. In this new version of our automation software, we will let John bring in the peaches in batches of his own choosing and will use the remaining peaches from the previous batch together with the new batch.

We get the incoming number of peaches from John and add it to the current number of peaches. Then, we print a message for each group of 20 peaches and say how many boxes we have shipped and how many peaches we have left, e.g., "2 boxes shipped, 54 peaches remaining". We would like to do this with a **while** loop. The loop will continue as we have a number of peaches that would fit at least one box. We will have another **while** loop that gets the next batch and quits if there is none. To achieve this, perform the following steps:

1. Create a new class and enter **PeachBoxCount** as the class name

2. Import the **java.util.Scanner** package:

3. Create a **numberOfBoxesShipped** variable and a **numberOfPeaches** variable.

4. In the **main()**, write an infinite **while** loop.

5. Use **System.out.print** to ask the user for the **incomingNumberOfPeaches**. If this is zero, **break** out of this infinite loop.

6. Add the incoming peaches to the existing peaches.

7. Write a **while** loop that continues as we have at least 20 peaches.

8. In the for loop, remove 20 peaches from **numberOfPeaches** and increment **numberOfBoxesShipped** by 1. Print these values.

9. Run the main program.

   The output should be similar to:

   ```
   Enter the number of peaches picked: 23
   1 boxes shipped, 3 peaches remaining
   Enter the number of peaches picked: 59
   2 boxes shipped, 42 peaches remaining
   3 boxes shipped, 22 peaches remaining
   4 boxes shipped, 2 peaches remaining
   Enter the number of peaches picked: 0
   ```

   Note

   The solution for this activity can be found on page 313.

Summary

In this lesson, we've covered some of the fundamental and important concepts in Java and programming by looking at some simple examples. Conditional statements and looping statements are normally essential to implementing logic.

In the next lesson, we will focus on a couple more fundamental concepts, such as functions, arrays, and strings. These concepts will help us in writing concise and reusable code.

Object-Oriented Programming

Learning Objectives

By the end of this lesson, you'll be able to:

- Explain the concept of classes and objects in Java
- Explain the four underlying principles of object-oriented programming
- Create simple classes and access them using objects in Java
- Implement inheritance in Java
- Experiment with method overloading and overriding in Java
- Create and use annotations in Java

Introduction

So far, we've looked at the basics of Java and how to use simple constructs such as **conditional** statements and looping statements, and how methods are implemented in Java. These basic ideas are very important to understand and are useful when building simple programs. However, to build and maintain large and complex programs, the basic types and constructs do not suffice. What makes Java really powerful is the fact that it is an object-oriented programming language. It allows you to build and integrate complex programs effectively, while maintaining a consistent structure, making it easy to scale, maintain, and reuse.

In this lesson, we will introduce a programming paradigm called object-oriented programming (OOP), which lies at the core of Java. We will have a look at how OOP is done in Java and how you can implement it to design better programs.

We will start this lesson with a definition of OOP and the principles underlying it, will look at OOP constructs called **classes** and **objects**, and will conclude the lesson by looking at a concept called **inheritance**.

We will write two simple OOP applications in Java: one to represent people who are normally found in a university, such as students, lecturers, and the staff, and the other to represent domestic animals in a farm. Let's get started!

Object-Oriented Principles

OOP is governed by four main principles, as follows. Throughout the rest of this lesson, we will delve further into each of these principles:

- **Inheritance**: We will learn how we can reuse code by using hierarchies of classes and inheriting behavior from derived classes

- **Encapsulation**: We will also look at how we can hide the implementation details from the outside world while providing a consistent interface to communicate with our objects through methods

- **Abstraction**: We will look at how we can focus on the important details of an object and ignore the other details

- **Polymorphism**: We will also have a look at how we can define abstract behaviors and let other classes provide implementations for these behaviors

Classes and Objects

A paradigm in programming is a style of writing programs. Different languages support different paradigms. A language can support more than one paradigm.

Object-Oriented Programming

Object-oriented programming, often referred to as OOP, is a style of programming in which we deal with objects. Objects are entities that have properties to hold their data and methods to manipulate the data.

Let's break this down into simpler terms.

In OOP, we primarily deal with objects and classes. An object is a representation of a real-world item. An example of an object is your car or yourself. An object has properties associated with it and actions it can perform. For example, your car has wheels, doors, an engine, and gears, which are all properties, and it can perform actions such as speeding, braking, and stopping, which are all called methods. The following diagram is an illustration of the properties and methods you have, as a person. Properties can sometimes be referred to as **fields**:

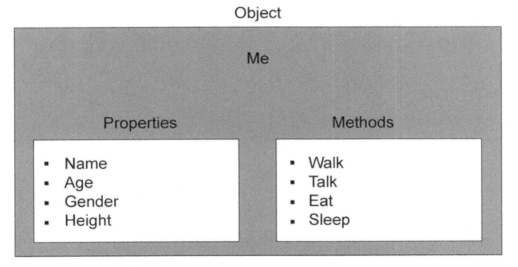

Figure 4.1: Representation of objects relating to humans

In OOP, we define classes as blueprints of our items and objects as instances of classes.

An example of a class is **Person** and an example of an object/instance of **Person** is a student or lecturer. These are specific example objects that belong to the **Person** class:

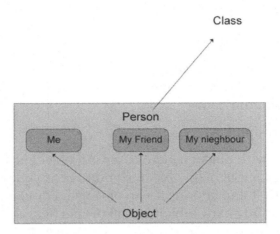

Figure 4.2 Representation of an instance of a class

In the preceding diagram, the **Person** class is used to represent all people, regardless of their gender, age, or height. From this class, we can create specific examples of people, as shown in the boxes inside the **Person** class.

In Java, we mainly deal with classes and objects, so it is very important that you understand the difference between the two.

> **Note**
>
> In Java, everything except primitive data types are objects.

Here is the format of a class definition in Java:

```
modifier class ClassName {
    //Body
}
```

A class definition in Java consists of the following parts:

- **Modifiers**: A class can be `public`, `private`, `protected`, or have no modifier. A `public` class is accessible from other classes in other packages. A `private` class is only accessible from within the class it is declared. A `protected` class member is accessible within all classes in the same package.
- **Class name**: The name should begin with an initial letter.
- **Body**: The class body is surrounded by braces, { }. This is where we define the properties and methods of the class.

Naming Conventions for Class Names

Naming conventions for classes in Java are as follows:

- Class names should use camelCase. That is, the first word should start with a capital letter and all of the inner words should have a capitalized first word, for example, `Cat`, `CatOwner`, and `House`.
- Class names should be nouns.
- Class names should be descriptive and should not be initials, unless they are widely known.

Here is an example of how the **Person** class would be defined:

```
public class Person {



}
```

The modifier is public, meaning that the class can be accessed from other Java packages. The class name is **Person**.

Here is a more robust example of the **Person** class with a few properties and methods:

```
public class Person {


    //Properties
    int age;
    int height;
    String name;


    //Methods
```

```
    public void walk(){

        //Do walking operations here

    }
    public void sleep(){

        //Do sleeping operations here

    }
    private void takeShower(){

        //Do take shower operations here

    }
}
```

These properties are used to hold the state of the object. That is, **age** holds the age of the current person, which can be different from that of the next person. **name** is used to hold the name of the current person, which will also be different from the next person. They answer the question: who is this person?

The methods are used to hold the logic of the class. That is, they answer the question: what can this person do? Methods can be private, public, or protected.

The operations in the methods can be as complex as your application needs. You can even call methods from other methods, as well as adding parameters to those methods.

Exercise 11: Working with Classes and Objects

Perform the following steps:

1. Open IntelliJ IDEA and create a file called **Person.java**.

2. Create a public class with the name **Person** with three properties, that is, **age**, **height**, and **name**. The **age** and **height** properties will hold integer values, whereas the **name** property will hold a string value:

    ```
    public class Person {

        //Properties
        int age;
        int height;
        String name;
    ```

3. Define three methods, that is, **walk()**, **sleep()**, and **takeShower()**. Write the print statements for each so that you can print out the text to the console when they are called:

```
//Methods
public void walk(){
    //Do walking operations here
    System.out.println("Walking...");
}
public void sleep(){
    //Do sleeping operations here
    System.out.println("Sleeping...");
}
private void takeShower(){
    //Do take shower operations here
    System.out.println("Taking a shower...");
}
```

4. Now, pass the **speed** parameter to the **walk()** method. If the **speed** is above 10, we print the output to the console, otherwise we don't:

```
public void walk(int speed){
    //Do walking operations here
    if (speed > 10)
{
        System.out.println("Walking...");
}
```

5. Now that we have the **Person** class, we can create objects for it using the **new** keyword. In the following code, we have created three objects:

```
Person me = new Person();
Person myNeighbour = new Person();
Person lecturer = new Person();
```

The **me** variable is now an object of the **Person** class. It represents a specific type of person, me.

With this object, we can do anything we wish, such as calling the **walk()** method, calling the **sleep()** method, and much more. We can do this as long as there are methods in the class. Later, we will look at how we can add all of this behavior to a class. This code will not have any output since we do not have the **main** method.

Exercise 12: Using the Person Class

To call the member functions of a class, perform the following steps:

1. Create a new class in IntelliJ called **PersonTest**.

2. Inside the **PersonTest** class, create the **main** method.

3. Inside the **main** method, create three objects of the **Person** class

    ```
    public static void main(String[] args){
    Person me = new Person();
    Person myNeighbour = new Person();
    Person lecturer = new Person();
    ```

4. Call the **walk()** method for the first object:

    ```
    me.walk(20);
    me.walk(5);
    me.sleep();
    ```

5. Run the class and observe the output:

    ```
    Walking...
    Sleeping…
    ```

6. Do the same using the **myNeighbour** and **lecturer** objects instead of **me**:

    ```
    myNeighbour.walk(20);
    myNeighbour.walk(5);
    myNeighbour.sleep();

    lecturer.walk(20);
    lecturer.walk(5);
    lecturer.sleep();
    }
    ```

7. Run the program again and observe the output:

    ```
    Walking...
    Sleeping...
    Walking...
    Sleeping...
    Walking...
    Sleeping...
    ```

In this example, we created a new class called **PersonTest** and inside it created three objects of the **Person** class. We then called the methods of the **me** object. From this program, it is evident that the **Person** class is a blueprint from which we can create as many objects as we wish. We can manipulate each of these objects separately as they are completely different and independent. We can pass these objects around as if they were just like any other variables, and can even pass them to other objects as parameters. This is the flexibility of object-oriented programming.

> **Note**
>
> We didn't call **me.takeShower()** because this method is declared private in the **Person** class. Private methods cannot be called outside their class.

Constructors

To be able to create an object of a class, we need a constructor. A constructor is called when you want to create an object of a class. When we create a class without a constructor, Java creates an empty default constructor for us that takes no parameters. If a class is created without a constructor, we can still instantiate it with the default constructor. A good example of this is the **Person** class that we used previously. When we wanted a new object of the **Person** class, we wrote the following:

```
Person me = new Person();
```

The default constructor is **Person()**, and it returns a new instance of the **Person** class. We then assign this returned instance to our variable, **me**.

A constructor is just like any other method, except for a few differences:

- A constructor has the same name as the class

- A constructor can be **public** or **private**

- A constructor doesn't return anything, even **void**

Let's look at an example. Let's create a simple constructor for our **Person** class:

```java
public class Person {
    //Properties
    int age;
    int height;
    String name;
    //Constructor
    public Person(int myAge){
        age = myAge;
    }

    //Methods
    public void walk(int speed){
        //Do walking operations here
        if (speed > 10)
            System.out.println("Walking...");
    }
    public void sleep(){
        //Do sleeping operations here
        System.out.println("Sleeping...");
    }
    private void takeShower(){
        //Do take shower operations here
        System.out.println("Taking a shower...");
    }
}
```

This constructor takes one argument, an integer called myAge, and assigns its value to the age property in the class. Remember that the constructor implicitly returns an instance of the class.

We can use the constructor to create the me object again, this time passing age:

```java
Person me = new Person(30);
```

The this Keyword

In our **Person** class, we saw the following line in our constructor:

```
age = myAge;
```

In this line, as we saw earlier, we are setting the **age** variable in our current object to the new value, **myAge**, which is passed in as a parameter. Sometimes, we wish to be explicit about the object we are referring to. When we want to refer to the properties in the current object we are dealing with, we use the **this** keyword. As an example, we could rewrite the preceding line as follows:

```
this.age = myAge;
```

In this new line, **this.age** is used to refer to the age property in the current object we are dealing with. **this** is used to access the current object's instance variables.

For example, in the preceding line, we are setting the current object's **age** to the value that's passed into the constructor.

In addition to referring to the current object, **this** can also be used to invoke a class' other constructors if you have more than one constructor.

In our **Person** class, we will create a second constructor that takes no parameter. If this constructor is invoked, it invokes the other constructor we created with a default value of 28:

```
//Constructor
public Person(int myAge){
    this.age = myAge;
}
public Person(){
    this(28);
}
```

Now, when the call of **Person me = new Person()** is made, the second constructor will call the first constructor with **myAge** set to 28. The first constructor will then set the current object's **age** to 28.

Activity 12: Creating a Simple Class in Java

Scenario: Let's imagine we want to create a program for an animal farm. In this program, we need to keep track of all the animals that are on the farm. To start with, we need a way to represent the animals. We will create an animal class to represent a single animal and then create instances of this class to represent the specific animals themselves.

Objective: We will create a Java class to represent animals and create instances of that class. By the end of this activity, we should have a simple `Animal` class and a few instances of that class.

Aim: To understand how to create classes and objects in Java.

Follow these steps to complete the activity

1. Create a new project in the IDE and name it `Animals`.

2. In the project, create a new file called `Animal.java` under the **src/** folder.

3. Create a class named `Animal` and add the instance variables `legs`, `ears`, `eyes`, `family`, and `name`.

4. Define a constructor with no parameters and initialize `legs` to 4, `ears` to 2, and `eyes` to 2.

5. Define another parameterized constructor which takes the `legs`, `ears`, and `eyes` as arguments.

6. Add getters and setters for `name` and `family`.

7. Create another file called `Animals.java`, define the `main` method, and create two objects of the `Animal` class.

8. Create another animal with two `legs`, two `ears`, and two `eyes`.

9. To set the animals' `name` and `family`, we will use the getters and setters we created in the class and print names of the animals.

The output should be similar to the following:

```
Cow
Goat
Anatidae
```

Figure 4.3: Output of the Animal class

> **Note**
>
> The solution for this activity can be found on page 314.

Activity 13: Writing a Calculator Class

For this activity you'll create a Calculator class that, given two operands and one operator, can execute the operation and return the result. This class will have one operate method which will execute the operation using the two operands. The operands and the operator will be fields in the class, set through the constructor.

With the Calculator class ready, write an application that executes some sample operations and prints the results to the console.

To complete this activity you'll need to:

1. Create a class **Calculator** with three fields: **double operand1**, **double operand2** and **String operator**. Add a constructor that sets all three fields.

2. In this class, add an **operate** method that will check what operator is ("+", "-", "x" or "/") and executes the correct operation, returning the result.

3. Add a **main** method to this class so that you can write a few sample cases and print the results.

> **Note**
>
> The solution for this activity can be found on page 318.

Inheritance

In this section, we will have a look at another important principle of OOP, called inheritance. Inheritance in OOP has the same meaning as it has in English. Let's look at an example by using our family trees. Our parents inherit from our grandparents. We then inherit from our parents, and finally, our children inherit, or will inherit, from us. Similarly, a class can inherit the properties of another class. These properties include methods and fields. Then, another class can still inherit from it, and so on. This forms what we call an **inheritance hierarchy**.

The class being inherited from is called the **superclass** or the **base** class, and the class that is inheriting is called the **subclass** or the **derived** class. In Java, a class can only inherit from one superclass.

Types of Inheritance

An example of inheritance is a management hierarchy in a company or in the government:

- **Single Level Inheritance**: In single level inheritance, a class inherits from only one other class:

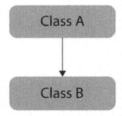

Figure 4.4: Representation of single level inheritance

- **Multi-level inheritance**: In multi-level inheritance, a class can inherit from another class that also inherits from another class:

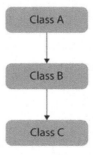

Figure 4.5: Representation of multi-level inheritance

- **Multiple inheritance**: Here, a class can inherit from more than one class:

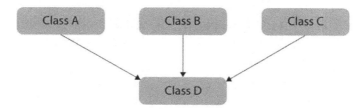

Figure 4.6: Representation of multiple inheritance

Multiple inheritance is not directly supported in Java, but can be achieved by using **interfaces**, which will be covered in the next lesson.

Importance of Inheritance in OOP

Let's go back to our **Person** class.

It is clear that there are common properties and actions that all people support, despite their gender or race. For example, in terms of properties, everyone has a name, and everyone has an age, height, and weight. With regard to common actions, all people sleep, all people eat, and all people breathe, among other things.

Instead of writing code for all of these properties and methods in all of our **Person** classes, we can define all of these common properties and actions in one class and let the other Person classes inherit from this class. That way, we won't have to rewrite the properties and methods in these subclasses. Therefore, inheritance allows us to write more concise code by reusing code.

The syntax for a class to inherit from another class is as follows:

```
class SubClassName extends SuperClassName {



}
```

We use the **extends** keyword to denote inheritance.

For example, if we wanted our **Student** class to extend the **Person** class, we would declare it like so:

```
public class Student extends Person {



}
```

In this **Student** class, we have access to the public properties and methods that we defined earlier in the **Person** class. When we create an instance of this **Student** class, we automatically have access to the methods we defined in the **Person** class earlier, such as **walk()** and **sleep()**. We don't need to recreate those methods anymore as our **Student** class is now a subclass of the **Person** class. We, however, don't have access to private methods such as **takeShower()**.

> **Note**
>
> Please note that a subclass only has access to the public properties and methods in its superclass. If a property or method is declared as private in the superclass, we cannot access it from the subclass. By default, the properties we declared are only accessible from classes in the same package, unless we specifically put the **public** modifier before them.

In our **Person** class, let's define some common properties and methods that all people have. Then, we will inherit these properties from this class to create other classes, such as **Student** and **Lecturer**:

```
public class Person {
    //Properties
    int age;
    int height;
    int weight;
    String name;
    //Constructors
    public Person(int myAge, int myHeight, int myWeight){
        this.age = myAge;
        this.height = myHeight;
        this.weight = myWeight;
    }
    public Person(){
        this(28, 10, 60);
    }
```

```
    //Methods
    public void walk(int speed){
        if (speed > 10)
            System.out.println("Walking...");
    }
    public void sleep(){
        System.out.println("Sleeping...");
    }
    public  void setName(String name){
        this.name = name;
    }
    public String getName(){
        return name;
    }
    public int getAge(){
        return age;
    }
    public int getHeight(){
        return height;
    }
    public int getWeight(){
        return weight;
    }
}
```

Here, we have defined four properties, two constructors, and seven methods. Can you explain what each method does? The methods are fairly simple for now so that we can focus on the core concepts of inheritance. We have also modified the constructors to take three parameters.

Let's create a **Student** class that inherits from this **Person** class, create an object of the class, and set the name of the student:

```
public class Student extends Person {
    public static void main(String[] args){
        Student student = new Student();
        student.setName("James Gosling");
    }
}
```

We have created a new **Student** class that inherits from the **Person** class. We have also created a new instance of the **Student** class and set its name. Note that we didn't redefine the **setName()** method in the **Student** class because it is already defined in the **Person** class. We can also call other methods on our **student** object:

```
public class Student extends Person {
    public static void main(String[] args){
        Student student = new Student();
            student.setName("James Gosling");
            student.walk(20);
        student.sleep();
        System.out.println(student.getName());
        System.out.println(student.getAge());
    }
}
```

Note that we did not create these methods in the **Student** class as they are already defined in the **Person** class from which the **Student** class inherits.

Implementing Inheritance in Java

Write down the expected output of the preceding program. Explain the output by looking at the program.

The solution was:

```
Walking...
Sleeping...
James Gosling
28
```

Let's define a **Lecturer** class that inherits from the same **Person** class:

```
public class Lecturer extends Person {
    public static void main(String[] args){
        Lecturer lecturer = new Lecturer();
        lecturer.setName("Prof. James Gosling");
        lecturer.walk(20);
        lecturer.sleep();
        System.out.println(lecturer.getName());
        System.out.println(lecturer.getAge());
    }
}
```

> **Note**
>
> Please note how Inheritance has helped us reduce the amount of code we write by reusing the same **Person** class. Without inheritance, we would have had to repeat the same methods and properties in all of our classes.

Activity 14: Creating a Calculator Using Inheritance

In the previous activity, you created a **Calculator** class that contained all the known operations in the same class. This makes this class harder to extend when you think about adding new operations. The operator method would grow indefinitely.

To make this better, you will use OOP practices to split the operator logic out of this class into its own class. In this activity you'll create a class Operator that defaults to the sum operation and then three other classes that implement the other three operations: subtraction, multiplication and division. This Operator class has a **matches** method that, given a String returns a boolean that is true if the String represents that operator or false if not.

With the operation logic in their own classes, write a new class called **CalculatorWithFixedOperators** with three fields: **double operand1**, **double operand2** and **operator** of type **Operator**. This class will have the same constructor that the previous calculator, but instead of storing the operator as a String, it will check for the operator classes using the matches method to determine the correct operator.

As the previous calculator, this calculator also has a method operate that returns a double, but instead of any login in there, it delegates the current operator, determined in the constructor.

To complete this activity you'll need to:

1. Create a class **Operator** that has one String field initialized in the constructor that represents the operator. This class should have a default constructor that represents the default operator, which is **sum**. The operator class should also have a method called operate that receives two doubles and return the result of the operator as a double. The default operation is sum.

2. Create three other classes: **Subtraction**, **Multiplication** and **Division**. They extend from Operator and override the **operate** method with each operation that they represent. They also need a no-argument constructor that calls super passing the operator that they represent.

3. Create a new class, called **CalculatorWithFixedOperators**. This class will contain four fields that are constants (finals) and represent the four possible operations. It should also have three other fields: **operand1** and **operator2** of type double and **operator** of type **Operator**. These other three fields will be initialized in the constructor that will receive the operands and the operator as a String. Using the match methods of the possible operators, determine which one will be set as the operator fields.

4. As the previous **Calculator** class, this one will also have an **operate** method, but it will only delegate to the **operator** instance.

5. Last, write a **main** method that calls the new calculator a few times, printing the results of the operation for each time.

> **Note**
>
> Rewriting the calculator to use more classes seems more complex than the initial code. But it abstracts some important behavior which opens some possibilities that will be explored in future activities.

> **Note**
>
> The solution for this activity can be found on page 319.

Overloading

The next principle of OOP we will discuss is called overloading. Overloading is a powerful concept in OOP that allows us to reuse method names as long as they have different signatures. A **method signature** is the method name, its parameters, and the order of the parameters:

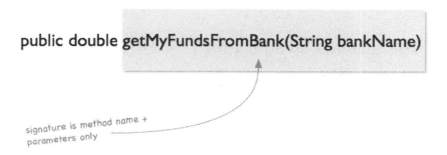

Figure 4.7: Representation of a method signature

The preceding is an example of a method that withdraws funds from a given bank name. The method returns a double and accepts a String parameter. The method signature here is the name of the **getMyFundsFromBank()** method and the String parameter **bankName**. The signature doesn't include the return type of the method, only the name and the parameters.

With overloading, we are able to define more than one method with the same method names but different parameters. This can be useful in defining methods that do the same thing but take different parameters.

Let's look at an example.

Let's define a class called **Sum** with three overloaded methods that add the parameters that are passed and returns the result:

```
public class Sum {

    //This sum takes two int parameters
    public int sum(int x, int y) {
        return (x + y);
    }


    //This sum takes three int parameters
    public int sum(int x, int y, int z) {
```

```
        return (x + y + z);
    }
    //This sum takes two double parameters
    public double sum(double x, double y) {
        return (x + y);
    }

    public static void main(String args[]) {
        Sum s = new Sum();
        System.out.println(s.sum(10, 20));
        System.out.println(s.sum(10, 20, 30));
        System.out.println(s.sum(10.5, 20.5));
    }
}
```

The output is as follows:

```
30
60
31.0
```

In this example, the sum() method is overloaded to take different parameters and return the sum. The method name is the same, but each of the methods takes a different set of parameters. This difference in the method signatures allows us to use the same name as many times as we wish.

You might be wondering about the benefits overloading brings to OOP. Imagine a scenario where we wouldn't be able to reuse a certain method name more than once, as in certain languages, such as C. For us to be able to accept different sets of parameters, we would need to come up with six different method names. Coming up with six different names for methods that essentially do the same thing is tiresome and painful when dealing with large programs. Overloading saves us from such scenarios.

Let's go back to our **Student** class and create two overloaded methods. In the first method, we will print a string to print "Going to class...", regardless of which day of the week it is. In the second method, we will pass the day of the week and check whether it is the weekend. If it is the weekend, we will print out a different string in comparison to the rest of the week. Here is how we will implement this:

```java
public class Student extends Person {
    //Add this
    public void goToClass(){
        System.out.println("Going to class...");
    }
    public void goToClass(int dayOfWeek){
        if (dayOfWeek == 6 || dayOfWeek == 7){
            System.out.println("It's the weekend! Not to going to class!");
        }else {
            System.out.println("Going to class...");
        }
    }
    public static void main(String[] args){

        Student student = new Student();
        student.setName("James Gosling");
        student.walk(20);
        student.sleep();
        System.out.println(student.getName());
        System.out.println(student.getAge());

        //Add this
        student.goToClass();
        student.goToClass(6);
    }
}
```

The output is as follows::

```
Walking...
Sleeping...
James Gosling
28
Going to class...
It's the weekend! Not to going to class!
```

Open the **Lecturer** class we created and add two overloaded methods, as follows:

- **teachClass()** prints out "Teaching a random class"
- **teachClass(String className)** prints out "**Teaching** " + **className**

Following is the code:

```
public void teachClass(){
    System.out.println("Teaching a random class.");
}
public void teachClass(String className){
    System.out.println("Teaching " + className);
}
```

We can overload the main method in a class, but once the program starts up, the JVM will only call **main(String[] args)**. We can call our overloaded **main** method from this **main** method. Here is an example:

```
public class Student {
    public static void main(String[] args){
        // Will be called by the JVM
    }
    public static void main(String[] args, String str1, int num){
        //Do some operations
    }
    public static void main(int num, int num1, String str){

    }
}
```

In this example, the `main` method is overloaded three times. However, when we run our program, the main method whose signature is `main(String[] args)` will be called. From anywhere in our code, we can then freely call the other main methods.

Constructor Overloading

Just like methods, constructors can be overloaded too. When the same constructors are declared with different parameters in the same class, this is known as **constructor overloading**. The compiler differentiates which constructor is to be called, depending on the number of parameters and their data types.

In our discussion on constructors, we created a second constructor for our `Person` class that takes `age`, `height`, and `weight` as parameters. We can have this constructor in the same class as the constructor that takes in no parameters. This is because the two constructors have a different signature and can hence be used side by side. Let's look at how we can do this:

```
//Constructors
public Person(){
    this(28, 10, 60);
}
//Overloaded constructor
public Person(int myAge, int myHeight, int myWeight){
    this.age = myAge;
    this.height = myHeight;
    this.weight = myWeight;
}
```

The two constructors have same name (the class name) but take different parameters.

Add a third constructor that takes `age`, `height`, `weight`, and `name`. Inside the constructor, set all the class variables to the passed parameters.

The code is as follows:

```
public Person(int myAge, int myHeight, int myWeight, String name){
    this.age = myAge;
    this.height = myHeight;
    this.weight = myWeight;
    this.name = name;
}
```

Polymorphism and Overriding

The next principle of OOP we will cover is called polymorphism. The term "**polymorphism**" stems from biology in that an organism can take many forms and stages. This term is also used in OOP in that sub-classes can define their unique behaviors yet still share some functionalities with their parent classes.

Let's illustrate this with an example.

In our **Person** example, we had a method, **walk**. In our **Student** class, which inherits from the **Person** class, we will redefine the same **walk** method, but now walking to class instead of just walking. In our **Lecturer** class, we will also redefine the same **walk** method and this time walk to the staff room instead of walking to class. This method must have the same signature and return type as the **walk** method in the superclass for this to be considered polymorphic. Here is what the implementation looks like in our **Student** class:

```
public class Student extends Person {

    ….

    public void walk(int speed){
        //Walk to class
        System.out.println("Walking to class ..");
    }
    ….…
}
```

When we call **student.walk(20)**, this method in our **Student** class will be called instead of the same method in the **Person** class. That is, we have provided a unique way to walk for our **Student** class that isn't the same for the **Lecturer** and **Person** classes.

In Java, we refer to such a method as overridden and the process as method overriding. The Java virtual machine (JVM) calls the appropriate method for the object that is referred.

The Difference between Overriding and Overloading

Let's have a look at the difference between method overloading and overriding:

- Method overloading deals with the notion of having two or more methods in the same class with the same name but different arguments:

```
void foo(int a)
void foo(int a, float b)
```

- Method overriding means having two methods with the same arguments, but different implementations. One of them would exist in the parent class, while another would exist in the child class:

```
class Parent {
    void foo(double d) {
        // do something
    }
}

class Child extends Parent {


    void foo(double d){
        // this method is overridden.
    }
}
```

Annotations

We will now cover another important topic that will help us write better Java programs.

Annotations are a way in which we can add metadata to our programs. This metadata can include information such as the version of a class we are developing. This is useful in scenarios where a class is deprecated or where we are overriding a certain method. Such metadata is not part of the program itself, but can help us catch errors or offer guidance. Annotations have no direct effect on the operation of the code they annotate.

Let's look at a scenario. How do we ensure that we are overriding a certain method and not creating another completely different method? When overriding a method, a single mistake such as using a different return type will cause the method to not be overridden anymore. Such a mistake is easy to make but can lead to software bugs later on if not taken care of early in the software development stages. How, then, do we enforce overriding? The answer, as you might have already guessed, is using annotations.

The @ character indicates to the compiler that what follows is an annotation.

Let's enforce overriding in our **Student** class with an annotation:

```
@Override
public void walk(int speed){
    //Walk to class
    System.out.println("Walking to class ..");
}
```

Note that we have added the **@Override** line above the method name to indicate that the method is overridden from the superclass. This annotation will be checked by the compiler when you're compiling the program and it will immediately know that we are trying to override this method. It will check whether this method exists in the superclass and whether the overriding has been done correctly. If it hasn't, it will report an error to indicate that the method is not correct. This, in a way, will have prevented us from making a mistake.

Java contains built-in annotations, and you can also create your own. Annotations can be applied to declarations of classes, properties, methods, and other program elements. When used on a declaration, each annotation appears, by convention, on its own line. Let's look at a few examples of the built-in annotations in Java:

Annotation	Use
@Override	Used to indicate that the element is meant to override an element from the superclass.
@Deprecated	Indicates that a certain method is deprecated and should no longer be used.

Table 4.1: Table with different annotations and their use

Creating Your Own Annotation Types

Annotations are created using the **interface** keyword. Let's declare an annotation so that we can add the author information of a class:

```
public @interface Author {
    String name();
    String date();
}
```

This annotation accepts the name of the author and the date. We can then use this annotation in our **Student** class:

```
@Author(name = "James Gosling", date = "1/1/1970")
public class Student extends Person {
}
```

You can replace the name and date with your values in the preceding example.

References

As you work with objects, it is important that you understand **references**. A reference is an address that indicates where an object's variables and methods are stored.

When we assign objects to variables or pass them to methods as parameters, we aren't actually passing the object itself or its copy – we are passing references to the objects themselves in memory.

To better understand how references work, let's illustrate this with an example.

Following is an example:

Create a new class called **Rectangle**, as follows:

```
public class Rectangle {

    int width;
    int height;

    public Rectangle(int width, int height){
        this.width = width;
        this.height = height;
    }
}
```

```java
public static void main(String[] args){
    Rectangle r1, r2;

    r1 = new Rectangle(100, 200);
    r2 = r1;

    r1.height = 300;
    r1.width = 400;
    System.out.println("r1: width= " + r1.width + ", height= " +
r1.height);
    System.out.println("r2: width= " + r2.width + ", height= " +
r2.height);


}
}
```

The output is as follows::

```
r1: width= 400, height= 300
r2: width= 400, height= 300
```

Here is a summary of what happens in the preceding program:

1. We create two variables, **r1** and **r2**, of type **Rectangle**.

2. A new **Rectangle** object is assigned to **r1**.

3. The value of **r1** is assigned to **r2**.

4. The width and height of **r2** are changed.

5. The values of the two objects are finally printed.

You might have expected the values of **r1** and **r2** to have different values. However, the output says otherwise. This is because when we used **r2** = **r1** , we created a reference from **r2** to **r1** instead of creating **r2** as a new object copied from **r1**. That is, **r2** points to the same object that was pointed to by **r1**. Either variable can be used to refer to the object and change its variables:

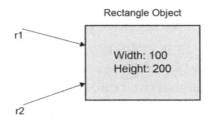

Figure 4.8: Representation of objects r1, r2

If you want **r2** to refer to a new object, use the following code:

```
r1 = new Rectangle(100, 200);
r2 = new Rectangle(300, 400);
```

References in Java become particularly important when arguments are passed to methods.

> **Note**
>
> There are no explicit pointers or pointer arithmetic in Java, as there is in C and C++. By using references, however, most pointer capabilities are duplicated without many of their drawbacks.

Activity 15: Understanding Inheritance and Polymorphism in Java

Scenario: Imagine we want our **Animals** class we created in Activity one to be more object oriented. That way, it would be easier to maintain it and scale it in the future in case our farm needs to.

Objective: We are going to create classes to inherit from our **Animals** class, implement overloaded and overridden methods, and create an annotation to version our classes.

Aim: To understand how to inherit from a class, overload and override methods, and create annotations in Java.

Procedure:

1. Open up the `Animals` project we created earlier.

2. In the project, create a new file named `Cat.java` in the `src/` folder.

3. Open `Cat.java` and inherit from the `Animals` class.

4. In it, create a new instance of the `Cat` class and set the family to "Cat", the name to "Puppy", `ears` to two, `eyes` to two, and `legs` to four. Don't redefine these methods and fields – instead, use the inherited ones from the `Animals` class.

5. Print the `family`, `name`, `ears`, `legs`, and `eyes`. What is the output?

> **Note**
>
> The solution for this activity can be found on page 322.

Summary

In this lesson, we have learned that classes are blueprints from which we can create objects, while objects are instances of a class and provide a specific implementation of that class. A class can be public, private, or protected. A class has a default constructor that takes no parameters. We can have user-defined constructors in Java. The **this** keyword is used to refer to the current instance of a class.

We then learned that inheritance is a property where a subclass inherits the properties of a superclass.

We went on to study overloading, polymorphism, annotation, and references in Java.

In the next lesson, we will have a look at the use of interfaces and the **Object** class in Java.

5

OOP in Depth

Learning Objectives

By the end of this lesson, you will be able to:

- Implement interfaces in Java
- Perform typecasting
- Utilize the **Object** class
- Work with abstract classes and methods

Introduction

In the previous lesson, we looked at the basics of object-oriented programming, such as classes and objects, inheritance, polymorphism, and overloading.

We saw how classes act as a blueprint from which we can create objects, and saw how methods define the behavior of a class while fields hold the state.

We looked at how a class can acquire properties from another class through inheritance to enable us to reuse code. Then, we learned how we can reuse a method name through overloading – that is, as long as they have different signatures. Finally, we had a look at how subclasses can redefine their own unique behavior by overriding methods from the superclass.

In this lesson, we will delve deeper into the principles of object-oriented programming and how to better structure our Java programs.

We will start with interfaces, which are constructs that allow us to define a generic behavior that any class can implement. We will then learn about a concept called **typecasting**, whereby we can change a variable from one type to another and back. In the same manner, we will deal with primitive data types as objects by using wrapper classes that are provided by Java. We will finish off with a detailed look at abstract classes and methods, which is a way to let users who are inheriting your class to run their own unique implementation.

In this lesson, we will walk through three activities by using the `Animal` class we created in the previous lesson. We will also be using our `Person` class to demonstrate some of these concepts.

Let's get started!

Interfaces

In Java, you can use interfaces to provide a set of methods that classes must implement for them to be conformant.

Let's take the example of our `Person` class. We want to define a set of actions that define the behavior of any person, regardless of their age or gender.

A few examples of these actions include sleeping, breathing, and moving/walking. We can place all of these common actions in an interface and let any class that claims to be a person implement them. A class that implements this interface is often referred to as being of the type `Person`.

In Java, we use the keyword interface to denote that the following block will be an interface. All the methods in an interface are empty and are not implemented. This is because any class that will implement this interface will provide its unique implementation details. Therefore, an interface is essentially a group of methods with no bodies.

Let's create an interface to define the behavior of a person:

```
public interface PersonBehavior {

    void breathe();

    void sleep();

    void walk(int speed);

}
```

This interface is called **PersonBehavior** and it contains three methods: one to breathe, another one to sleep, and one to walk at a given speed. Every class that implements this interface will have to also implement these three methods.

We use the **implements** keyword after a class name, followed by the interface name, when we want to implement a given interface.

Let's see this with an example. We will create a new class called **Doctor** to represent doctors. This class will implement the **PersonBehavior** interface:

```
public class Doctor implements PersonBehavior {


}
```

Because we have stated that we want to conform to the **PersonBehavior** interface, the compiler will give us an error if we don't implement the three methods in the interface:

```
public class Doctor implements PersonBehavior {

    @Override
    public void breathe() {


    }
    @Override
    public void sleep() {


    }
    @Override
```

```java
    public void walk(int speed) {


    }
```

We use the **@Override** annotation to indicate that this method is from the interface. Inside these methods, we are free to perform any kind of operations that are relevant to our **Doctor** class.

In the same spirit, we can also create an **Engineer** class that implements the same interface:

```java
public class Engineer implements PersonBehavior {

    @Override
    public void breathe() {


    }
    @Override
    public void sleep() {


    }
    @Override
    public void walk(int speed) {


    }
}
```

In *Lesson 1, Introduction to Java*, we mentioned abstraction as one of the underlying principles of OOP. Abstraction is a way for us to provide a consistent interface to our classes.

Let's use a mobile phone as an example. With a mobile phone, you are able to call and text your friends. When calling, you press the call button and immediately get connected to a friend. That call button forms an interface between you and your friend. We don't really know what happens when we press the button because all those details are abstracted (hidden) from us.

You will often hear the term **API**, which stands for Application Programming Interface. It is a way for different software to speak to each other in harmony. An example is when you want to log in to an app using Facebook or Google. The application will call the Facebook or Google API. The Facebook API will then define the rules to be followed to log in.

A class in Java can implement more than one interface. These extra interfaces are separated by a comma. The class must provide implementations for all the methods it promises to implement in the interfaces:

```
public class ClassName implements  InterfaceA, InterfaceB, InterfaceC {



}
```

Use Case: Listeners

One of the most important uses of interfaces is creating listeners for conditions or events in your programs. Basically, a listener notifies you of any state changes when an action takes place. Listeners are also called callbacks – a term that stems from procedural languages.

For example, an event listener could be called when a button is clicked or hovered over.

This kind of event-driven programming is popular for making Android apps using Java.

Imagine that we want to know when a person walks or sleeps so that we can perform some other actions. We can achieve this by using an interface that listens for such events. We will look at this in the following exercise.

Exercise 13: Implementing Interfaces

We are going to create an interface called **PersonListener** that listens for two events: **onPersonWalking** and **onPersonSleeping**. When the **walk(int speed)** method is called, we will dispatch the **onPersonWalking** event, and when **sleep()** is called, **onPersonSleeping** will be called:

1. Create an interface called **PersonListener** and paste the following code inside it:

```
public interface PersonListener {
    void onPersonWalking();
    void onPersonSleeping();
}
```

2. Open our **Doctor** class and add the **PersonListener** interface after the **PersonBehavior** interface, separated by a comma:

```
public class Doctor implements PersonBehavior, PersonListener {
```

3. Implement the two methods in our **PersonListener** interface. When the doctor walks, we will perform some actions and raise the **onPersonWalking** event to let other listeners know that the doctor is walking. When the doctor sleeps, we shall raise the **onPersonSleeping** event. Modify the **walk()** and **sleep()** methods to look like this:

```
@Override
public void breathe() {

}
@Override
public void sleep() {
    //TODO: Do other operations here
    // then raise event
    this.onPersonSleeping();
}
@Override
public void walk(int speed) {
    //TODO: Do other operations here
    // then raise event
    this.onPersonWalking();
}
@Override
public void onPersonWalking() {
    System.out.println("Event: onPersonWalking");
}
@Override
public void onPersonSleeping() {
    System.out.println("Event: onPersonSleeping");
}
```

4. Add the main method to test our code by calling **walk()** and **sleep()**:

```
public static void main(String[] args){
    Doctor myDoctor = new Doctor();
    myDoctor.walk(20);
    myDoctor.sleep();
}
```

5. Run the **Doctor** class and see the output in the console. You should see something like this:

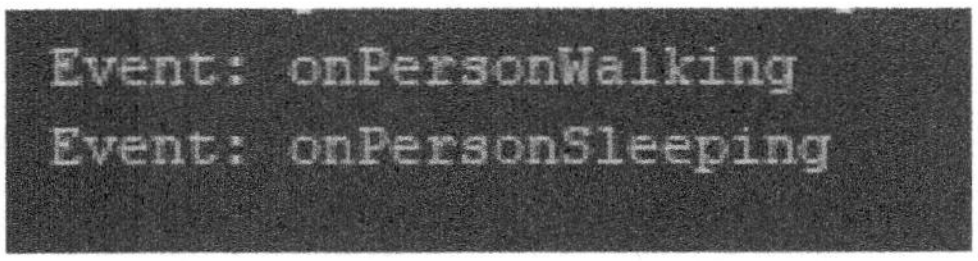

Figure 5.1: Output of the Doctor class

The full **Doctor** class is as follows:

```java
public class Doctor implements PersonBehavior, PersonListener {

    public static void main(String[] args){
        Doctor myDoctor = new Doctor();

        myDoctor.walk(20);
        myDoctor.sleep();
    }
    @Override
    public void breathe() {

    }
    @Override
    public void sleep() {
        //TODO: Do other operations here
        // then raise event
        this.onPersonSleeping();
    }
    @Override
    public void walk(int speed) {
        //TODO: Do other operations here
        // then raise event
        this.onPersonWalking();
    }
    @Override
    public void onPersonWalking() {
        System.out.println("Event: onPersonWalking");
    }
    @Override
```

```
        public void onPersonSleeping() {
            System.out.println("Event: onPersonSleeping");
        }
    }
```

> **Note**
>
> Since a class can implement more than one interface, we can use interfaces in Java to simulate multiple inheritance.

Activity 16: Creating and Implementing Interfaces in Java

Scenario: In our animal farm from the previous lesson, we wish to have common actions that all animals must possess, regardless of their type. We want to also know when an animal has moved or made any sound. A movement can help us keep track of where each animal is and the sound can be indicative of distress.

Objective: We are going to implement two interfaces: one that holds two actions that all animals must possess, **move()** and **makeSound()**, and the other that listens for movement and sound from the animals.

Aim: To understand how to create interfaces in Java and implement them.

These steps will help you complete this activity:

1. Open your **Animals** project from the previous lesson.

2. Create a new interface called **AnimalBehavior**.

3. In this, create two methods: **void move()** and **void makeSound()**

4. Create another interface called **AnimalListener** with **onAnimalMoved()** and **onAnimalSound()** method.

5. Create a new public class called **Cow** and implement the **AnimalBehavior** and **AnimalListener** interface.

6. Create instance variable sound and **movementType** in **Cow** class.

7. Override the **move()** such that the **movementType** is "Walking" and the **onAnimalMoved()** method is called.

8. Override the **makeSound()** such that **movementType** is "Moo" and the **onAnimalMoved()** method is called.

9. Override the **onAnimalMoved()** and **inAnimalMadeSound()** methods.

10. Create a **main()** to test the code.

The output should be similar to the following:

```
Animal moved: Walking
Sound made: Move
```

> **Note**
>
> The solution for this activity can be found on page 323.

Typecasting

We have already seen how, when we write **int a = 10**, **a** is of integer data type, which is usually 32 bits in size. When we write **char c = 'a'**, **c** has a data type of character. These data types were referred to as primitive types because they can be used to hold simple information.

Objects also have types. The type of an object is often the class of that object. For example, when we create an object such as **Doctor myDoctor = new Doctor()**, the **myDoctor** object is of type **Doctor**. The **myDoctor** variable is often referred to as a reference type. As we discussed earlier, this is because the **myDoctor** variable doesn't hold the object itself. Rather, it holds the reference to the object in memory.

Typecasting is a way for us to change the class or interface from one type to another. It's important to note that only classes or interfaces (together, these are called types) that belong to the same superclass or implement the same interface, that is, they have a parent-child relationship, can be cast or converted into each other.

Let's go back to our **Person** example. We created the **Student** class, which inherits from this class. This essentially means that the **Student** class is in the **Person** family and so is any other class that inherits from the **Person** class:

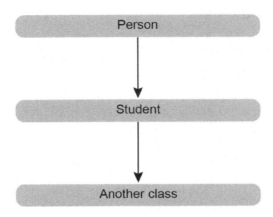

Figure 5.2: Inheriting the subclass from the base class

We typecast in Java by using brackets before the object:

```
Student student = new Student();

Person person = (Person)student;
```

In this example, we have created an object of type **Student** called **student**. We then typecast it to a **Person** by using the **(Person)student** statement. This statement labels **student** as a **Person** type instead of **Student** type. This type of typecasting, where we label the subclass as a superclass, is called upcasting. This operation doesn't change the original object; it only labels it as a different type.

Upcasting reduces the number of methods we have access to. For example, the **student** variable cannot access the methods and fields in the **Student** class anymore.

We convert **student** back to the **Student** type by performing downcasting:

```
Student student = new Student();

Person person = (Person)student;

Student newStudent = (Student)person;
```

Downcasting is the conversion of a superclass type into a subclass type. This operation gives us access to the methods and fields in the subclass. For example, **newStudent** now has access to all the methods in the **Student** class.

For downcasting to work, the object must have originally been of the subclass type. For example, the following operation is not possible:

```
Student student = new Student();

Person person = (Person)student;

Lecturer lecturer = (Lecturer) person;
```

If you try to run this program, you will get the following exception:

Exception in thread "main" java.lang.ClassCastException: Class Student cannot be cast to class Lecturer (Student and Lecturer are in unnamed module of loader 'app')
    at Student.main(Student.java:11)

Figure 5.3: Exception message while downcasting

This is because **person** was not originally a **Lecturer** type, but rather a **Student** type. We will talk more about exceptions in the upcoming lessons.

To avoid such kinds of exceptions, you can use the **instanceof** operator to first check whether an object is of a given type:

```
if (person instanceof  Lecturer) {

  Lecturer lecturer() = (Lecturer) person;

}
```

The **instanceof** operator returns **true** if **person** was originally of type **Lecturer**, or returns false otherwise.

Activity 17: Using instanceof and Typecasting

On previous activity, you used interface to declare common methods around salary and tax on the Employee interface. With the expansion of JavaWorks limited, salespeople started to get commission. That means that now, you'll need to write a new class: **SalesWithCommission**. This class will extends from **Sales**, which means it has all the behavior that employees have but will also have an additional method: **getCommission**. This new method returns the gross sales of this employee (which will be passed in the constructor) times the sales commission, which is 15% for all.

As part of this activity, you'll also write a class that has a method that generates employees. This will serve as the **datasource** for this and other activities. This **EmployeeLoader** class will have one method: **getEmployee()**, which returns an Employee. Inside this method, you can use any means to return a newly generated employee. Using the **java.util.Random** class might help you to accomplish this and still get consistency if you need it.

With your data source and the new **SalesWithCommission**, you'll write an application that will call the **EmployeeLoader.getEmployee** method a few times using a **for** loop. With each generated employee, it will print their net salary and the tax they pay. It will also check if the employee is an instance of **SalesWithCommission**, cast it and print his commission.

To complete this activity you'll need to:

1. Create a **SalesWithCommission** class that extends **Sales**. Add a constructor that receives the gross sales as double and store it as a field. Also add a method called **getCommission** which returns a double that is the gross sales times 15% (0.15).

2. Create another class that will work as a data source, generating employees. This class has one method **getEmployee()** that will create an instance of one of the implementations of Employee and return it. The method return type should be Employee.

3. Write an application that calls **getEmployee()** repeatedly inside a **for** loop and print the information about the Employee salary and tax. And if the employee is an instance of **SalesWithCommission**, also print his commission.

> **Note**
>
> The solution for this activity can be found on page 325.

The Object Class

Java provides a special class called **Object**, from which all classes implicitly inherit. You don't have to manually inherit from this class because the compiler does that for you. **Object** is the superclass of all classes:

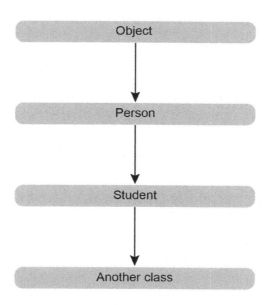

Figure 5.4: Superclass Object

This means that any class in Java can be upcast to **Object**:

```
Object object = (Object)person;

Object object1 = (Object)student;
```

Likewise, you can downcast to the original class:

```
Person newPerson = (Person)object;

Student newStudent  = (Student)object1;
```

You can use this **Object** class when you want to pass around objects whose type you don't know. It's also used when the JVM wants to perform garbage collection.

Autoboxing and Unboxing

Sometimes, we need to deal with primitive types in methods that only accept objects. A good example of this is when we want to store integers in an ArrayList (which we will discuss later). This class, **ArrayList**, only accepts objects, and not primitives. Fortunately, Java provides all primitive types as classes. Wrapper classes can hold primitive values and we can manipulate them as if they were normal classes.

An example of the **Integer** class, which can hold an **int** is as follows:

```
Integer a = new Integer(1);
```

We can also skip the **new** keyword and the compiler will implicitly wrap it for us:

```
Integer a = 1;
```

We can then use the object as if it was any other object. We can upcast it to **Object** and then downcast it back to an **Integer**.

This operation of converting a primitive type into an object (reference type) is referred to as autoboxing.

We can also convert the object back into a primitive type:

```
Integer a = 1;
int b = a;
```

Here, the **b** primitive is assigned the value of **a**, which is 1. This operation of converting a reference type back to a primitive is called unboxing. The compiler performs autoboxing and unboxing automatically for us.

In addition to **Integer**, Java also provides the following wrapper classes for the following primitives:

Primitive	Wrapper class
int	Integer
char	Character
double	Double
float	Float
boolean	Boolean
byte	Byte

Table 5.1: Table representing the wrapper classes for primitives

Activity 18: Understanding Typecasting in Java

Scenario: Let's understand typecasting concepts using our **Animal** classes we have been working with.

Objective: We are going to create a test class for our **Animal** class, and upcast and downcast the **Cow** and **Cat** classes.

Aim: Internalize the concepts of typecasting.

These steps will help you complete this activity:

Perform the following steps:

1. Open the **Animals** project.

2. Create a new class called **AnimalTest** and, inside it, create the **main** method

3. In the **main()** method create an object of the **Cat** and **Cow** classes.

4. Print the owner of the **Cat** object.

5. Upcast the object of **Cat** class to **Animal** and try to print the owner once more. Notice the error.

6. Print the sound of the object of **Cow** class.

7. Upcast the object of **Cow** class to **Animal** and try to print the owner once more. Notice the error.

8. Downcast the object of Animal class to the new object of **Cat** class and print the owner again.

    The output should be similar to this:

Figure 5.5: Output of the AnimalTest class

> **Note**
>
> The solution for this activity can be found on page 327.

Abstract Classes and Methods

Earlier, we discussed interfaces and how they can be useful when we wish to have a contract with our classes on the methods they have to implement. We then saw how we can only cast classes that share the same hierarchy tree.

Java also allows us to have classes with abstract methods that all classes inheriting from it must implement. Such a class is referred to as an **abstract class** and is denoted by using the **abstract** keyword after the access modifier.

When we declare a class as **abstract**, any class inheriting from it must implement the **abstract** methods in it. We cannot instantiate abstract classes:

```
public abstract class AbstractPerson {

        //this class is abstract and cannot be instantiated

}
```

Because **abstract** classes are still classes in the first place, they can have a logic and state of their own. This gives them more advantages compared to interfaces whose methods are empty. In addition, once we inherit from an **abstract** class, we can perform typecasting along that class hierarchy.

Java also allows us to have **abstract methods**. Abstract methods do not contain a body, and any class inheriting from their class must implement them too. In addition, any class that contains at least one **abstract** method must also be declared as **abstract**.

We use the **abstract** keyword after the access modifier to declare a method **abstract**.

When we inherit from an **abstract** class, we have to implement all the **abstract** methods in it:

```
public class SubClass extends  AbstractPerson {

        //TODO: implement all methods in AbstractPerson

}
```

Activity 19: Implementing Abstract Classes and Methods in Java

Scenario: Imagine that you have been tasked by the local hospital to build a piece of software to manage the different types of people who use the facility. You have to find a way to represent the doctors, nurses, and patients.

Objective: We are going to create three classes: one that's abstract, to represent any person, another one to represent the doctor, and finally, one to represent the patient. All of the classes are going to inherit from the abstract person class.

Aim: To understand these concepts of **abstract** classes and methods in Java.

These steps will help you complete the activity:

1. Create a new project called **Hospital** and open it.

2. Inside the **src** folder, create an abstract class called **Person**:

    ```
    public abstract class Patient {


    }
    ```

3. Create an **abstract** method that returns the type of person in the hospital. Name this method String **getPersonType()**, returning a String:

    ```
    public abstract String getPersonType();
    ```

    We have finished our **abstract** class and method. Now, we will continue to inherit from it and implement this **abstract** method.

4. Create a new class called **Doctor** that inherits from the **Person** class:

    ```
    public class Doctor extends Patient {
    }
    ```

5. Override the **getPersonType** abstract method in our **Doctor** class. Return the "**Arzt**" string. This is German for doctor:

    ```
    @Override
    public String getPersonType() {
        return "Arzt";
    }
    ```

6. Create another class called **Patient** to represent the patients in the hospital. Similarly, make sure that the class inherits from **Person** and overrides the **getPersonType** method. Return "**Kranke**". This is German for patient:

    ```
    public class People extends Patient{
        @Override
        public String getPersonType() {
            return "Kranke";
        }
    }
    ```

    Now we have two classes, we will test our code using a third test class.

7. Create a third class called **HospitalTest**. We will use this class to test the two classes we created previously.

8. Inside the **HospitalTest** class, create the **main** method:

```
public class HospitalTest {
    public static void main(String[] args){


    }
}
```

9. Inside the **main** method, create an instance of **Doctor** and another instance of **Patient**:

```
Doctor doctor = new Doctor();
People people = new People();
```

10. Try calling the **getPersonType** method for each of the objects and print it out to the console. What is the output?

```
String str = doctor.getPersonType();
String str1 = patient.getPersonType();
System.out.println(str);
System.out.println(str1);
```

The output is as follows:

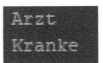

Figure 5.6: Output on calling getPersonType()

> **Note**
>
> The solution for this activity can be found on page 329.

Activity 20: Use abstract class to Encapsulate Common Logic

JavaWorks keeps growing. Now that they have many employees, they noticed that salary variation is not supported for the application you've built before. So far every Engineer had to have the same salary as all others. Same with Managers, Sales and Sales with commission people. To solve that, you're going to use an abstract class that encapsulates the logic to calculate net salary, based on the tax. For that to work, the abstract class will have a constructor that receives the gross salary. It will not implement the **getTax()** method, delegating that to the subclasses. With new subclasses for the generic employees that receive the gross salary as an argument for the constructor.

You'll also add a new method to the **EmployeeLoader**, **getEmployeeWithSalary()**, that will generate a new generic employee with a randomly generated gross salary.

And last, on your application, you'll do just like you did before, print the salary information and tax, and if the employee is an instance of **GenericSalesWithCommission**, also print his commission.

To complete this activity, you'll need to:

1. Create an abstract class **GenericEmployee** that has a constructor that receives the gross salary and stores that in a field. It should implement the Employee interface and have two methods: **getGrossSalary()** and **getNetSalary()**. The first will just return the value passed into the constructor. The latter will return the gross salary minus the result of calling **getTax()** method.

2. Create a new generic version of each type of employee: **GenericEngineer**, **GenericManager**, **GenericSales**, and **GenericSalesWithCommission**. They all need a constructor that receives gross salary and pass it to the super constructor. They also need to implement the **getTax()** method, returning the correct tax value for each class. Remember to also receive the gross sales on the **GenericSalesWithCommission** class, and add the method that calculates the commission.

3. Add a new method **getEmployeeWithSalary** to your **EmployeeLoader** class. This method will generate a random salary between 70,000 and 120,000 and assign to the newly created employee before returning it. Remember to also provide a gross sales when creating a **GenericSalesWithCommission** employee.

4. Write an application that calls the **getEmployeeWithSalary** method multiple times from inside a **for** loop. This method will work like the one in the previous activity: print the net salary and tax for all employees. If the employee is an instance of **GenericSalesWithCommission** also print his commission.

> **Note**
>
> The solution for this activity can be found on page 331.

Summary

In this lesson, we have learned that interfaces are a way for us to define a set of methods that all classes implementing them must provide specific implementations for. Interfaces can be used to implement events and listeners in your code when a specific action occurs.

We then learned that typecasting is a way for us to change a variable of one type to another type, as long as they are on the same hierarchy tree or implement a common interface.

We also looked at the use of the **instanceof** operator and the **Object** class in Java, and learned the concepts of autoboxing, unboxing, abstract classes, and abstract methods in Java.

In the next lesson, we will look at a few common classes and data structures that come with Java.

6

Data Structures, Arrays, and Strings

Learning Objectives

By the end of this lesson, you will be able to:

- Create and manipulate various data structures such as arrays
- Describe the fundamentals behind algorithms for programming
- Write simple sorting programs for arrays
- Input and perform operations on strings

Introduction

This is the last topic in our discussion on OOP. So far, we have already looked at classes and objects and how we can use classes as blueprints to create multiple objects. We saw how we can use methods to hold the logic of our classes and fields to hold the state. We've discussed how classes can inherit some properties from other classes to allow easy reusability of code.

We've also looked at polymorphism, or how a class can redefine the implementation of a method inherited from the superclass; and overloading, or how we can have more than one method using the same name, as long as they have different signatures. We've also discussed functions or methods.

We've looked at typecasting and interfaces in our previous lesson and how typecasting is a way for us to change an object from one type to another, as long as they are on the same hierarchy tree. We talked about upcasting and downcasting. Interfaces, on the other hand, are a way for us to define generic behaviors that our classes can provide specific implementations of their own.

In this section, we will look at a few common classes that come with Java. These are classes that you will find yourself using on a daily basis, and therefore it's important that you understand them. We will also talk about data structures and discuss common data structures that come with Java. Remember that Java is a wide language and that this list will not be exhaustive. Do find time to look at the official Java specification to learn more about the other classes you have at your disposal. Throughout this lesson, we will be introducing a topic, giving sample programs to illustrate the concepts, and then we'll finish with an exercise.

Data Structures and Algorithms

An algorithm is a set of instructions that should be followed to achieve an end goal. They are specific to computing, but we often talk about algorithms to accomplish a certain task in a computer program. When we write computer programs, we generally implement algorithms. For example, when we wish to sort an array or list of numbers, we usually come up with an algorithm to do so. It is a core concept in computer science and important for any good programmer to understand. We have algorithms for sorting, searching, graph problems, string processing, and many more. Java comes with a number of algorithms already implemented for you. However, we still have the scope to define our own.

A data structure is a way to store and organize data in order to facilitate access and modifications. An example of a data structure is an array used to hold several items of the same type or a map used to hold key-value pairs. No single data structure works well for all purposes, and so it is important to know their strengths and limitations. Java has a number of predefined data structures for storing and modifying different kinds of data types. We will also cover some of them in the coming sections.

Sorting different types of data is a common task in a computer program.

Arrays

We touched upon arrays in *Lesson 3, Control Flow*, when we were looking at looping, but it's worth taking an even closer look because they are powerful tools. An array is a collection of ordered items. It is used to hold several items of the same type. An example of an array in Java could be **{1, 2, 3, 4, 5, 6, 7}**, which is holding the integers 1 through 7. The number of items in this array is 7. An array can also hold strings or other objects as follows:

```
{"John","Paul","George",  "Ringo"}
```

We can access an item from an array by using its index. An index is the location of the item in the array. Elements in an array are indexed from **0**. That is, the first number is at index **0**, the second number is at index **1**, the third number is at index **2**, and so on. In our first example array, the last number is at index **6**.

For us to be able to access an element from the array, we use **myArray[0]** to access the first item in **myArray**, **myArray[1]** to access the second item, and so on to **myArray[6]** to access the seventh item.

Java allows us to define arrays of primitive types and objects such as reference types.

Arrays also have a size, which is the number of items in that array. In Java, when we create an array, we must specify its size. This size cannot be changed once the array has been created.

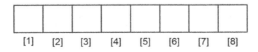

Figure 6.1: An empty array

Creating and Initializing an Array

To create an array, you need to declare the name of the array, the type of elements it will contain, and its size as follows:

```
int[] myArray = new int[10];
```

We use the square brackets [ ] to indicate an array. In this example, we are creating an array of integers that holds 10 items, indexed from 0 to 9. We specify the number of items so that Java can reserve enough memory for the elements. We also use the **new** keyword to indicate a new array.

For example, to declare array of 10 doubles, use this:

```
double[] myArray = new double[10];
```

To declare array of 10 Boolean values, use this:

```
boolean[] myArray = new boolean[10];
```

To declare array of 10 **Person** objects, use this:

```
Person[] people = new Person[10];
```

You can also create an array and at the same time declare the items in the array (initialization):

```
int[] myArray = {0, 1, 2, 3, 4, 5, 6, 7, 8, 9};
```

Accessing Elements

To access array elements, we use the index enclosed in square brackets. For example, to access the fourth element, we use **myArray[3]**, to access the tenth element, we use **myArray[9]**.

Here's an example:

```
int first_element = myArray[0];
int last_element = myArray[9];
```

To get the length of the array, we use the **length** property. It returns an integer that is the number of items in the array:

```
int length = myArray. length;
```

If the array has no items, **length** will be 0. We can use the **length** and a loop to insert items into the array.

Exercise 14: Creating an Array Using a Loop

It can be useful to use control flow commands to create long arrays. Here we will use a **for** loop to create an array of numbers from 0-9.

1. Create a new class with **DataStr** as the class name and set up the **main** method as follows:

```
public class DataStr {
public static void main(String[] args){
}
```

2. Create an array of integers of length 10 as follows:

```
int[] myArray = new int[10];
```

3. Initialize a **for** loop with a variable starting at zero, with loop incrementing one with each iteration and the condition being less than the array length:

```
for (int i = 0; i < myArray.length; i++)
```

4. Insert item **i** into the array:

```
{
myArray[i] = i;
}
```

5. Use a similar loop construct to print out the loop:

```
for (int i = 0; i < myArray.length; i++){
System.out.println(myArray[i]);
}
```

The full code should look as follows:

```
public class DataStr {
    public static void main(String[] args){
        int[] myArray = new int[10];
        for (int i = 0; i < myArray.length; i++){
            myArray[i] = i;
        }
        for (int i = 0; i < myArray.length; i++){
            System.out.println(myArray[i]);
        }
    }
}
```

Your output should be as follows:

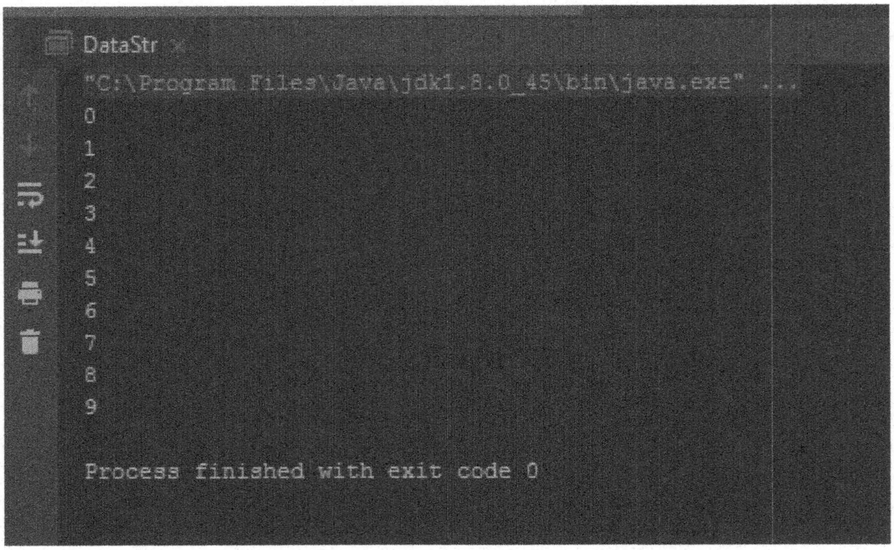

Figure 6.2: Output of the DataStr class

In this exercise, we used the first **for** loop to insert items into **myArray** and the second to print out the items.

As we discussed previously, we can replace the second **for** loop with a **for-each** loop, which is much shorter and makes the code easier to read:

```
for (int i : myArray) {
System.out.println(i);
}
```

Java does automatic bound checking for us - if you have created an array of size N and use an index whose value is less than 0 or greater than N-1, your program will terminate with an **ArrayOutOfBoundsException** exception.

Exercise 15: Searching for a Number in an Array

In this exercise, you will check whether the number entered by the user is present in the array or not. To do this, perform the following steps:

1. Define a new class called **NumberSearch** and include the **main** method in it:

```
public class NumberSearch {
public static void main(String[] args){
}
}
```

2. Ensure that you import this package at the top, which is for reading values from the input devices:

```
import java.util.Scanner;
```

3. Declare an array sample that store the integers 2, 4, 7, 98, 32, 77, 81, 62, 45, 71:

```
int [] sample = { 2, 4, 7, 98, 32, 77, 81, 62, 45, 71 };
```

4. Read a number from the user:

```
Scanner sc = new Scanner(System.in);
System.out.print("Enter the number you want to find: ");
int ele = sc.nextInt();
```

5. Check whether the **ele** variable matches any of the items in the array sample. To do this we iterate through the loop and check whether each element of the array matches the element entered by the user:

```
for (int i = 0; i < 10; i++) {
  if (sample[i] == ele) {
    System.out.println("Match found at element " + i);
    break;
  }
  else
    {
    System.out.println("Match not found");
    break;
    }
}
```

Your output should be similar to this:

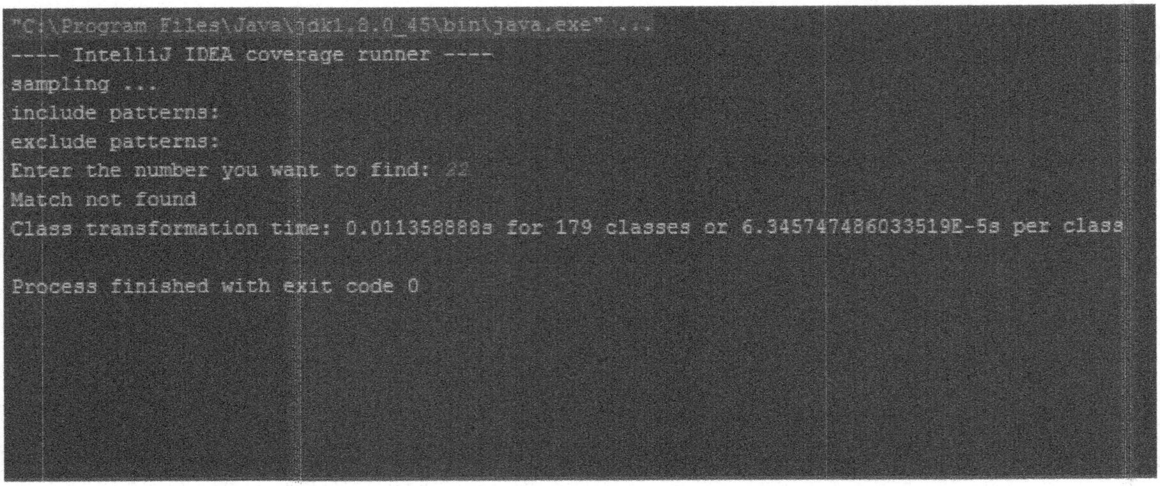

```
"C:\Program Files\Java\jdk1.8.0_45\bin\java.exe" ...
---- IntelliJ IDEA coverage runner ----
sampling ...
include patterns:
exclude patterns:
Enter the number you want to find: 22
Match not found
Class transformation time: 0.011358888s for 179 classes or 6.345747486033519E-5s per class

Process finished with exit code 0
```

Figure 6.3: Output of the NumberSearch class

Activity 21: Finding the Smallest Number in an Array

In this activity, we will take an array of 20 unsorted numbers and loop through the array to find the smallest number.

The steps are as follows:

1. Create a class called **ExampleArray** and create the **main** method.

2. Create an array made up of 20 floating points as follows:

   14, 28, 15, 89, 46, 25, 94, 33, 82, 11, 37, 59, 68, 27, 16, 45, 24, 33, 72, 51

3. Create a **for-each** loop through the array and find the minimum element in the array.

4. Print out the minimum float.

> **Note**
>
> The solution for this activity can be found on page 335.

Activity 22: Calculator with Array of Operators

In this activity you'll change your calculator to be more dynamic and make it easier to add new operators. For that, instead of making all possible operators a different field, you'll add them into an array and use a for-loop to determine what operator to use.

To complete this activity you'll need to:

1. Create a class **Operators** that will contain the logic of determining what operator to use based out of a String. In this class create a public constant field **default_ operator** that is going to be an instance of the **Operators** class. Then create another constant field called **operators** of type array of **Operators** and initialize it with an instance of each of the operators you have.

2. In the **Operators** class, add a public static method called **findOperator** that receives the operator as a String and return an instance of **Operators**. Inside it iterate over the possible operators array and, using the matches method for each operator, return the selected operator, or the default one if it didn't match any of them.

3. Create a new **CalculatorWithDynamicOperator** class with three fields: **operand1** and **operator2** as double and **operator** of type **Operators**.

4. Add a constructor that receives three parameters: operand1 and operand2 of type double and operator as a String. In the constructor, instead of having an if-else to select the operator, use the **Operators.findOperator** method to set the operator field.

5. Add a **main** method where you call the **Calculator** class multiple times and print the results.

> **Note**
>
> The solution for this activity can be found on page 336.

Two-Dimensional Arrays

The arrays we have looked so far are referred to as one-dimensional because all the elements can be considered to be on one row. We can also declare arrays that have both columns and rows, just like a matrix or grid. Multidimensional arrays are arrays of one-dimensional arrays we saw earlier. That is, you can consider one of the rows as a one-dimensional array and then the columns are multiple one-dimensional arrays.

When describing a multidimensional array, we say the array is a M-by-N multidimensional array to denote that the array has M rows each of N length, for example, an array of 6 by 7:

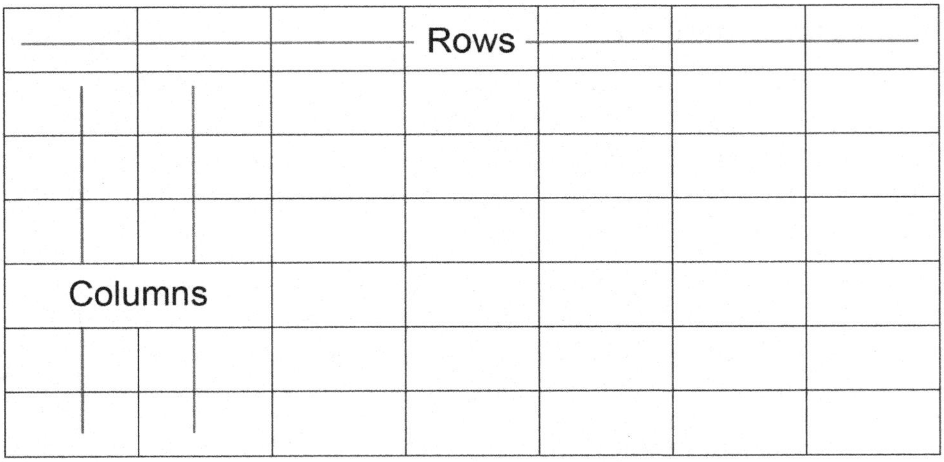

Figure 6.4: Graphical representation of a multi-dimensional array

In java, to create a two-dimensional array, we use the double square brackets, `[M]` `[N ]`. This notation creates a M-by-N array. We can then refer to an individual item in the array by using the notation `[ i ] [ j ]` to access the element in the ith row and j^{th} column.

To create an 8-by-10 multidimensional array of doubles we do the following:

```
double[][] a = new double[8][10];
```

Java initializes all the numeric types to zeros and the Booleans to false. We could also loop through the array and initialize each item manually to a value of our choice:

```
double[][] a = new double[8][10];
for (int i = 0; i < 8; i++)
for (int j = 0; j < 10; j++)
a[i][j] = 0.0;
```

Exercise 16: Printing a Simple Two-Dimensional Array

To print a simple two-dimensional array, perform the following steps:

1. Set up the **main** method in a new class file known as **Twoarray**:

    ```java
    public class Twoarray {
        public static void main(String args[]) {
        }
    }
    ```

2. Define the **arr** array by adding elements to the array:

    ```java
    int arr[][] = {{1,2,3}, {4,5,6}, {7,8,9}};
    ```

3. Create a nested **for** loop. The outer **for** loop is to print the elements row-wise, and the inner **for** loop is to print the elements column-wise:

    ```java
    System.out.print("The Array is :\n");
    for (int i = 0; i < 3; i++) {
        for (int j = 0; j < 3; j++) {
            System.out.print(arr[i][j] + "  ");
        }
        System.out.println();
    }
    ```

4. Run the program. Your output should be similar to this:

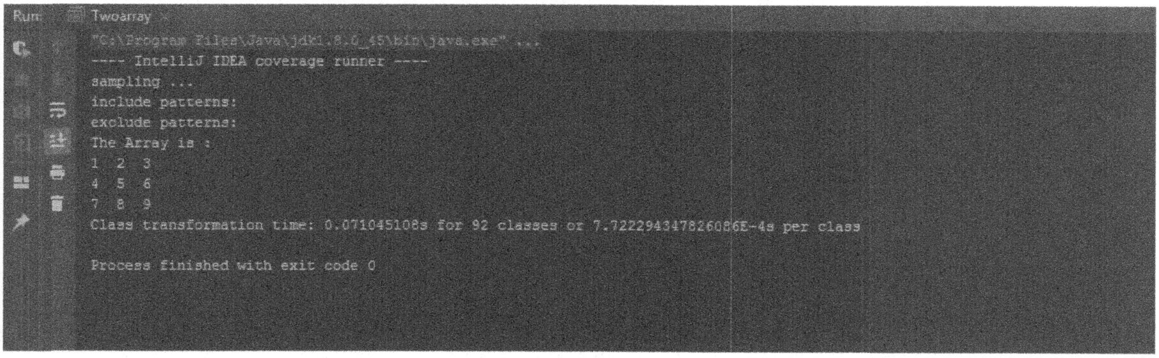

Figure 6.5: Output of the Twoarray class

Most of the rest of the operations with arrays remain pretty much the same as with one-dimensional arrays. One important detail to remember is that in a multidimensional array, using **a[i]** returns a row that is a one-dimensional array. You have to use a second index to access the exact location you wish, **a[i][j]**.

> **Note**
>
> Java also allows you to create higher-order dimensional arrays, but dealing with them becomes complex. This is because our human brain can easily comprehend three-dimensional arrays but higher-order ones become hard to visualize.

Exercise 17: Creating a Three-Dimensional Array

Here we will create a three-dimensional **(x,y,z)** array of integers and initialize each element to the product of its row, column, and depth (x * y * z) indices.

1. Create a new class called **Threearray** and set up the **main** method:

```java
public class Threearray
{
    public static void main(String args[])
    {
    }
}
```

2. Declare an **arr** array of dimension **[2][2][2]**:

```java
int arr[][][] = new int[2][2][2];
```

3. Declare the variables for iteration:

```java
int i, j, k, num=1;
```

4. Create three **for** loops nested within each other, in order to write values into the three-dimensional array:

```
for(i=0; i<2; i++)
  {
    for(j=0; j<2; j++)
      {
        for(k=0; k<2; k++)
          {
          arr[i][j][k] = no;
          no++;
      }
    }
  }
```

5. Print the elements out of the array using the three **for** loops that are nested within each other:

```
for(i=0; i<2; i++)
  {
  for(j=0; j<2; j++)
    {
      for(k=0; k<2; k++)
      {
      System.out.print(arr[i][j][k]+ "\t");
      }
    System.out.println();
    }
  System.out.println();
  }
}
}
}
}
}
```

The full code should look like this:

```
public class Threearray
{
    public static void main(String args[])
    {
        int arr[][][] = new int[2][2][2];
        int i, j, k, num=1;

        for(i=0; i<2; i++)
        {
            for(j=0; j<2; j++)
            {
                for(k=0; k<2; k++)
                {
                    arr[i][j][k] = num;
                    num++;
                }
            }
        }

        for(i=0; i<2; i++)
        {
            for(j=0; j<2; j++)
            {
                for(k=0; k<2; k++)
                {
                    System.out.print(arr[i][j][k]+ "\t");
                }
                System.out.println();
            }
            System.out.println();
        }
    }
}
```

The output is as follows:

```
1    2
3    4

5    6
7    8

Class transformation time: 0.054165701s for 106 classes or 5.10997179245283E-4s per class

Process finished with exit code 0
```

Figure 6.6: Output of the Threearray class

The Arrays Class in Java

Java provides the **Arrays** class, which provides static methods we can use with our arrays. It is often easier to use this class because we have access to methods to sort, search, and much more. This class is available in the **java.util.Arrays** package, so before we work with it, place this line at the top of any file you want to use it:

```
import java.util.Arrays;
```

In the following code, we can see how to use the **Arrays** class and a few methods that we have at our disposal. All the methods are explained after the snippet:

```java
import java.util.Arrays;

class ArraysExample {

public static void main(String[] args) {

double[] myArray = {0.0, 1.0, 2.0, 3.0, 4.0, 5.0, 6.0, 7.0, 8.0, 9.0};

System.out.println(Arrays.toString (myArray));

Arrays.sort(myArray);

System.out.println(Arrays.toString (myArray));

Arrays.sort(myArray);

int index = Arrays.binarySearch(myArray,7.0);

System.out.println("Position of 7.0 is: " + index);

}

}
```

This is the output:

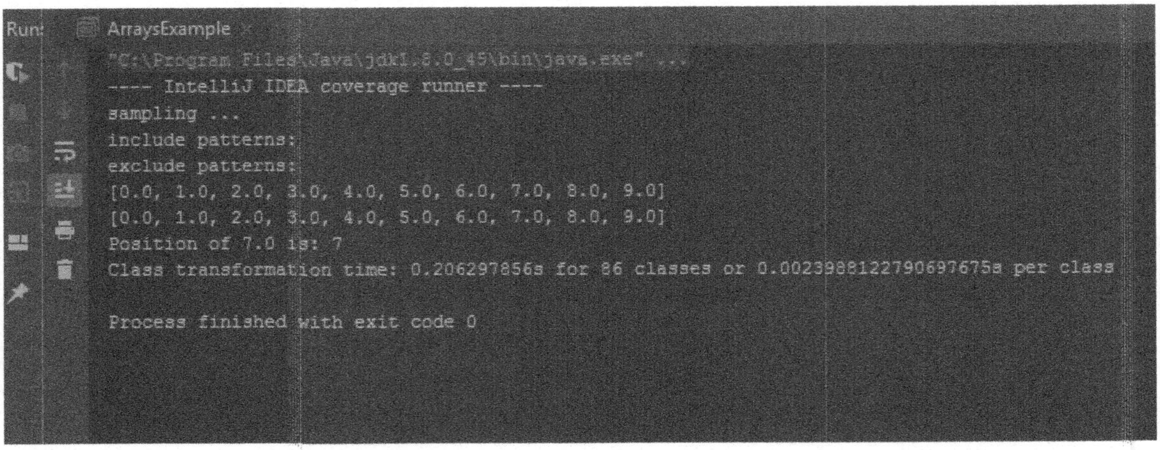

Figure 6.7: Output of the ArraysExample class

In this program, we have three example uses of the **Arrays** class. In the first example, we see how we can use **Arrays.toString()** to easily print out the elements of an array without the need of the **for** loop we were using earlier. In the second example, we saw how we can use **Arrays.sort()** to quickly sort an array. If we were to implement such a method on our own, we would use many more lines and be prone to making a lot of errors in the process.

In the last example, we sort the arrays and then search for 7.0 by using **Arrays.binarySearch()**, which uses a searching algorithm called **binary search**.

> **Note**
>
> **Arrays.sort()** uses an algorithm called double-pivot quicksort to sort large arrays. For smaller arrays, it uses a combination of Insertion sort and Merge sort. It is better to trust that **Arrays.sort()** is optimized to each use case instead of implementing your own sorting algorithm. **Arrays.binarySearch()** uses an algorithm called binary search to look for an item in the array. It first requires that the array be sorted, and that is why we called **Arrays.sort()** first. Binary search splits the sorted array into two equal halves recursively until it can no longer divide the array, at which point that value is the answer.

Insertion sort

Sorting is one of the fundamental applications of algorithms in computer science. Insertion sort is a classic example of a sorting algorithm, and although it is inefficient it is a good starting point when looking at arrays and the sorting problem. The steps in the algorithm are as follows:

1. Take the first element in the array and assume it is already sorted since it is only one.

2. Pick the second element in the array. Compare it with the first element. If it is greater that the first element, then the two items are already sorted. If it is smaller than the first element, swap the two elements so that they are sorted.

3. Take the third element. Compare it with the second element in the already sorted subarray. If smaller then swap the two. The compare it again with the first element. If it is smaller, then swap the two again so that it is the first. The three elements will now be sorted.

4. Take the fourth element and repeat this process, swapping if it smaller than its left neighbor, otherwise leaving it where it is.

5. Repeat this process for the rest of the items in the array.

6. The resultant array will be sorted.

Example

Take the array [3, 5, 8, 1, 9]:

1. Let's take the first element and assume it is sorted: [3].

2. Take the second element, 5. Since it is greater than 3, we leave the array as it is: [3, 5].

3. Take the third element, 8. It is greater than 5, so there's no swapping here either: [3, 5, 8].

4. Take the fourth element, 1. Since it is smaller than 8, we swap 8 and 1 to have: [3, 5, 1, 8].

5. Since 1 is still smaller than 5, we swap the two again: [3, 1, 5, 8].

6. 1 is still smaller than 3. We swap again: [1, 3, 5, 8].

7. It is now the smallest.

8. Take the last element, 9. It is greater than 8, so there's no swapping.

9. The whole array is now sorted : `[1, 3, 5, 8, 9]`.

Exercise 18: Implementing Insertion Sort

In this exercise, we will implement the insertion sort.

1. Create a new class called **InsertionSort**, and inside this class, create the **main** method:

```
public class InsertionSort {
public static void main(String[] args){
}
}
```

2. Inside our **main** method, create a sample array of random integers and pass it to our **sort** method. Use the following array, [1, 3, 354, 64, 364, 64, 3, 4, 74, 2, 46]:

```
int[] arr = {1, 3,354,64,364,64, 3,4 ,74,2 , 46};
System.out.println("Array before sorting is as follows: ");
System.out.println(Arrays.toString(arr));
```

3. After calling **sort()** with our array, use a **foreach** loop to print each of the items in the sorted array with a space in a single line:

```
sort(arr);
        System.out.print("Array after sort looks as follows: ");
        for (int i : arr) {
            System.out.print(i + " ");
        }
    }
}
```

4. Create a public static method called **sort()** that takes an array of integers and returns **void**. This is the method that will have our sorting algorithm:

```
public static void sort(int[] arr){
}
```

Inside the **sort** method, implement the algorithm illustrated earlier.

5. Define the integer **num** as the length of the array in the **sort()** method:

```
int num = arr.length;
```

6. Create a **for** loop that executes until **i** has reached the length of the array. Inside the loop, create the algorithm that compares the numbers: **k** will be an integer defined by the index **i**, and **j** will be index **i-1**. Add a **while** loop inside the **for** loop that switches the integers at **i** and **i-1** with the following conditions: **j** is greater or equal to **0** and the integer at index **j** is greater than **k**:

```
for (int i = 1; i < num; i++) {
        int k = arr[i];
        int j = i - 1;
    while (j>= 0 && arr[j] > k) {
        arr[j + 1] = arr[j];
        j = j - 1;
    }
    arr[j + 1] = k;
    }
}
```

The completed code looks as follows:

```
import java.util.Arrays;
public class InsertionSort {
    public static void sort(int[] arr) {
        int num = arr.length;
        for (int i = 1; i < num; i++) {
            int k = arr[i];
            int j = i - 1;
        while (j>= 0 && arr[j] > k) {
            arr[j + 1] = arr[j];
            j = j - 1;
        }
        arr[j + 1] = k;
        }
    }
    public static void main(String[] args) {
        int[] arr = {1, 3, 354, 64, 364, 64, 3, 4, 74, 2, 46};
        System.out.println("Array before sorting is as follows: ");
        System.out.println(Arrays.toString(arr));
        sort(arr);
        System.out.print("Array after sort looks as follows: ");
        for (int i : arr) {
```

```
                    System.out.print(i + " ");
            }
        }
    }
```

The output is as follows:

```
Array before sorting is as follows:
[1, 3, 354, 64, 364, 64, 3, 4, 74, 2, 46]
Array after sort looks as follows: 1 2 3 3 4 46 64 64 74 354 364
```

Figure 6.8: Output of the InsertionSort class

Java makes it easy for us to deal with commonly used data structures such as lists, stacks, queues, and maps. It comes with the Java collections framework that provides easy-to-use APIs when dealing with such data structures. A good example is when we want to sort the elements in an array or want to search for a particular element in the array. Instead of rewriting such methods from scratch on our own, Java comes with methods that we can apply to our collections, as long as they conform to the requirements of the collections framework. The classes of the collections framework can hold objects of any type.

We will now look at a common class in the collections framework called **ArrayList**. Sometimes we wish to store elements but are not sure of the number of items we are expecting. We need a data structure to which we can add as many items as we wish and remove some when we need to. The arrays we have seen so far require us to specify the number of items when creating it. After that, we cannot change the size of that array unless we create a whole new array. An ArrayList is a dynamic list that can grow and shrink as needed; they are created with an initial size and when we add or remove an item, the size is automatically enlarged or shrank as needed.

Creating an ArrayList and Adding Elements

When creating an **ArrayList**, you need to specify the type of objects to be stored. Array lists only support storage of reference types (that is, objects) and don't support primitive types. However, since Java provides **wrapper classes** for all the primitive types, you can use the wrapper classes to store the primitives in an ArrayList. To append an item to the end of the list, we use the **add()** method with the object to be added as a parameter. ArrayList also has a method to get the number of items in the list called **size()**. The method returns an integer, which is the number of items in the list:

```
import java.util.ArrayList;

public class Person {

public static void main(String[] args){
```

```
Person john=new Person();
//Initial size of 0
ArrayList<Integer> myArrayList = new ArrayList<>();
System.out.println("Size of myArrayList: "+myArrayList.size());

//Initial size of 5
ArrayList<Integer> myArrayList1 = new ArrayList<>(5);
myArrayList1.add(5);System.out.println("Size of myArrayList1: "+myArrayList1.
size());
//List of Person objectsArrayList<Person> people = new ArrayList<>();
people.add(john);System.out.println("Size of people: "+people.size());
 }
}
```

The output is as follows:

```
Size of myArrayList: 0
Size of myArrayList1: 1
Size of people: 1
```

Figure 6.9: Output of the Person class

In the first example, we create an **ArrayList** of size 0 called **myArrayList** holding **Integer** types. In the second example, we create an **ArrayList** of size 5 of **Integer** types. Although the initial size is 5, when we add more items, the list will increase in size automatically. In the last example, we create an **ArrayList** of **Person** objects. From these three examples, the following should be adhered to when creating an array list:

1. Import the **ArrayList** class from the **java.util** package.

2. Specify the data type of the objects between <>.

3. Specify the name of the list.

4. Use the **new** keyword to create a new instance of **ArrayList**.

Following are some ways to add elements to the ArrayList:

```
myArrayList.add( new Integer(1));
```

```
myArrayList1.add(1);
```

```
people.add(new Person());
```

In the first example, we create a new **Integer** object and add it to the list. The new object will be appended to the end of the list. In the second line, we inserted 1 but because **ArrayList** accepts only objects, the JVM will **autobox** the 1 to an integer instance with a value of 1 instead. In the last example, we also create a new object of the **Person** class and appended it to the list. We might also wish to insert the element at a specific index instead of appending at the end of the list in the same class. Here we specify the index to insert the object and the object to be inserted:

```
myArrayList1.add(1, 8);
```

```
System.out.println("Elements of myArrayList1: " +myArrayList1.toString());
```

The output is as follows:

```
Size of myArrayList: 0
Elements of myArrayList1: [5, 8]
Size of myArrayList1: 2
Size of people: 1
```

Figure 6.10: Output after adding an element to the list

> **Note**
>
> Inserting an object at an index less that 0 or greater than the size of the array list will result in an **IndexOutOfBoundsException** and your program will crash. Always check the size of the list before specifying the index to insert.

Replacing and Removing Elements

ArrayList also allows us to replace an element at a specified location with a new element. Append the following in the previous code and observe the output:

```
myArrayList1.set(1, 3);
```

```
System.out.println("Elements of myArrayList1 after replacing the element: "
+myArrayList1.toString());
```

Here's the output:

```
Size of myArrayList: 0
Elements of myArrayListl after replacing the element: [5, 8]
Elements of myArrayListl: [5, 3]
Size of myArrayListl: 2
Size of people: 1
```

Figure 6.11: List after replacing the element

Here we are replacing the element at index 2 with a new **Integer** object with a value of 3. This method also throws **IndexOutOfBoundsException** if we try to replace the element at an index greater than the size of the list or an index below zero.

If you also wish to remove a single element or all of the elements, ArrayList supports that too:

```
//Remove at element at index 1

myArrayList1.remove(1);

System.out.println("Elements of myArrayList1 after removing the element: "
+myArrayList1.toString());

//Remove all the elements in the list

myArrayList1.clear();

System.out.println("Elements of myArrayList1 after clearing the list: "
+myArrayList1.toString());
```

Here's the output:

```
Size of myArrayList: 0
Elements of myArrayListl after replacing the element: [5, 8]
Elements of myArrayListl: [5, 3]
Elements of myArrayListl after removing the element: [5]
Elements of myArrayListl after clearing the list: []
Size of myArrayListl: 0
Size of people: 1
```

Figure 6.12: List after clearing all elements

To get an element at a specific index, use the **get()** method, passing in the index. The method returns an object:

```
myArrayList1.add(10);

Integer one = myArrayList1.get(0);

System.out.println("Element at given index: "+one);
```

The output is as follows:

```
Size of myArrayList: 0
Elements of myArrayList1 after replacing the element: [5, 8]
Elements of myArrayList1: [5, 3]
Elements of myArrayList1 after removing the element: [5]
Elements of myArrayList1 after clearing the list: []
Size of myArrayList1: 0
Size of people: 1
Element at given index: 10
```

Figure 6.13: Output of the element at the given index

This method will also throw **IndexOutOfBoundsException** if the index passed is invalid. To avoid the exception, always check the size of the list first. Consider the following example:

```
Integer two = myArrayList1.get(1);
```

```
Exception in thread "main" java.lang.IndexOutOfBoundsException: Index 1 out of bounds for length 1 <3 internal calls>
    at java.base/java.util.Objects.checkIndex(Objects.java:372)
    at java.base/java.util.ArrayList.get(ArrayList.java:458)
    at Person.main(Person.java:31)
```

Figure 6.14: IndexOutOfBounds exception message

Exercise 19: Adding, Removing, and Replacing Elements in an Array

Arrays are basic, but useful ways of storing information. In this exercise we will look at how to add and subtract elements in a list of students:

1. Import the **ArrayList** and **List** class for **java.util**:

    ```
    import java.util.ArrayList;
    import java.util.List;
    ```

2. Create a **public** class and the **main** method:

    ```
    public class StudentList {
        public static void main(String[] args) {
    ```

3. Define the students **List** as new ArrayList that contains strings:

```
List<String> students = new ArrayList<>();
```

4. Add the names of four students:

```
students.add("Diana");
students.add("Florence");
students.add("Mary");
students.add("Betty");
```

5. Print out the array and remove the last student:

```
System.out.println(students);
students.remove("Betty");
```

6. Print out the array:

```
System.out.println(students);
```

7. Replace the first student (at index 0):

```
students.set(0, "Jean");
```

8. Print out the array:

```
System.out.println(students);
    }
}
```

The output is as follows:

```
List of students: [Diana, Florence, Mary, Betty]
List of students after removing elements: [Diana, Florence, Mary]
List of students after replacing name: [Jean, Florence, Mary]
```

Figure 6.15: Output of the StudentList class

Iterators

The collections framework also provides iterators that we can use to loop through the elements of an **ArrayList**. Iterators are like pointers to the items in the list. We can use iterators to see if there is a next element in the list and then retrieve it. Consider iterators as loops for the collections framework. We can use the **array.iterator()** object with **hasNext()** to loop through an array.

Exercise 20: Iterating through an ArrayList

In this exercise, we will create an **ArrayList** of the cities in the world and use an iterator to print out the cities in the whole **ArrayList** one at a time:

1. Import the ArrayList and the **Iterator** packages:

```
import java.util.ArrayList;
import java.util.Iterator;
```

2. Create a **public** class and the **main** method:

```
public class Cities {
public static void main(String[] args){
```

3. Create a new array and add the city names:

```
ArrayList<String> cities = new ArrayList<>();
cities.add( "London");
cities.add( "New York");
cities.add( "Tokyo");
cities.add( "Nairobi");
cities.add( "Sydney");
```

4. Define an iterator containing strings:

```
Iterator<String> citiesIterator = cities.iterator();
```

5. Loop through the iterator with **hasNext()**, printing out each city with **next()**:

```
while (citiesIterator.hasNext()){
String city = citiesIterator.next();
System.out.println(city);
}
}
}
```

The output is as follows:

Figure 6.16: Output of the Cities class

In this class, we created a new ArrayList holding strings. We then inserted a few names and created an iterator called **citiesIterator**. Classes in the collections framework support the **iterator()** method, which returns an iterator to use with the collection. The iterator has the **hasNext()** method, which returns true if there is another element in the list after where we currently are, and a **next()** method that returns that next object. **next()** returns an object instance and then implicitly downcasts it to a string because our **citiesIterator** was declared to hold string types: `Iterator<String> citiesIterator`.

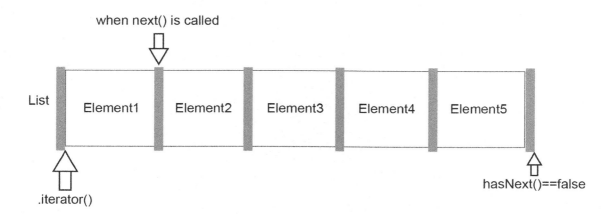

Figure 6.17: Working of next() and hasNext()

Instead of using iterators for looping, we can also use a normal **for** loop to achieve the same goal:

```
for (int i = 0; i < cities.size(); i++){
String name = cities.get(i);
System.out .println(name);
}
```

The output is as follows:

Figure 6.18: Output of the Cities class using a for loop

Here, we are using the **size()** method to check the size of the list and **get()** to retrieve an element at a given index. There is no need to cast the object to string as Java already knows we are dealing with a list of strings.

Similarly, we can use a **for-each** loop, which is more concise but achieves the same goal:

```
for (String city : cities) {
System.out.println(city);
}
```

The output is as follows:

Figure 6.19: Output of the Cities class using a for-each loop

Activity 23: Working with ArrayList

We have several students we wish to keep track in our program. However, we are not sure of the exact number currently but expect the number to change as more and more students use our program. We also wish to also be able to loop over our students and print their names. We will create an ArrayList of objects and use an iterator to loop over the ArrayList:

These steps will help you complete the activity:

1. Import **ArrayList** and **Iterator** from **java.util**.

2. Create a new class called **StudentsArray**.

3. In the **main** method, define an **ArrayList** of **Student** objects. Insert four student instances, instantiated with the different kinds of constructors we created earlier.

4. Create an iterator for your list and print the name of each student.

5. Finally, clear all the objects from the **ArrayList**.

The output will be as follows:

Figure 6.20: Output of the StudentsArray class

> **Note**
>
> ArrayList is an important class to know, as you will find yourself using it in your day-to-day life. The class has more capabilities not covered here, such as swapping two elements, sorting the items, and much more.

> **Note**
>
> The solution for this activity can be found on page 338.

Strings

Java has the string data type, which is used to represent a sequence of characters. String is one of the fundamental data types in Java and you will encounter it in almost all programs.

A string is simply a sequence of characters. "Hello World", "London", and "Toyota" are all examples of strings in Java. Strings are objects in Java and not primitive types. They are immutable, that is, once they are created, they cannot be modified. Therefore, the methods we will consider in the following sections only create new string objects that contain the result of the operation but don't modify the original string object.

Creating a String

We use double quotes to denote a string, compared to single quotes for a char:

```
public class StringsDemo {
    public static void main(String[] args) {
        String hello="Hello World";
        System.out.println(hello);
    }
}
```

The output is as follows:

Figure 6.21: Output of the StringsDemo class

The **hello** object is now a string and is immutable. We can use delimiters in strings, such as **\n** to represent a newline, **\t** to present a tab, or **\r** to represent a return:

```
String data = '\t'+ "Hello"+ '\n'+" World";

System.out.println(data);
```

The output is as follows:

```
        Hello
World
```

Figure 6.22: Output using delimiters

We have a tab before **Hello** and then a newline before **World**, which prints **World** on the next line.

Concatenation

We can combine more than one string literal in a process commonly referred to as concatenation. We use the **+** symbol to concatenate two strings as follows:

```
String str = "Hello " + "World";

System.out.println(str);
```

The output is as follows:

```
Hello World
```

Concatenation is often used when we want to substitute a value that will be calculated at runtime. The code will look as follows:

```
String userName = getUserName(); // get the username from an external
location like database or input field

System.out.println( " Welcome " + userName);
```

In the first line, we get **userName** from a method that we haven't defined here. Then we print out a welcome message, substituting the **userName** with **userName** we got earlier.

Concatenation is also important when we want to represent a string that spans more than one line:

```
String quote = "I have a dream that " +

"all Java programmers will " +

"one day be free from " +

"all computer bugs!";

System.out.println(quote);
```

Here is the output:

```
I have a dream that all Java programmers will one day be free from all computer bugs!
```

Figure 6.23: Concatenated string

In addition to the **+** symbol, Java also provides the **concat()** method for concatenating two string literals:

```
String wiseSaying = "Java programmers are " . concat("wise and
knowledgeable").concat("." );

System.out.println(wiseSaying);
```

Here is the output:

```
Java programmers are wise and knowledgeable.
```

Figure 6.24: Concatenated string using concat()

String Length and Characters

String provides the **length()** method to get the number of characters in a string. The number of characters is the count of all the valid java characters, including newlines, spaces, and tabs:

```
String saying = "To be or not to be, that is the question."

int num = saying.length();

System.out.println(num);
```

Here is the output:

```
4
```

To access a character at a given index, use the **charAt(i)**. This method takes the index of the character you want and returns a char of it:

```
char c = quote.charAt(7);

System.out.println(c);
```

Here is the output:

```
r
```

Calling **charAt(i)** with an index greater than the number of characters in the string or a negative number will cause your program to crash with the **StringIndexOutOfBoundsException** exception:

```
char d = wiseSaying.charAt(-3);
```

```
Exception in thread "main" java.lang.StringIndexOutOfBoundsException: String index out of range: -3
    at java.base/java.lang.StringLatin1.charAt(StringLatin1.java:47)
    at java.base/java.lang.String.charAt(String.java:693)
    at Strings.main(Strings.java:24)
```

Figure 6.25: **StringIndexOutOfBoundsException message**

We can also convert a string to an array of chars by using the **getChars()** method. This method returns an array of chars that we can use. We can convert the whole string or part of the string:

```
char[] chars = new char [quote.length()];

quote.getChars(0, quote.length(), chars, 0);

System.out.println(Arrays.toString (chars));
```

The output is as follows:

Figure 6.26: Characters array

Activity 24: Input a String and Output Its Length and as an Array

In order to check that names being inputted into a system aren't too long, we can use some of the features mentioned previously to count the length of a name. In this activity, you will write a program that will input a name and then export the length of the name and the first initial.

The steps are as follows:

1. Import the **java.util.Scanner** package.

2. Create a public class called **nameTell** and a **main** method.

3. Use the **Scanner** and **nextLine** to input a string at the prompt **"Enter your name:"**.

4. Count the length of the string and find the first character.

5. Print the output as follows:

```
Your name has 10 letters including spaces.
The first letter is: J
```

The output will be as follows:

```
Enter your name: David

Your name has 5 letters including spaces.

The first letter is: D
```

Figure 6.27: Output of the NameTell class

> **Note**
>
> The solution for this activity can be found on page 340.

Activity 25: Calculator Reads from Input

With all the calculator logic encapsulated we will write a command line calculator where you give the operator, the two operands and it will show you the result. A command line application like that starts with a while loop that never ends. Then reads the input from the user and makes decisions based on that.

For this activity you'll write an application that has only two choices: exit or execute an operation. If the user types **Q** (or **q**), the application will exit the loop and finish. Anything else will be considered an operation. You'll use the **Operators.findOperator** method to find and operator, then request to more inputs from the user. Each will be converted to a double (using **Double.parse** or **Scanner.nextDouble**). Operate on them using the Operator found and print the result to the console.

Because of the infinite loop, the application will start over, asking for another user action.

To complete this activity you'll have to:

1. Create a new class called **CommandLineCalculator** with a **main** method in it.

2. Use an infinite loop to keep the application running until the user asks to exit.

3. Collect the user input to decide which action to execute. If the action is **Q** or **q**, exit the loop.

4. If the action is anything else, find an operator and request two other inputs that will be the operands covering them to double.

5. Call the **operate** method on the Operator found and print the result to the console.

> **Note**
>
> The solution for this activity can be found on page 341.

Conversion

Sometimes we might wish to convert a given type to a string so we can print it out, or we might want to convert a string to a given type. An example is when we wish to convert the string "**100**" to the integer **100**, or convert the integer **100** to string "**100**".

Concatenating a primitive data type to a string using the **+** operator will return a string representation of that item.

For example, this is how to convert between an integer and a string:

```
String str1 = "100";
Integer number = Integer.parseInt(str1);
String str2 = number.toString();
System.out.println(str2);
```

The output is as follows:

```
100
```

Here we used the **parseInt()** method to get the integer value of the string, and then used the **toString()** method to convert the integer back to a string.

To convert an integer to a string, we concatenate it with an empty String "":

```
int a = 100;
String str = "" + a;
```

The output is as follows:

```
100
```

> **Note**
>
> Every object in Java has a string representation. Java provides the **toString()** method in the **Object** superclass, which we can override in our classes to provide a string representation of our classes. String representations are important when we want to print our class in string format.

Comparing Strings and Parts of Strings

The **String** class supports a number of methods for comparing strings and portions of strings.

Comparing two strings for equality:

```
String data= "Hello";
String data1 = "Hello";
if (data == data1){
System. out .println("Equal");
}else{
System. out .println("Not Equal");
}
```

The output is as follows:

```
Equal
```

Return **true** if this string ends with or begins with a given substring:

```
boolean value= data.endsWith( "ne");
System.out.println(value);
boolean value1 = data.startsWith("He");
System.out.println(value);
```

The output is as follows:

```
False
True
```

StringBuilder

We have stated that strings are immutable, that is, once they are declared they cannot be modified. However, sometimes we wish to modify a string. In such cases, we use the **StringBuilder** class. **StringBuilder** is just like a normal string except it is modifiable. **StringBuilder** also provides extra methods, such as **capacity()**, which returns the capacity allocated for it, and **reverse()**, which reverses the characters in it. StringBuilder also supports the same methods in the **String** class, such as **length()** and **toString()**.

Exercise 21: Working with StringBuilder

This exercise will append three strings to create one, then print out its length, capacity, and reverse:

1. Create a public class called **StringBuilderExample**, then create a **main** method:

   ```
   import java.lang.StringBuilder;
   public class StringBuilder {

   public static void main(String[] args) {
   ```

2. Create a new **StringBuilder()** object called **stringbuilder**:

   ```
   StringBuilder stringBuilder = new StringBuilder();
   ```

3. Append three phrases:

```
stringBuilder.append( "Java programmers " );
stringBuilder.append( "are wise " );
stringBuilder.append( "and knowledgeable");
```

4. Print out the string using the **\n** as a line break:

```
System.out.println("The string is \n" + stringBuilder.toString());
```

5. Find the length of the string and print it:

```
int len = stringBuilder.length();
System.out.println("The length of the string is: " + len);
```

6. Find the capacity of the string and print it:

```
int capacity = stringBuilder.capacity();
System.out.println("The capacity of the string is: " + capacity);
```

7. Reverse the string and print it out using the line break:

```
stringBuilder.reverse();
        System.out.println("The string reversed is: \n" + stringBuilder);
}
}
```

Here is the output:

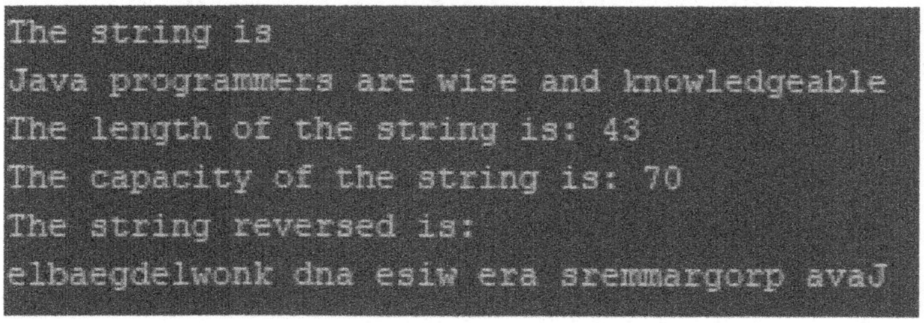

Figure 6.28: Output of StringBuilder class

In this exercise, we created a new instance of **StringBuilder** with the default capacity of 16. We then inserted a few strings and then printed out the entire string. We also got the number of characters in the builder by using **length()**. We then got the capacity of **StringBuilder**. The capacity is the number of characters allocated for **StringBuilder**. It is usually higher than or equal to the length of the builder. We finally reversed all the characters in the builder and then print it out. In the last print out, we didn't use **stringBuilder.toString()** because Java implicitly does that for us.

Activity 26: Removing Duplicate Characters from a String

In order to create secure passkeys, we have decided that we need to create lines of strings that do not contain duplicate characters. In this activity, you will be creating a program that takes in a string, removes any duplicate characters, and then prints out the result.

One way of doing this is to loop through all the characters of the string and for each character, we loop through the string again, checking if the character already exists. If we find a duplicate, we immediately remove it. This algorithm is a brute-force approach and not the best when it comes to running time. In fact, its running time is exponential.

These steps will help you complete the activity:

1. Create a new class named **Unique** and inside it create a **main** method. Leave it empty for now.

2. Create a new method **removeDups** called that takes and returns a string. This is where our algorithm will go. This method should be **public** and **static**.

3. Inside the method, check whether the string is null, empty, or has a length of 1. If any of these cases are true, then just return the original string since there checking is not needed.

4. Create a string called **result** that is empty. This will be unique string to be returned.

5. Create **for** loop from 0 to the length of the string passed into the method.

6. Inside the **for** loop, get the character at the current index of the string. Name the variable **c**.

7. Also create a boolean called **isDuplicate** and initialize it to **false**. When we encounter a duplicate, we will change it to **true**.

8. Create another nested **for** loop from 0 to the **length()** of result.

9. Inside the **for** loop, also get the character at the current index of result. Name it **d**.

10. Compare **c** and **d**. If they are equal, then set **isDuplicate** to true and **break**.

11. Close the inner **for** loop and go inside the first **for** loop.

12. Check if **isDuplicate** is **false**. If it is, then append **c** to result.

13. Go outside the first **for** loop and return the result. That concludes our algorithm.

14. Go back to our empty **main** method. Create a few test strings of the following:

    ```
    aaaaaaa
    aaabbbbb
    abcdefgh
    Ju780iu6G768
    ```

15. Pass the strings to our method and print out the result returned from the method.

16. Check the result. Duplicate characters should be removed in the returned strings.

    The output should look like this:

Figure 6.29: Expected output of Unique class

> **Note**
>
> The solution for this activity can be found on page 342.

Summary

This lesson brings us to the end of our discussion on the core principles of object-oriented programming. In this lesson, we have looked at data types, algorithms, and strings.

We've seen how an array is an ordered collection of items of the same type. Arrays are declared with square brackets, **[ ]**, and their size cannot be modified. Java provides the **Arrays** class from the collections framework that has extra methods we can use on arrays.

We also saw the concept of **Arraylist** and string. Java provides the **StringBuilder** class, which is basically a modifiable string. **stringbuilder** has **length** and **capacity** functions.

The Java Collections Framework and Generics

Learning Objectives

By the end of this lesson, you will be able to:

- Use collections to process data
- Compare objects in different ways
- Sort collections of objects
- Use collections to build efficient algorithms
- Use the best-suited collection for each use case

Introduction

In previous lessons, you learned how objects can be grouped together in arrays to help you process data in batches. Arrays are really useful but the fact that they have a static length makes them hard to deal with when loading an unknown amount of data. Also, accessing objects in the array requires you to know the array's index, otherwise traversing the whole array is necessary to find the object. You also learned briefly about ArrayList, which behaves like an array that can dynamically change its size to support more advanced use cases.

In this lesson, you'll learn how ArrayList actually works. You'll also learn about the Java Collections Framework, which includes some more advanced data structures for some more advanced use cases. As part of this journey, you'll also learn how to iterate on many data structures, compare objects in many different ways, and sort collections in an efficient way.

You'll also learn about generics, which is a powerful way of getting help from the compiler on using collections and other special classes.

Reading Data from Files

Before we begin, let's go through some fundamentals that we're going to be using in the next sections of this lesson.

Binary versus Text Files

There are many types of files in your computer: executable files, configuration files, data files, and so on. Files can be split into two basic groups: binary and text.

Binary files are used when human interaction with the files will only be indirect, such as executing an application (an executable file), or a spreadsheet file that loads inside Excel. If you try to look inside these files, you'll see a bunch of unreadable characters. This type of file is very useful because they can be made compact to take up less space and be structured so that computers can read them quickly.

Text files, on the other hand, contain readable characters. If you open them with a text editor, you can see what's in there. Not all of them are meant for humans to read and some formats are almost impossible to understand. But the majority of text files can be read and easily edited by humans.

CSV Files

A comma-separated value (CSV) file is a very common type of text file that is used to transport data between systems. CSVs are useful because they are easy to generate and easy to read. The structure of such a file is very simple:

- One record per line.

- The first line is the header.

- Each record is a long string where values are separated from others using a comma (values can also be separated by other delimiters).

The following is a piece of a file that was extracted from the sample data we'll be using:

```
id,name,email
10,Bill Gates,william.gates@microsoft.com
30,Jeff Bezos,jeff.bezos@amazon.com
20,Marc Benioff,marc.benioff@salesforce.com
```

Reading Files in Java

Java has two basic sets of classes that are used to read files: **Stream**, to read binary files, and **Reader**, to read text files. The most interesting part of how the **io** package is designed is that **Stream** and **Reader** can be combined to incrementally add functionality on top of each other. This capability is called piping because it resembles the process of connecting multiple pipes to one another.

We're going to be using a simple example to explain these, along with the help of **FileReader** and **BufferedReader**.

FileReader reads characters one at a time. **BufferedReader** can buffer these characters to read one line at a time. That simplifies things for us when reading a CSV because we can just create a **FileReader** instance, then wrap it with **BufferedReader**, and then read line by line from the CSV file:

Figure 7.1: Illustration of the process of reading from a CSV file

Exercise 22: Reading a CSV File

In this exercise, you'll use **FileReader** and **BufferedReader** to read lines from a CSV file, split them, and process them like a record:

1. Create a file called **ReadCSVFile.java** and add a class with the same name, and add a **main** method to it:

```
public class ReadCSVFile {
    public static void main(String [] args) throws IOException {
```

2. To start, you need to add a String variable that will get the name of the file to be loaded from the command-line argument:

```
String fileName = args[0];
```

3. Then, you create a new **FileReader** and pipe it into **BufferedReader** inside a try-with-resource, as in the following code:

```
FileReader fileReader = new FileReader(fileName);
try (BufferedReader reader = new BufferedReader(fileReader)) {
```

4. Now that you have a file open to read, you can read it line by line. **BufferedReader** will give you a new line all the way to the end of the file. When the file ends, it will return **null**. Because of that, we can declare a variable line and set it in the **while** condition. Then, we need to immediately check whether it's null. We also need a variable that will count the number of lines we read from the file:

```
String line;
int lineCounter = -1;
while ( (line = reader.readLine()) != null ) {
```

5. Inside the loop, you increment the line count and ignore line zero, which is the header. That's why we initialized **lineCounter** with **-1** instead of zero:

```
lineCounter++;
// Ignore the header
if (lineCounter == 0) {
  continue;
}
```

6. Finally, you split the line using the **split** method from the **String** class. That method receives a separator, which in our case is a comma:

```
String [] split = line.split(",");
System.out.printf("%d - %s\n", lineCounter, split[1]);
```

> **Note**
>
> You can see how **FileReader** is passed into **BufferedReader** and then never accessed again. That's because we only want the lines and we don't care about the intermediate process of transforming characters into lines.

Congratulations! You wrote an application that can read and parse a CSV. Feel free to dig deeper into this code and understand what happens when you change the initial line count value.

The output is as follows:

```
1 - Bill Gates
2 - Jeff Bezos
3 - Marc Benioff
4 - Bill Gates
5 - Jeff Bezos
6 - Sundar Pichai
7 - Jeff Bezos
8 - Larry Ellison
9 - Marc Benioff
10 - Larry Ellison
11 - Jeff Bezos
12 - Bill Gates
13 - Sundar Pichai
14 - Jeff Bezos
15 - Sundar Pichai
16 - Marc Benioff
17 - Larry Ellison
18 - Marc Benioff
19 - Jeff Bezos
20 - Marc Benioff
21 - Bill Gates
22 - Sundar Pichai
23 - Larry Ellison
24 - Bill Gates
```

```
25 - Larry Ellison
26 - Jeff Bezos
27 - Sundar Pichai
```

Building a CSV Reader

Now that you know how to read data from a CSV, we can start thinking about abstracting that logic away into its own pipe. Just like **BufferedReader** allows you to read a text file line-by-line, the CSV reader allows you to read a CSV file record by record. It builds on top of the **BufferedReader** functionality and adds the logic of splitting the line using a comma as the separator. The following diagram shows how our new pipeline will look with the CSV reader:

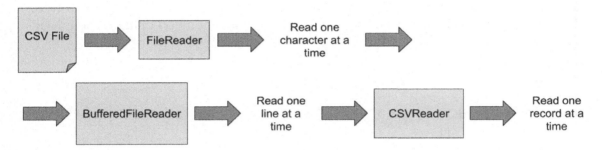

Figure 7.2: CSVReader can be added to the chain to read records one by one

Exercise 23: Building a CSV Reader

In this exercise, we'll follow the piping pattern and build a simple **CSVReader** that we'll be using throughout the rest of this lesson:

1. Create a new file called **CSVReader.java** and open it in your editor.

2. In this file, create a public class that is called **CSVReader** and implements the **Closeable** interface:

   ```
   public class CSVReader implements Closeable {
   ```

3. Add two fields, one field to store **BufferedReader** as **final** where we're going to read from, and another to store the line count:

   ```
   private final BufferedReader reader;
   private int lineCount = 0;
   ```

4. Create a constructor that receives **BufferedReader** and set it to the field. This constructor will also read and discard the first line of the passed-in reader, since that is the header and we don't care about them in this lesson:

```
public CSVReader(BufferedReader reader) throws IOException {
    this.reader = reader;

    // Ignores the header
    reader.readLine();
}
```

5. Implement the **close** method by just calling the **close** method from the underlying reader:

```
public void close() throws IOException {
    this.reader.close();
}
```

6. Just as **BufferedReader** has a **readLine** method, our **CSVReader** class will have a **readRecord** method, which will read the line from **BufferedReader** and then return that string, split by a comma. In this method, we'll keep track of how many lines we have read so far. We also need to check whether the reader returned a line or not since it can return null, which means it's finished reading the file and has no more lines to give us. If that's the case, we'll just follow the same pattern and return null:

```
public String[] readRow() throws IOException {
    String line = reader.readLine();
    if (line == null) {
        return null;
    }
    lineCount++;

    return line.split(",");
}
```

> **Note**
>
> In a more elaborate implementation, we could store the header to expose extra functionalities for the user of the class, such as fetch value by header name. We could also do some tidying and validation on the line to ensure no extra spaces are wrapping the values and that they contain the expected amount of values (same as the header count).

7. Expose **linecount** with a getter:

```
public int getLineCount() {
    return lineCount;
}
```

8. Now your new **CSVReader** is ready to be used! Create a new file called **UseCSVReaderSample.java**, with a class of the same name and a **main** method:

```
public class UseCSVReaderSample {
    public static void main (String [] args) throws IOException {
```

9. Following the same pattern we used before to read the lines from the CSV, now you can use your **CSVReader** class to read from the CSV file, adding the following to your **main** method:

```
String fileName = args[0];
FileReader fileReader = new FileReader(fileName);
BufferedReader reader = new BufferedReader(fileReader);
try (CSVReader csvReader = new CSVReader(reader)) {
    String[] row;
    while ( (row = csvReader.readRow()) != null ) {
        System.out.printf("%d - %s\n", csvReader.getLineCount(), row[1]);
    }
}
```

> **Note**
>
> From the preceding snippet, you can see that your code is now much simpler. It's focused on delivering the business logic (printing the second value with line count) and doesn't care about reading a CSV. This is a great practical example of how to create your readers to abstract away logic about processing the data coming from files.

10. For the code to compile, you'll need to add the imports from the **java.io** package:

```
import java.io.BufferedReader;
import java.io.FileReader;
import java.io.IOException;
```

The output is as follows:

```
 1 - Bill Gates
 2 - Jeff Bezos
 3 - Marc Benioff
 4 - Bill Gates
 5 - Jeff Bezos
 6 - Sundar Pichai
 7 - Jeff Bezos
 8 - Larry Ellison
 9 - Marc Benioff
10 - Larry Ellison
11 - Jeff Bezos
12 - Bill Gates
13 - Sundar Pichai
14 - Jeff Bezos
15 - Sundar Pichai
16 - Marc Benioff
17 - Larry Ellison
18 - Marc Benioff
19 - Jeff Bezos
20 - Marc Benioff
21 - Bill Gates
22 - Sundar Pichai
23 - Larry Ellison
24 - Bill Gates
25 - Larry Ellison
26 - Jeff Bezos
27 - Sundar Pichai
```

Arrays

As you have already learned from previous lessons, arrays are really powerful, but their static nature makes things difficult. Suppose you have a piece of code that loads users from some database or CSV file. The amount of data that will come from the database or file is unknown until you finish loading all the data. If you're using an array, you would have to resize the array on each record read. That would be too expensive because arrays can't be resized; they need to be copied over and over.

The following is some code that illustrates resizing an array:

```
// Increase array size by one
// Create new array
User[] newUsers = new User[users.length + 1];
// Copy data over
System.arraycopy(users, 0, newUsers, 0, users.length);
// Switch
users = newUsers;
```

To be more efficient, you could initialize the array with a specified capacity and trim the array after finishing reading all the records to ensure that it doesn't contain any extra empty rows in it. You would also need to ensure that the array has enough capacity while you're adding new records into it. If not, you'll have to make a new array with enough room and copy data over.

Exercise 24: Reading Users from a CSV File into an Array

In this exercise, you'll learn how to use an array to store an unlimited amount of data coming from a data source. In our case, we'll be using the same users CSV that we've been using throughout the previous sections:

1. Create a file called **User.java** and add a class with the same name. This class will have three fields: **id**, **name**, and **email**. It will also have a constructor that can initialize it with all three values. We'll use this class to represent a **User**:

```
public class User {
  public int id;
  public String name;
  public String email;
  public User(int id, String name, String email) {
    this.id = id;
    this.name = name;
    this.email = email;
  }
}
```

2. At the beginning of the **User** class, add a **static** method that will create a user from values coming as an array of strings. This will be useful when creating a **User** from the values read from a CSV:

```
public static User fromValues(String [] values) {
  int id = Integer.parseInt(values[0]);
  String name = values[1];
  String email = values[2];
  return new User(id, name, email);
}
```

3. Create another file called **IncreaseOnEachRead.java** and add a class with the same name and a **main** method that will pass the first argument from the command line to another method called **loadUsers**. Then, print the number of users loaded, like so:

```
public class IncreaseOnEachRead {
  public static final void main (String [] args) throws Exception {
    User[] users = loadUsers(args[0]);
    System.out.println(users.length);
  }
}
```

4. In this same file, add another method called **loadUsers**, which will return an array of users and receive a String called **fileToRead**, which will be the path to the CSV file to read:

```
public static User[] loadUsers(String fileToReadFrom) throws Exception {
```

5. In this method, start by creating an empty users array and returning it at the end:

```
User[] users = new User[0];
return users;
```

6. Between those two lines, add the logic to read the CSV record by record using your **CSVReader**. For each record, increase the size of the array by one and then add a newly created **User** to the last position on the array:

```
BufferedReader lineReader = new BufferedReader(new
FileReader(fileToReadFrom));
try (CSVReader reader = new CSVReader(lineReader)) {
  String [] row = null;
  while ( (row = reader.readRow()) != null) {
    // Increase array size by one
    // Create new array
    User[] newUsers = new User[users.length + 1];
```

```
        // Copy data over
        System.arraycopy(users, 0, newUsers, 0, users.length);
        // Swap
        users = newUsers;

        users[users.length - 1] = User.userFromRow(row);
    }
}
```

The output is as follows:

27

You now can read from the CSV file and have a reference to all users loaded from it. This implements the approach of increasing the array on each record read. How would you go about implementing the more efficient approach of initializing the array with some capacity and increasing it as needed and trimming it at the end?

Activity 27: Read Users from CSV Using Array with Initial Capacity

In this activity you're going to read users from the CSV similar to how you did in the previous exercise, but instead of growing the array on every read, create the array with an initial capacity and grow it as necessary. At the end, you'll need to check if the array has empty spaces left and shrink it to return an array with exact size as the number of users loaded.

To complete this activity you'll need to:

1. Initialize an array with an initial capacity.

2. Read the CSV from the path passed in from the command line in a loop, create users and add them to the array.

3. Keep track of how many users you loaded in a variable.

4. Before adding Users to the array, you'll need to check the size of the array and grow it if necessary.

5. At the end, shrink the array as necessary to return the exact number of users loaded.

> **Note**
>
> The solution for this activity can be found on page 345.

The Java Collections Framework

When building complex applications, you need to manipulate collections of objects in different ways. Initially, the core Java library was limited to only three options: Array, Vector, and Hashtable. All of them are powerful in their own way, but with time, it became clear that wasn't enough. People started building their own frameworks to deal with more complex use cases such as grouping, sorting, and comparing.

The Java Collections Framework was added to Java Standard Edition to reduce programming effort and improve the performance and interoperability of Java applications by providing data structures and algorithms that are efficient and easy to use. This set of interfaces and implementing classes were designed to provide an easy way for Java developers to build APIs that could be shared and reused.

Vectors

Vectors solve the problem of arrays being static. They provide a dynamic and scalable way of storing many objects. They grow as you add new elements, can be prepared to receive large numbers of elements, and it is easy to iterate over elements.

To take care of the internal array without having to resize it unnecessarily, a vector initializes it with some capacity and keeps track of what position the last element was added to using a pointer value, which is just an integer that marks that position. By default, the initial capacity is 10. When you add more than the capacity of the array, the internal array is copied over to a new one that is bigger by some factor, leaving more empty space open so that you can add extra elements. The copying process is just like you did manually with the array in *Exercise 24: Reading Users from a CSV File into an Array*. The following is an illustration of how that works:

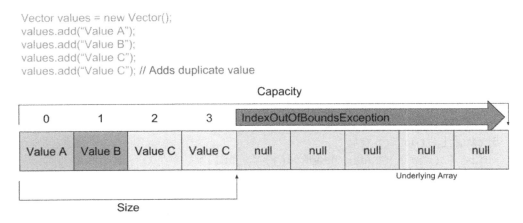

Figure 7.3: Illustration of Vectors

Using vectors was the way to get dynamic arrays in Java before the Java Collections Framework. However, there were two major problems:

- Lack of a defined interface that was easy to understand and extend

- Fully synchronized, which means it is protected against multi-threaded code

After the Java Collections Framework, vectors were retrofitted to comply with the new interfaces, solving the first problem.

Exercise 25: Reading Users from a CSV File into a Vector

Since a vector solves the problem of growing and shrinking as needed, in this exercise, we'll rewrite the previous exercise, but instead of handling the size of the array, we'll delegate to a vector. We'll also start building a **UsersLoader** class, which we'll share in all the future exercises:

1. Create a file called **UsersLoader.java** and add a class with the same name in it:

   ```
   public class UsersLoader {
   }
   ```

2. You'll use this class to add the shared methods so that you can load users from CSV files in future lessons. The first one you'll write is going to load users from a CSV into a vector. Add a public static method that returns a Vector. In this method, instantiate **Vector** and return it at the end:

   ```
   private static Vector loadUsersInVector(String pathToFile)
       throws IOException {
     Vector users = new Vector();
     return users;
   }
   ```

3. Between creating **Vector** and returning it, load the data from the CSV and add it to **Vector**:

   ```
   BufferedReader lineReader = new BufferedReader(new
   FileReader(pathToFile));
   try (CSVReader reader = new CSVReader(lineReader)) {
     String [] row = null;
     while ( (row = reader.readRow()) != null) {
       users.add(User.fromValues(row));
     }
   }
   ```

4. Add the imports that are required for this file to compile:

```
import java.io.BufferedReader;
import java.io.FileReader;
import java.io.IOException;
import java.util.Vector;
```

5. Create a file called **ReadUsersIntoVector.java** and add a class with the same name and a **main** method in it:

```
public class ReadUsersIntoVector {
  public static void main (String [] args) throws IOException {
  }
}
```

6. In the **main** method, similar to what we did in the array case, call the method that loads users from a CSV into **Vector** and then print the size of **Vector**. In this case, use the **loadUsersInVector()** method we created in the previous step:

```
Vector users = UserLoader.loadUsersInVector(args[0]);
System.out.println(users.size());
```

7. Add the imports for this file to compile:

```
import java.io.IOException;
import java.util.Vector;
```

The output is as follows:

```
27
```

Congratulations on finishing one more exercise! This time, you can see that your code is much simpler since most of the logic of loading the CSV, splitting it into values, creating a user, and resizing arrays is now abstracted away.

Activity 28: Reading a Real Dataset Using Vector

In this activity you'll download a CSV with income information from the United States census and do some calculation over the values in the file.

To start, go to this page: https://github.com/TrainingByPackt/Java-Fundamentals/tree/master/Lesson07/data. To download the CSV you can click on **Adult_Data**. It will open the data file in the browser. Download the file and save it to some place in your computer. The extension is irrelevant but you'll need to remember the name of the file and the path.

You can read more about the format of the data in the website or just by opening it as a text file. Two things to keep in mind while working with this file:

- There's an extra empty line at the end of the file
- This file has no header line

Create an application that will calculate the minimum, maximum and average wage in this file. After reading all rows, your application should print these results. To accomplish this you'll need to:

1. Load all wages from the file into a Vector of integers using your **CSVReader**. You can modify your **CSVReader** to support files without headers.

2. Iterate over the values in the Vector and keep track of three values: minimum, maximum and sum.

3. Print the results at the end. Remember, the average is just the sum divided by the size of the Vector.

> **Note**
>
> The solution for this activity can be found on page 347.

Iterating over Collections

When working with arrays, you have two ways of iterating over them: you can use a **for** loop with an index:

```
for (int i = 0; i < values.length; i++) {
    System.out.printf("%d - %s\n", i, values[i]);
}
```

You can also iterate using a **for-each** loop, where you don't have access to the index of the element:

```
for (String value : values) {
    System.out.println(value);
}
```

When you need to iterate over a vector, you can use the loop with an index, just like an array:

```
for (int i = 0; i < values.size(); i++) {
  String value = (String) values.get(i);
  System.out.printf("%d - %s\n", i, value);
}
```

You can also use **Vector** in a **for-each** loop, just like an array:

```
for (Object value : values) {
  System.out.println(value);
}
```

This works because **Vector** implements **Iterable**. Iterable is a simple interface that tells the compiler that the instance can be used in a **for-each** loop. In fact, you could change your **CSVReader** to implement Iterable and then use it in a **for-each** loop, just like in the following code:

```
try (IterableCSVReader csvReader = new IterableCSVReader(reader)) {
  for (Object rowAsObject : csvReader) {
    User user = User.fromValues((String[]) rowAsObject);
    System.out.println(user.name);
  }
}
```

Iterable is a very simple interface; it has only one method that you need to implement: **iterator()**. That method returns an iterator. An iterator is another simple interface that only has two methods to implement:

- **hasNext()**: Returns **true** if the iterator still has elements to return.

- **next()**: Fetches the next record and returns it. It will throw an exception if **hasNext()** returns **false** before calling this.

An iterator represents a simple way of getting things out of a collection. But it also has another method that is important in some more advanced contexts, **remove()**, which removes the current element that was just fetched from calling **next()**.

This **remove** method is important because when you're iterating on a collection, you cannot modify it. This means that if you write a **for-each** loop to read elements from the vector and then inside this loop you call **remove(Object)** to remove an element from it, **ConcurrentModificationException** would be thrown. So, if you want to iterate over a collection using a loop and in this loop you need to remove an element from vector, you'll have to use an iterator.

You must be thinking, "why would it be designed to work like this?" Because Java is a multi-threaded language. You won't learn how to create threads or use them in this book because it's an advanced topic. But the idea behind multi-threading is that a piece of data in memory can be accessed by two pieces of code at the exact same time. This is possible because of the multi-core capabilities of modern computers. With collections and arrays, you have to be very careful when working on multi-threaded applications. The following is an illustration of how that happens:

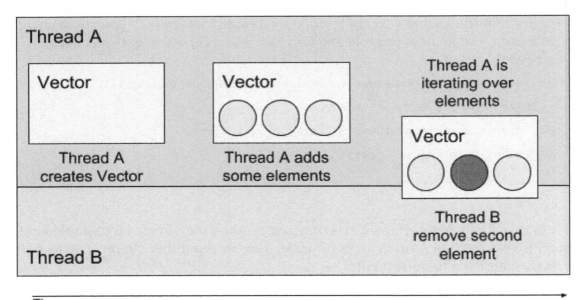

Figure 7.4: Illustration of how ConcurrentModificationException occurs

`ConcurrentModificationException` is more common than we expect. The following is a sample for loop using an iterator that avoids this problem:

```
for (Iterator it = values.iterator(); it.hasNext();) {
  String value = (String) it.next();
  if (value.equals("Value B")) {
    it.remove();
  }
}
```

Activity 29: Iterating on a Vector of Users

Now that you have a method to load all users from the CSV file, and you know how to iterate on a vector, write an application that prints the names and emails of all users in the file. To complete this activity, you'll need to follow these steps:

1. Create a new Java application that loads data from a CSV file in a vector. The file will be specified from the command line.

2. Iterate over the users in the vector and print a string that is a concatenation of their names and emails.

> **Note**
>
> The solution for this activity can be found on page 349.

Hashtable

Arrays and vectors are great when dealing with many objects that are to be processed in sequence. But when you have a group of objects that need to be indexed by a key, for example, some kind of identification, then they become cumbersome.

Enter hashtables. They are a very old data structure that was created to solve exactly this problem: given a value, quickly identifying it and finding it in an array. To solve this, hash tables use a hashing function to uniquely identify objects. From that hash, they can use another function (normally a remainder of a division) to store the values in an array. That makes the process of adding an element to the table deterministic and fetching it very fast. The following is an illustration of the process of how a value gets stored in a hashtable:

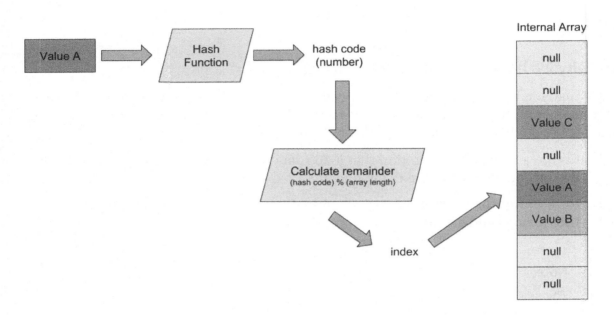

Figure 7.5: The process behind storing and fetching a value from a hash table

A hashtable uses an array to internally store an entry, which represents a key-value pair. When you put a pair in the hashtable, you provide the key and the value. The key is used to find where in the array the entry will be stored. Then, an entry holding the key and value is created and stored in the position specified.

To fetch the value, you pass in the key from which the hash is calculated and the entry can be quickly found in the array.

An interesting feature you get for free from this process is de-duplication. Because adding a value with the same key will generate the same hash, when you do that, it will overwrite whatever was stored in there previously.

Just as with vectors, the **Hashtable** class was added to Java before the Collections Framework. It suffered from the same two problems that vectors suffered from: lack of defined interfaces and being fully synchronized. It also breaks the Java naming convention by not following CamelCase for word separation.

Also, as with vectors, after the introduction of the Collections Framework, hashtables was retrofitted to comply with the new interfaces, making them a seamless part of the framework.

Exercise 26: Writing an Application that Finds a User by Email

In this exercise, you'll write an application that reads the users from a specified CSV file into a hashtable, using their email as a key. They then receive an email address from the command line and search for it in the hashtable, printing its information or a friendly message if this isn't found:

1. In your **UsersLoader.java** file, add a new method that will load users into a hashtable using the email as a key. Create a **Hashtable** at the beginning and return it at the end:

   ```
   public static Hashtable loadUsersInHashtableByEmail(String pathToFile)
       throws IOException {
     Hashtable users = new Hashtable();
     return users;
   }
   ```

2. Between creating **Hashtable** and returning it, load the users from the CSV and put them in **Hashtable** using **email** as the key:

   ```
   BufferedReader lineReader = new BufferedReader(new
   FileReader(pathToFile));
   try (CSVReader reader = new CSVReader(lineReader)) {
     String [] row = null;
     while ( (row = reader.readRow()) != null) {
       User user = User.fromValues(row);
       users.put(user.email, user);
     }
   }
   ```

3. Import **Hashtable** so that the file compiles correctly:

   ```
   import java.util.Hashtable;
   ```

4. Create a file called **FindUserHashtable.java** and add a class with the same name and add a **main** method:

```
public class FindUserHashtable {
  public static void main(String [] args) throws IOException {
  }
}
```

5. In your **main** method, load the users into a **Hashtable** using the method we created in the previous steps and print the number of users found:

```
Hashtable users = UsersLoader.loadUsersInHashtableByEmail(args[0]);
System.out.printf("Loaded %d unique users.\n", users.size());
```

6. Print some text to inform the user that you're waiting for them to type in an email address:

```
System.out.print("Type a user email: ");
```

7. Read the input from the user by using **Scanner**:

```
try (Scanner userInput = new Scanner(System.in)) {
   String email = userInput.nextLine();
```

8. Check whether the email address is in **Hashtable**. If not, print a friendly message and exit the application:

```
if (!users.containsKey(email)) {
  // User email not in file
  System.out.printf("Sorry, user with email %s not found.\n", email);
  return;
}
```

9. If found, print some information about the user that was found:

```
User user = (User) users.get(email);
System.out.printf("User with email '%s' found!", email);
System.out.printf(" ID: %d, Name: %s", user.id, user.name);
```

10. Add the necessary imports:

```
import java.io.IOException;
import java.util.Hashtable;
import java.util.Scanner;
```

This is the output in the first case:

```
Loaded 5 unique users.
Type a user email: william.gates@microsoft.com
User with email 'william.gates@microsoft.com' found! ID: 10, Name: Bill
Gates
```

This is the output in the second case:

```
Loaded 5 unique users.
Type a user email: randomstring
Sorry, user with email randomstring not found.
```

Congratulations! In this exercise, you used **Hashtable** to quickly find a user by email address.

Activity 30: Using a Hashtable to Group Data

One very common usage of Hashtable, is to group records based on some key. In this activity you'll use this to calculate the minimum, maximum and average wages from the file downloaded on the previous activity.

If you haven't already, go to this page: https://github.com/TrainingByPackt/Java-Fundamentals/tree/master/Lesson07/data. To download the CSV you can click on **Adult_Data**. As explained before, this file contains income data from the United States census.

There are many attributes that are associated with each wage. For this exercise, you'll group the records by the education attribute. Then, as you did before, print the minimum, maximum and average wages, but now, for each grouped set wages.

To complete this activity you'll need to:

1. Load the **adult.data** CSV file using the **CSVReader**. This time, you'll load the data into a Hashtable where the keys are Strings and the values are Vectors of integers. The key is going to be the education attribute and in the vector, you'll store all the wages associated with that education.

2. With all the wages grouped inside the Hashtable, now you can iterate over the entries, key-value pairs, and do the same calculation you did in the previous activity.

3. For each entry, print the minimum, maximum and average wages for each education level found in the file.

> **Note**
>
> The solution for this activity can be found on page 351.

Generics

Classes that work with other classes in a generic way, like Vector, didn't have a way to explicitly tell the compiler that only one type was accepted. Because of that, it uses Object everywhere and runtime checks like **instanceof** and casting were necessary everywhere.

To solve this problem, Generic was introduced in Java 5. In this section you'll understand better the problem, the solution and how to use it.

What was the Problem?

When declaring an array, you tell the compiler what type of data goes inside the array. If you try to add something else in there, it won't compile. Look at the following code:

```
// This compiles and work

User[] usersArray = new User[1];

usersArray[0] = user;


// This wouldn't compile

// usersArray[0] = "Not a user";


/* If you uncomment the last line and try to compile, you would get the
following error: */


File.java:15: error: incompatible types: String cannot be converted to User
        usersArray[0] = "Not a user";
                        ^
```

Let's say you try to do something similar with **Vector**, like the following:

```
Vector usersVector = new Vector();
usersVector.add(user); // This compiles
usersVector.add("Not a user"); // This also compiles
```

The compiler will not help you at all. The same thing goes for **Hashtable**:

```
Hashtable usersTable = new Hashtable();
usersTable.put(user.id, user); // This compiles
usersTable.put("Not a number", "Not a user"); // This also compiles
```

This also occurs when fetching data. When fetching from an array, the compiler knows what type of data is in there, so you don't need to cast it:

```
User userFromArray = usersArray[0];
```

To fetch data from a collection, you need to cast data. A simple example is adding the following code after adding the two elements to the previous **usersVector**:

```
User userFromVector = (User) usersVector.get(1);
```

It will compile, but it will throw a **ClassCastException** at runtime:

```
Exception in thread "main" java.lang.ClassCastException: java.lang.String
cannot be cast to User
```

This was a big source of bugs for a long time in the Java world. And then generics came along and changed everything.

Generics is a way for you to tell the compiler that a generic class will only work with a specified type. Let's have a look at what this means:

- **Generic class**: A generic class is a class that has a generic functionality which works with different types, like a Vector, that can store any type of object.

- **Specified type**: With generics, when you instantiate a generic class, you specify what type that generic class will be used with. For example, you can specify that you only want to store users in your Vector.

- **Compiler**: It is important to highlight that a generic is a compile time-only feature. There's no information about generic type definition at runtime. At runtime, everything behaves like it was before generics.

Generic classes have a special declaration that exposes how many types it requires. Some generic classes require multiple types, but most only require one. In the Javadocs for generic classes, there's a special angle brackets arguments list that specifies how many type parameters it requires, such as in **<T, R>**. The following is a screenshot of the Javadoc for **java.util.Map**, which is one of the interfaces in the Collections Framework:

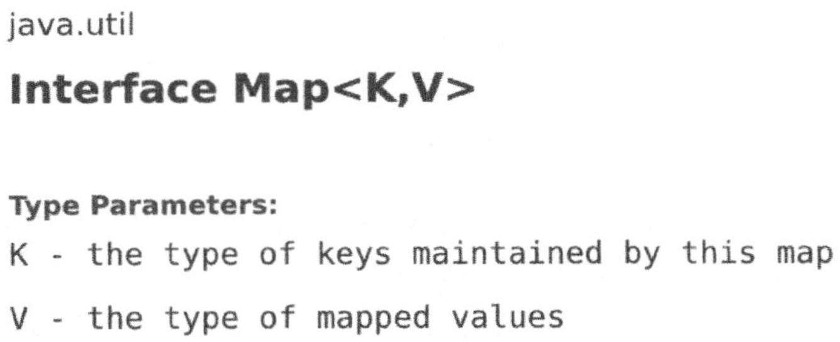

java.util

Interface Map<K,V>

Type Parameters:

K - the type of keys maintained by this map

V - the type of mapped values

Figure 7.6: Screenshot of the Javadoc for java.util.Map, where it shows the generic type declaration

How to Use Generics

To use generics, when declaring an instance of a generic class, you specify what type will be used for that instance using angle brackets. The following is how you declare a vector that only handles users:

```
Vector<User> usersVector = new Vector<>();
```

For a hashtable, you need to specify the types for the key and value. For a hashtable that would store users with their IDs as keys, the declaration would look as follows:

```
Hashtable<Integer, User> usersTable = new Hashtable<>();
```

Just declaring the generic types with the correct parameters will solve the problems we described earlier. For example, let's say you are declaring a vector so that it only handles users. You would try and add a String to it, as in the following code:

```
usersVector.add("Not a user");
```

However, this would result in a compilation error:

```
File.java:23: error: no suitable method found for add(String)
        usersVector.add("Not a user");
            ^
```

Now that the compiler ensures that nothing except users will be added to the vector, you can fetch data from it without having to cast it. The compiler will automatically convert the type for you:

```
// No casting needed anymore
User userFromVector = usersVector.get(0);
```

Exercise 27: Finding a User by Text in a Name or Email

In this exercise, you'll write an application that reads users from a CSV file into a vector like you did before. You'll then be asked for a string that will be used to filter the users. The application will print some information about all the users that contained the passed-in string in their name or email:

1. Open your **UsersLoader.java** file and set all the methods to use generic versions of collections. Your **loadUsersInHashtableByEmail** should look as follows (only showing the lines that have changed):

```
public static Hashtable<String, User> loadUsersInHashtableByEmail(String pathToFile)
    throws IOException {
  Hashtable<String, User> users = new Hashtable<>();
  // Unchanged lines
}
```

Your **loadUsersInVector** should look as follows (only showing lines that have changed):

```
public static Vector<User> loadUsersInVector(String pathToFile) throws IOException{
  Vector<User> users = new Vector<>();
  // Unchanged lines
}
```

> **Note:**
>
> You don't have to change other places where you called these methods because using them as the non-generic version still works.

2. Create a file named **FindByStringWithGenerics.java** and add a class with the same name and a **main** method, like so:

```java
public class FindByStringWithGenerics {
  public static void main (String [] args) throws IOException {
  }
}
```

3. Add a call to the **loadUsersInVector** method to your **main** method, storing the value in a vector with the specified generic type. Print the number of users loaded:

```java
Vector<User> users = UsersLoader.loadUsersInVector(args[0]);
System.out.printf("Loaded %d users.\n", users.size());
```

4. After that, ask the user to type a string and store that in a variable after transforming it to lowercase:

```java
System.out.print("Type a string to search for: ");
// Read user input from command line
try (Scanner userInput = new Scanner(System.in)) {
  String toFind = userInput.nextLine().toLowerCase();
}
```

5. Inside the try-with-resource block, create a variable to count the number of users found. Then, iterate over the users from the vector we loaded previously and search for the string in the email and name for each user, making sure to set all strings to lowercase:

```java
int totalFound = 0;
for (User user : users) {
  if (user.email.toLowerCase().contains(toFind)
        ||user.name.toLowerCase().contains(toFind)) {
    System.out.printf("Found user: %s",user.name);
    System.out.printf(" Email: %s\n", user.email);
    totalFound++;
  }
}
```

6. Finally, if **totalFound** is zero, meaning no users were found, print a friendly message. Otherwise, print the number of users you found:

```java
if (totalFound == 0) {
  System.out.printf("No user found with string '%s'\n", toFind);
} else {
  System.out.printf("Found %d users with '%s'\n", totalFound, toFind);
}
```

Here's the output of the first case:

```
Loaded 27 users.
Type a string to search for: will
Found user: Bill Gates Email: william.gates@microsoft.com
Found user: Bill Gates Email: william.gates@microsoft.com
Found user: Bill Gates Email: william.gates@microsoft.com
Found user: Bill Gates Email: william.gates@microsoft.com
Found user: Bill Gates Email: william.gates@microsoft.com
Found 5 users with 'will'
```

Here's the output of the second case:

```
Loaded 27 users.
Type a string to search for: randomstring
No user found with string 'randomstring'
```

Congratulations! Now you understand how generics can help you write safe and easy code using your collections.

Sorting and Comparing

In our day-to-day lives, we compare things all the time: cold/hot, short/tall, thin/thick, big/small. Objects can be compared using different spectrums. You can compare them by color, size, weight, volume, height, width, and so on. When comparing two objects, you're normally interested in finding which one is more something (or less something) than the other or whether they are equal on whatever measure you're using.

There are two basic scenarios where comparing objects is important: finding the maximum (or minimum) and sorting.

When finding the maximum or minimum, you compare all objects with each other and then pick the winner in whatever regard you were looking at. Everything else can be ignored. You don't need to keep track of the others, as long as you can be sure you're not infinitely comparing the same two objects over and over again.

Sorting, on the other hand, is more complicated. You have to keep track of all the elements that you have compared so far and you also need to make sure that you keep them sorted along the way.

The Collections Framework includes a few interfaces, classes, and algorithms that can help you with all of this.

Comparables and Comparators

In Java, there is an interface that describes how objects can be compared to each other. The **java.lang.Comparable** interface is a generic interface that has only one method that needs to be implemented: **compareTo(T)**. From the Javadocs, **compareTo** should return "a negative integer, zero, or a positive integer as this object is less than, equal to, or greater than the specified object".

To understand how it works, let's take a String as an example. String implements **java.lang.Comparable<String>**, which means you can compare two strings, like so:

```
"A".compareTo("B") < 0 // -> true
"B".compareTo("A") > 0 // -> true
```

If the first object on the comparison is "less" than the second, then it will return a negative number (it can be any number and the size means nothing). If both are the same, then it will return zero. If the first is more than the second, then it will return a positive number (again, size means nothing).

That's all well and good until you stumble onto something such as the following:

```
"a".compareTo("B") < 0 // -> false
```

When you go to read the String Javadoc, its **compareTo** method says that it "compares two strings lexicographically". This means that it uses the character code to check which string comes first. The difference here is that the character codes have all the uppercase letters first, then all the lowercase ones. Because of that, "A" comes after "B", since B's character code is before A's.

But what if we want to compare strings alphabetically and not lexicographically? As mentioned before, objects can be compared in many different spectrums. Because of that, Java provides another interface that can be used to compare two objects: **java.util.Comparator**. Classes can implement a comparator using the most common use case, like numbers can be compared using their natural order. Then, we can create another class that implements **Comparator** to compare objects using some other custom algorithm.

Exercise 28: Creating a Comparator that Compares Strings Alphabetically

In this exercise, you'll create a class that implements **java.util.Comparator<String>** and can be used to compare strings alphabetically, and not lexicographically:

1. Create a file called **AlphabeticComparator.java** and add a class with the same name that implements **java.util.Comparator<String>** (don't forget the import):

    ```
    import java.util.Comparator;

    public class AlphabeticComparator implements Comparator<String> {
      public int compare(String first, String second) {
      }
    }
    ```

2. In the **compareTo** method, you just turn both strings into lowercase and then compare them:

    ```
    return first.toLowerCase().compareTo(second.toLowerCase());
    ```

3. Create a new file called **UseAlphabeticComparator.java** and add a class with the same name with a **main** method in so that you can test your new comparator:

    ```
    public class UseAlphabeticComparator {
      public static void main (String [] args) {
      }
    }
    ```

4. Now instantiate your class and write some test cases to make sure that your class is working as expected:

    ```
    AlphabeticComparator comparator = new AlphabeticComparator();
    System.out.println(comparator.compare("A", "B") < 0); // -> true
    System.out.println(comparator.compare("B", "A") > 0); // -> true
    System.out.println(comparator.compare("a", "B") < 0); // -> true
    System.out.println(comparator.compare("b", "A") > 0); // -> true
    System.out.println(comparator.compare("a", "b") < 0); // -> true
    System.out.println(comparator.compare("b", "a") > 0); // -> true
    ```

The output is as follows:

```
true
true
true
true
true
true
```

Congratulations! You wrote your first comparator. Now, let's move on and see what else you can do with Comparables and Comparators.

Sorting

When you have collections of objects, it's very common to want to sort them in some way or other. Being able to compare two objects is the basis for all sorting algorithms. Now that you know how to compare objects, it's time to use that to add sorting logic to your applications.

There are many sorting algorithms out there, each one with its own strengths and weaknesses. For simplicity, we'll discuss only two: bubble sort, because of its simplicity, and merge sort, because of its stable performance, which is why it was picked by the Java core implementers.

Bubble Sort

The most naive sorting algorithm is bubble sort, but it's also the simplest to understand and implement. It works by iterating over each element and comparing it with the next element. If it finds two elements that are not sorted, it swaps them and moves on to the next. When it gets to the end of the array, it checks how many elements were swapped. It continues this cycle until the number of swapped elements in a cycle is zero, which means that the whole array or collection has been sorted.

The following is an illustration of how sorting an array with seven elements using bubble sort would happen:

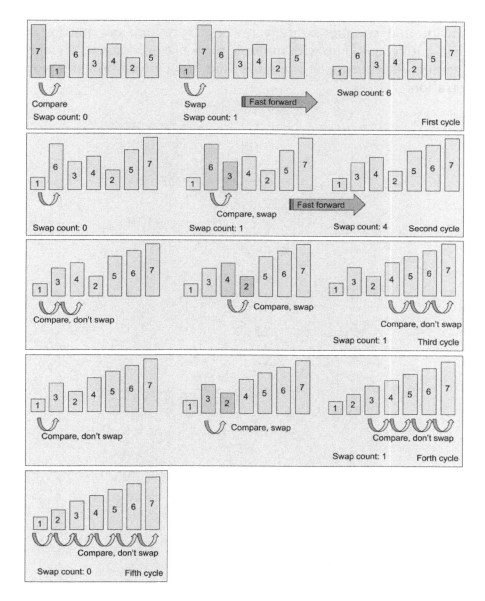

Figure 7.7: Illustration showing how bubble sort works

Bubble sort is very space efficient since it doesn't need any extra arrays or a place to store variables. However, it uses a lot of iterations and comparisons. In the example from the illustration, there's a total of 30 comparisons and 12 swaps.

Merge Sort

Bubble sort works, but as you may have noticed, it is really naive and it feels like there are a lot of wasted cycles. Merge sort, on the other hand, is much more efficient and is based on the divide-and-conquer strategy. It works by recursively splitting the array/collection in half until you end up with multiple pairs of one element. Then, it merges them back together while sorting at the same time. You can see how this works in the following illustration:

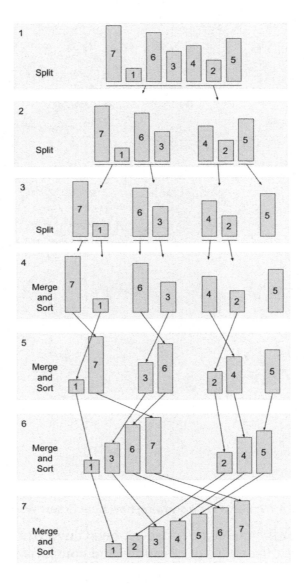

Figure 7.8: Illustration of the merge sort algorithm

In comparison to bubble sort, the number of comparisons for merge sort is much smaller – only 13 for the illustrated example. It uses more memory space since every merge step needs an extra array to store the data that is being merged.

One good thing that is not explicit in the preceding illustration is that merge sort has stable performance since it will always execute the same amount of steps; it doesn't matter how shuffled or sorted the data is. Compared to bubble sort, the number of swaps can get very high if you get a situation where the array/collection is sorted backwards.

Stability is very important for a core library such as the Collections Framework, and that's why merge sort was the algorithm that was picked as the implementation for sorting in the `java.util.Collections` utility class.

Activity 31: Sorting Users

Write three user comparators: one to compare by ID, one to compare by name, and one to compare by email. Then, write an application that loads the unique users and prints the users sorted by a field that was picked from an input from the command line. To complete this activity, you will need to follow these steps:

1. Write three classes that implement `java.util.Comparator<User>`. One that compares by ID, one that compares by name, and one that compares by email.

2. Load the users from the CSV using the method that returns a **Hashtable** instance so that you have a collection with unique users.

3. Load the values from **Hashtable** into a vector so that you can keep them in a specified order.

4. Read input from the command line to decide what field will be used to sort.

5. Use the correct comparator to sort the vector using the `java.util.Collections` sort method.

6. Print the users.

> **Note**
>
> The solution for this activity can be found on page 354.

Data Structures

The most fundamental part of building applications is processing data. The way you store the data is influenced by the way you'll need to read and process it. Data structures define the way you store data. Different data structures optimize for different use cases. So far, we have mentioned two ways of accessing data:

- Sequentially, as with an array or vector
- Key-value pairs, as with a hashtable

> **Note**
>
> In the following sections, we'll discuss the basic data structure of interfaces that have been added to the Collections Framework and how they differ from each other. We'll also dive deeper into each implementation and the use cases they solve.

Collection

This is the most generic interface that is the base for all collections except Map. The documentation describes it as representing a collection of objects called elements. It declares the basic interface for all collections with the following most important methods:

- **add(Element)**: Adds an element to the collection
- **clear()**: Removes all elements from the collection
- **contains(Object)**: Checks whether an object is in the collection
- **remove(Object)**: Removes the specified element from the collection, if present
- **size()**: Returns the number of elements stored in the collection

List

The list interface represents a sequential collection of elements that can grow indefinitely. Elements in a list can be accessed by their index, which is the position that they were put in, but can change if elements are added between other elements.

When iterating over a list, the order that the elements will be fetched in is deterministic and will always be based on the order of their indexes, just like an array.

As we mentioned previously, Vector was retrofitted to support the Collections Framework and it implements the list interface. Let's take a look at the other implementations that are available.

`List` extends `Collection`, so it inherits all the methods we mentioned previously and adds some other important methods, mostly associated with position-based access:

- `add(int, Element)`: Adds an element at the specified position
- `get(int)`: Returns the element at the specified position
- `indexOf(Object)`: Returns the index of the object or `-1` if not present in the collection
- `set(int, Element)`: Replaces the element at the specified position
- `subList(int, int)`: Creates a sublist from the original list

ArrayList

Just like Vector, ArrayList wraps an array and takes care of scaling it as needed, behaving just like a dynamic array. The major difference between the two is that vectors are fully synchronized. This means that they protect you from concurrent access (multi-threaded applications). It also means that on non-concurrent applications, which occurs in the majority of the cases, Vector is slower because of the locking mechanisms that are added to it. For that reason, it is recommended that you use ArrayList, unless you really need a synchronized list.

As we mentioned previously, for all purposes, ArrayList and Vector can be used interchangeably. Their functionality is the same and both implement the same interfaces.

LinkedList

LinkedList is an implementation of List that does not store elements in an underlying array, like ArrayList or Vector. It wraps each value in another object called a node. A node is an internal class that contains two references to other nodes (the next node and the previous node) and the value being stored for that element. This type of list is known as a double-linked list because each node is linked twice, once in each direction: from the previous to the next and from the next to the previous.

Internally, LinkedList stores a reference to the first and last nodes, so it can only traverse the list starting from the beginning or the end. It is not good for random or position-based access as with arrays, ArrayLists, and vectors, but it is good when adding an undetermined number of elements very fast.

LinkedList also stores a variable that keeps track of the size of the list. That way, it doesn't have to traverse the list every time to check the size.

The following illustration shows how LinkedList is implemented:

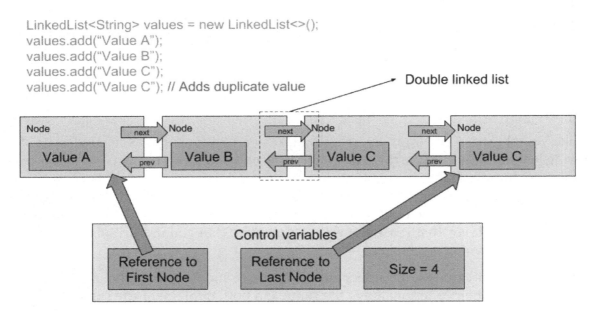

Figure 7.9: How LinkedList works under the hood

Map

When you need to store elements associated with keys, you use Maps. As we saw previously, Hashtable is a powerful mechanism for indexing objects by some key, and after the addition of the Collections Framework, Hashtable was retrofitted to implement Map.

The most fundamental property of maps is that they cannot contain duplicate keys.

Maps are powerful because they allow you to see the dataset from three different perspectives: keys, values, and key-value pairs. After adding your elements to a map, you can iterate over them from any of those three perspectives, giving you extra flexibility when fetching data from it.

The most important methods in the **Map** interface are as follows:

- **clear()**: Remove all keys and values from the map
- **containsKey(Object)**: Check whether the key is present in the map
- **containsValue(Object)**: Check whether the value is present in the map
- **entrySet()**: Return a set of entries with all the key-value pairs in the map
- **get(Object)**: Return the value associated with the specified key if present
- **getOrDefault(Object, Value)**: Return the value associated with the specified key if present, otherwise return the specified value
- **keySet()**: A set containing all keys in the map
- **put(Key, Value)**: Add or replace a key-value pair
- **putIfAbsent(Key, Value)**: Same as the previous method, but won't replace if the key is already present
- **size()**: The number of key-value pairs in this map
- **values()**: Return a collection with all the values present in this map

HashMap

Just like **Hashtable**, **HashMap** implements a hash table to store the entries of key-value pairs, and it works exactly the same way. Just as Vector is to ArraySet, Hashtable is so to **HashMap**. **Hashtable** existed before the Map interface, so HashMap was created as a non-synchronous implementation of the hash table.

As we mentioned before, hash tables, and consequently HashMap, are very fast to find elements by key. They are great to use as an in-memory cache where you load data that's been keyed by some field, like you did in *Exercise 26: Writing an Application that Finds a User by Email*.

TreeMap

TreeMap is an implementation of Map that can keep key-value pairs sorted by key or by a specified comparator.

As the name implies, TreeMap uses a tree as the underlying storage mechanism. Trees are very special data structures that are used to keep data sorted as insertions happen and at the same time, fetch data with very few iterations. The following illustration shows what a tree looks like and how a fetch operation can quickly find an element, even in very large trees:

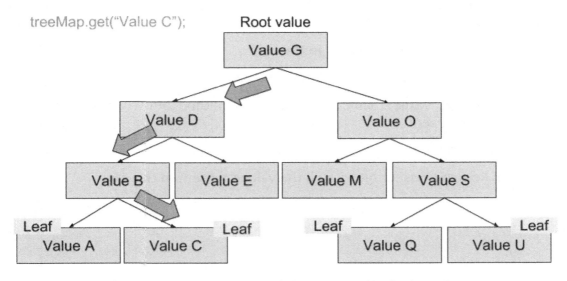

Figure 7.10: A tree data structure being traversed to fetch an element

Trees have nodes that represent the branches. Everything starts from a root node and expands into multiple branches. At the ends of the leaf nodes, there are nodes with no children. TreeMap implements a specific type of tree called a red-black tree, which is a binary tree, so each node can have only two children.

LinkedHashMap

The name of the `LinkedHashMap` class is a bit cryptic because internally it uses two data structures to support some use cases that HashMap didn't support: a hash table and a linked list. The hash table is used to quickly add and fetch elements from the map. The linked list is used when iterating over the entries by whatever means: key, value, or key-value pair. This gives it the ability to iterate over the entries in a deterministic order, which is whatever order they were inserted in.

Set

The main characteristic of sets is that they contain no duplicate elements. Sets are useful when you want to collect elements and at the same time eliminate duplicate values.

Another important characteristic about sets is that the order that you fetch elements from them varies based on the implementation. This means that if you want to eliminate duplicates, you have to think about how you're going to read them afterward.

All set implementations in the Collections Framework are based on their corresponding Map implementation. The only difference is that they handle the values in the set as the keys in the map.

HashSet

By far the most common of all the sets, HashSet uses a HashMap as the underlying storage mechanism. It stores its elements in a random order, based on the hashing function used in HashMap.

TreeSet

Backed by a TreeMap, `TreeSet` is really useful when you want to store unique elements sorted by their natural order (comparables) or using a comparator.

LinkedHashSet

Backed by `LinkedHashMap`, `LinkedHashSet` will keep the insertion order and remove duplicates as you add them to the set. It has the same advantages as LinkedHashSet: fast insertion and fetching like HashSet, and fast iteration like LinkedList.

Exercise 29: Using TreeSet to Print Sorted Users

In *Activity 31: Sorting Users*, you wrote three comparators that can be used to sort users. Let's use them and TreeSet to make an application that prints the sorted users in a much more efficient way:

1. Add a method to your **UsersLoader** class that can load the users into **Set**:

```java
public static void loadUsersIntoSet(String pathToFile, Set<User> usersSet)
    throws IOException {
  FileReader fileReader = new FileReader(pathToFile);
  BufferedReader lineReader = new BufferedReader(fileReader);
  try(CSVReader reader = new CSVReader(lineReader)) {
    String [] row = null;
    while ( (row = reader.readRow()) != null) {
      usersSet.add(User.fromValues(row));
    }
  }
}
```

2. Import **Set** as follows:

```java
java.util.Set;
```

3. Create a new file called **SortUsersTreeSet.java** and add a class with the same name and add a **main** method:

```java
public class SortUsersTreeSet {
  public static void main (String [] args) throws IOException {
  }
}
```

4. Read from the command line what field we'll sort by:

```java
Scanner reader = new Scanner(System.in);
System.out.print("Type a field to sort by: ");
String input = reader.nextLine();
Comparator<User> comparator;
switch(input) {
  case "id":
    comparator = new ByIdComparator();
    break;
  case "name":
    comparator = new ByNameComparator();
    break;
  case "email":
```

```
      comparator = new ByEmailComparator();
      break;
    default:
      System.out.printf("Sorry, invalid option: %s\n", input);
      return;
  }
  System.out.printf("Sorting by %s\n", input);
```

5. Create a **TreeSet** of users using the specified comparator, load the users into it with your new method, and then print the loaded users to the command line:

```
TreeSet<User> users = new TreeSet<>(comparator);
UsersLoader.loadUsersIntoSet(args[0], users);
for (User user : users) {
  System.out.printf("%d - %s, %s\n", user.id, user.name, user.email);
}
```

Here's the output of the first case:

```
Type a field to sort by: address
Sorry, invalid option: address
```

Here's the output of the second case

```
Type a field to sort by: email
Sorting by email
30 - Jeff Bezos, jeff.bezos@amazon.com
50 - Larry Ellison, lawrence.ellison@oracle.com
20 - Marc Benioff, marc.benioff@salesforce.com
40 - Sundar Pichai, sundar.pichai@google.com
10 - Bill Gates, william.gates@microsoft.com
```

Here's the output of the third case

```
Type a field to sort by: id
Sorting by id
10 - Bill Gates, william.gates@microsoft.com
20 - Marc Benioff, marc.benioff@salesforce.com
30 - Jeff Bezos, jeff.bezos@amazon.com
40 - Sundar Pichai, sundar.pichai@google.com
50 - Larry Ellison, lawrence.ellison@oracle.com
```

Here's the output of the fourth case

```
Type a field to sort by: name
Sorting by name
10 - Bill Gates, william.gates@microsoft.com
30 - Jeff Bezos, jeff.bezos@amazon.com
50 - Larry Ellison, lawrence.ellison@oracle.com
20 - Marc Benioff, marc.benioff@salesforce.com
40 - Sundar Pichai, sundar.pichai@google.com
```

Congratulations! In this exercise, you used TreeSet to sort and eliminate duplicate elements while loading them from the CSV file, all at the same time.

Queue

Queues are a special data structure that respect the First In, First Out (FIFO) pattern. This means that it keeps the elements in order of insertion and can return the elements starting from the first inserted one while adding elements to the end. That way, new work can be enqueued at the end of the queue while work to be processed gets dequeued from the front. The following is an illustration of this process:

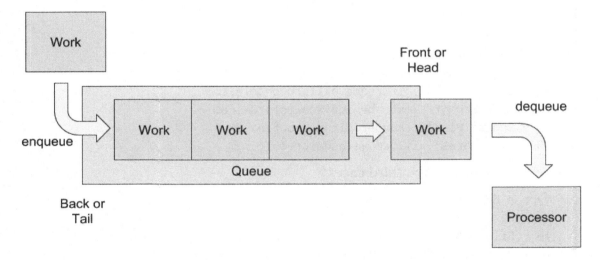

Figure 7.11: A queue that stores work to be processed

In the Collections Framework, a queue is represented by the **java.util.Queue** interface. To enqueue an element, you can use **add(E)** or **offer(E)**. The first will throw an exception if the queue is full, while the second will just return **true** or **false**, telling you whether the operation was successful or not. It also has methods to dequeue elements or just check what's at the front of the queue. **remove()** will return and remove the element at the front or throw an exception if the queue is empty. **poll()** will return the element and remove it or return null if the queue is empty. **element()** and **peek()** work the same way, but only return the element without removing it from the queue, the first throwing an exception and the latter returning null if the queue is empty.

java.util.Deque is an interface that extends **java.util.Queue** with extra methods that allow elements to be added, removed, or peeked at on both sides of the queue.

java.util.LinkedList is an implementation of **java.util.Queue** and **java.util.Deque** that also implements **java.util.List**.

java.util.ArrayDeque

The implementation of Queue and Deque uses an array as the underlying data store. The array grows automatically to support the data that's added to it.

java.util.PriorityQueue

The implementation of Queue uses a heap to keep elements in sort order. The order can be given by the element if it implements **java.lang.Comparable** or by a passed-in comparator. A heap is a specialized type of tree that keeps elements sorted, similar to **TreeMap**. This implementation of queue is great for processing elements that need to be processed in some priority.

Exercise 30: Fake Email Sender

In this exercise, you will simulate the process of sending emails to users using one processor. For this, you'll write two applications: one that simulates sending the email and one that reads from the CSV and invokes the first one for each user. The constraint that forces you to use a queue is that only one process can run at a time. This means that while the users are loaded from the CSV, you'll enqueue them and send emails whenever possible:

1. Create a file called **EmailSender.java** with a class and a **main** method in it. To simulate sending the email, the class will sleep for a random amount of time, up to one second:

```
System.out.printf("Sending email to %s...\n", args[0]);
Thread.sleep(new Random().nextInt(1000));
System.out.printf("Email sent to %s!\n", args[0]);
```

2. Create another file called **SendAllEmails.java** with a class and a **main** method.

```
public class SendAllEmails {
```

3. Add a **static** field called **runningProcess**. This will represent the send email process that is running:

```
private static Process runningProcess = null;
```

4. Create a **static** method that will try to initiate the process of sending an email by dequeuing an element from the queue, if the process is available:

```
private static void sendEmailWhenReady(ArrayDeque<String> queue)
    throws Exception {
  // If running, return
  if (runningProcess != null && runningProcess.isAlive()) {
    System.out.print(".");
    return;
  }

  System.out.print("\nSending email");
  String email = queue.poll();
  String classpath = System.getProperty("java.class.path");
  String[] command = new String[]{
    "java", "-cp", classpath, "EmailSender", email
  };
  runningProcess = Runtime.getRuntime().exec(command);
}
```

5. In the **main** method, create an **ArrayDeque** of strings that will represent the queue of emails to send to:

```
ArrayDeque<String> queue = new ArrayDeque<>();
```

6. Open the CSV to read each row from it. You can do this by using **CSVReader**:

```
FileReader fileReader = new FileReader(args[0]);
BufferedReader bufferedReader = new BufferedReader(fileReader);
try (CSVReader reader = new CSVReader(bufferedReader)) {
  String[] row;
  while ( (row = reader.readRow()) != null) {
    User user = User.fromValues(row);
  }
}
```

7. With the user loaded, we can add its email to the queue and try to send an email immediately:

```
queue.offer(user.email);
sendEmailWhenReady(queue);
```

8. Because reading from a file is, in general, very fast, we'll simulate a slow read by adding some sleep time:

```
Thread.sleep(100);
```

9. Outside the try-with-resources block, that is, after we've finished reading all users from the file, we need to ensure we drain the queue. For that, we can use a **while** loop that runs while the queue is not empty:

```
while (!queue.isEmpty()) {
   sendEmailWhenReady(queue);

   // Wait before checking again
   Thread.sleep(100);
}
```

> **Note**
>
> In this case, it is important to not use 100% of the CPU while you sleep. This is very common when processing elements from a queue, like in this case.

10. Now you can just wait for the last send email process to finish, following a similar pattern: check and wait while sleeping:

```
while (runningProcess.isAlive()) {
   System.out.print(".");
   Thread.sleep(100);
}
System.out.println("\nDone sending emails!");
```

Congratulations! You wrote an application that simulates the sending of emails using constrained resources (one process only). This application is ignoring the fact that users are duplicated in the file. It also ignores the output of the send email process. How would you implement a duplicate send detector and avoid that issue? How do you think the output of the send process affects the decision of duplicate avoidance?

Properties of Collections

When picking a data structure to solve a problem, you'll have to consider the following things:

- Ordering - If order is important when accessing the data, what order the data will be accessed?

- Uniqueness - Does it matter if you have the same element multiple times inside the collection? How do you define uniqueness?

- Nullables - Can values be null? If mapping key to values, is the null key valid? Does it make sense to use null in either?

Use the following table to determine what collection better suits your use case:

Collection	Ordering	Uniqueness	Nulls
ArrayList	Based on index	Allows Duplicate	Allows nulls.
Vector	Based on index	Allows Duplicate	Allows nulls.
LinkedList	Based on index	Allows Duplicate	Allows nulls
HashMap	No ordering guarantee	No duplicate keys. Allows duplicate values.	Allows null key. Allows null values.
TreeMap	Sorted Naturally by Key	No duplicate keys. Allows duplicate values.	Allows null key. Allows null values.
LinkedHashSet	Order of insertion	No duplicate keys. Allows duplicate values.	Allows null key. Allows null values.
HashSet	No ordering guarantee	De-duplicate elements	Allows nulls
TreeSet	Sorted Naturally	De-duplicate elements	Not allowed
LinkedHashSet	Order of insertion	De-duplicate elements	Allows nulls
ArrayDeque	Order of insertion	Allows duplicate	Not allowed
PriorityQueue	Sorted Naturally	Allows duplicate	Not allowed

Table 7.1: Table representing the properties on collections

Note

"Sorted naturally" means that it will sort based on the element (or key) if the element implements **Comparable** or using a passed-in comparator.

Summary

When developing applications, processing data is one of the most fundamental tasks. In this lesson, you learned how to read and parse data from files so that you're able to process them as part of your application. You also learned how to compare objects so that you can sort them in different ways.

As part of processing data, you learned how to store data using basic and advanced data structures. Knowing how to efficiently process data is very important so that you avoid resource contention scenarios such as running out of memory, or requiring too much processing or time to execute the task at hand. A big part of processing data efficiently is about picking the right data structures and algorithms for the right problems. All the new tools that you have added to your belt will help you make the correct decisions when building your Java applications.

In the next lesson, we will have a look at some advanced data structures.

8

Advanced Data Structures in Java

Learning Objectives

By the end of this lesson, you will be able to:

- Implement a linked list
- Implement a Binary Search Tree
- Use enumerations to handle constants better
- Explain the logic behind uniqueness in HashSet

Introduction

In the previous lessons, you learned about various data structures in Java, such as lists, sets, and maps. You also learned about how to iterate on the many data structures, compare objects in many different ways; and sort these collections in an efficient way.

In this lesson, you will learn the implementation details of advanced data structures such as linked lists and binary search trees. As we progress, you'll also learn about a powerful concept called enumerations and explore how to use them effectively instead of constants. At the end of the lesson, you will gain an understanding of the magic and mystery behind `equals()` and `hashCode()`.

Implementing a Custom Linked List

A list has two implementations:

- **ArrayList**: This is implemented using arrays as the underlying data structure. It comes with the same limitations as arrays.

- **Linked List**: Elements in linked lists are distributed across the memory, contrary to in an array, where they are contiguous.

Disadvantages of ArrayList

Disadvantages of ArrayList are as follows:

- Though ArrayList is dynamic and the size need not be mentioned during creation. However as the size of arrays is fixed, therefore ArrayLists often need to be implicitly resized when more elements are added to the list. Resizing follows the procedure of creating a new array and adding all the elements of the previous array into a new array.

- Inserting a new element at the end of the ArrayList is often faster than adding in between, however, it's expensive when elements are added in between the list, because room has to be created for the new elements, and to create room existing elements have to shift.

- Deleting the last element of the ArrayList is often faster, however, it's expensive when elements are deleted in between, because the element has to be adjusted, shifting elements to the left.

Advantages of Linked List over Arrays

The following are the advantages of linked lists over arrays:

- Dynamic sizing, as the size is not fixed, there are no resizing problems. Every node holds a reference to the next.

- Adding and deleting elements at random places within a linked list, is much simpler as compared to vectors and arrays.

In this topic, you will learn how to build a custom linked list for specific purposes. By doing this, we will appreciate the power of linked list and understand the implementation details as well.

Here is a diagrammatic representation of a linked list:

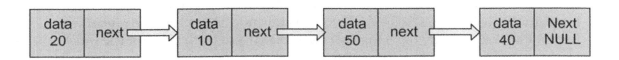

Figure 8.1: Representation of a linked list

Dynamic memory allocation is a popular application of linked lists. Other applications of linked lists include implementation of data structures such as stacks, various implementations of queues, graphs, trees and so on.

Exercise 31: Adding Elements to a Linked list

Let's create a simple linked list that allows us to add integers, and print the elements in the list:

1. Create a class **SimpleIntLinkedList** as follow:

   ```
   public class SimpleIntLinkedList
   {
   ```

2. Create another class **Node** that represents each element in a linked list. Each node will have data (an Integer value) that it needs to hold; and it will have a reference to the next **Node**. Implement getters and setter for the data and the **next** variable:

   ```
   static class Node {
   Integer data;
   Node next;
   Node(Integer d) {
   data = d;
   ```

```
next = null;
}
Node getNext() {
return next;
}
void setNext(Node node) {
next = node;
}
Object getData() {
return data;
}
}
```

3. Implement the **add(Object item)** method so that any item/object can be added into this list. Construct a new **Node** object by passing the **newItem = new Node(item)** item. Start with the **head** node, and move towards the end of the list, visiting each node. In the last node, set the next node as our newly created node (**newItem**). Increment the index by invoking **incrementIndex()** to keep track of the index:

```
// appends the specified element to the end of this list.
    public void add(Integer element) {
        // create a new node
        Node newNode = new Node(element);
        //if head node is empty, create a new node and assign it to Head
        //increment index and return
        if (head == null) {
            head = newNode;
            return;
        }

        Node currentNode = head;

        while (currentNode.getNext() != null) {
                currentNode = currentNode.getNext();
        }
        // set the new node as next node of current
        currentNode.setNext(newNode);

    }
```

4. Implement a **toString()** method to represent this object. Starting from the **head** node, iterate all the nodes until the last node is found. On each iteration, construct a string representation of an Integer stored in each node. The representation will look similar to this: **[Input1,Input2,Input3]**

```
public String toString() {
  String delim = ",";
  StringBuffer stringBuf = new StringBuffer();
  if (head == null)
    return "LINKED LIST is empty";

  Node currentNode = head;
  while (currentNode != null) {
    stringBuf.append(currentNode.getData());
    currentNode = currentNode.getNext();
    if (currentNode != null)
      stringBuf.append(delim);
    }
  return stringBuf.toString();
}
```

5. Create a member attribute of type **Node** (pointing to the **head** node) for the **SimpleIntLinkedList**. In the **main** method, create an object of **SimpleIntLinkedList** and add five integers one after the other (13, 39, 41, 93, 98) into it respectively. Print the **SimpleIntLinkedList** object.

```
Node head;
public static void main(String[] args) {
  SimpleLinkedList list = new SimpleLinkedList();
  list.add(13);
  list.add(39);
  list.add(41);
  list.add(93);
  list.add(98);
  System.out.println(list);
  }
}
```

The output will be as follows:

```
[13, 39, 41, 93, 98]
```

Activity 32: Creating a Custom Linked List in Java

In our exercise, we created a Linked list that could take Integer values. As an activity, let's create a custom linked list that can take any object into it and display all the elements added to the list. Additionally, let's add two more methods to get and remove the values from the linked list.

These steps will help you complete this activity:

1. Create a class name **SimpleObjLinkedList** and create a member attribute of type Node (pointing to the head node). Add a member attribute of type **int** (pointing to the current index or position in a node)

2. Create a class Node that represents each element in a Linked List. Each node will have an object that it needs to hold and it will have the reference to the next Node. The **LinkedList** class will have a reference to the head node and will be able to traverse to the next Node by using **Node.getNext()**. Because **head** is the first element, we could traverse to the next element by moving next in the **current** node. Like this, we could traverse till the last element of the list.

3. Implement the **add(Object item)** method so that any item/object could be added to this list. Construct a new **Node** object by passing the **newItem = new Node(item)** item. Starting at the **head** node, crawl to the end of the list. In the last node, set the **next** node as our newly created node (**newItem**). Increment the index.

4. Implement the **get(Integer index)** method to retrieve the item from the list based on the index. Index must not be less than 0. Write logic to crawl to the specified index and identify the node and return the value from the node.

5. Implement the **remove(Integer index)** method to remove the item from the list based on the index. Write logic to crawl to the one node before the specified index and identify the node. In this node, set the next as **getNext()**.Return true if the element was found and deleted. If element not found, return false.

6. Implement a **toString()** method to represent this object. Starting from head Node, iterate all the nodes until the last node is found. On each iteration construct a string representation of the object stored in each node.

7. Write a **main** method and add create an object of **SimpleObjLinkedList** and add five Strings one after the other ("INPUT-1", "INPUT-2", "INPUT-3", "INPUT-4","INPUT-5") into it respectively. Print the **SimpleObjLinkedList** object. In the main method, get the item from the list using **get(2)** and print the value of the item retrieved, also remove the item from the list **remove(2)** and print the value of the list. One element should have been deleted from the list.

The output will be as follows:

```
[INPUT-1  ,INPUT-2 ,INPUT-3 ,INPUT-4 ,INPUT-5 ]
INPUT-3
[INPUT-1  ,INPUT-2 ,INPUT-3 ,INPUT-5 ]
```

> **Note**
>
> The solution for this activity can be found on page 356.

Drawbacks of Linked List

The drawbacks of linked lists are as follows:

- The only way to access elements is starting from the first element, and moving sequentially; accessing an element at random is not possible.

- Searching is slow.

- Linked lists require extra space in the memory.

Implementing Binary Search Tree

We already had a brief look at trees in *Lesson 7, The Java Collections Framework and Generics* let's look at a special implementation of trees known as **binary search trees (BSTs)**.

To understand BSTs, let's take a look at what binary tree is. A tree in which each node in the tree has at most two child nodes, is a **binary tree**.

A BST is a special implementation of a binary tree, where the left-child node is always less than or equal to the parent node, and the right-child node is always greater than or equal to the parent node. This unique structure of the binary search tree makes it easier to add, delete, and search for elements of the tree. The following diagram represents a BST:

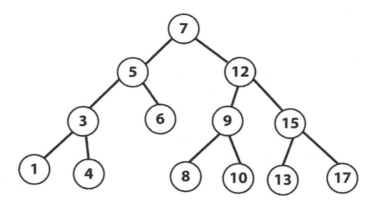

Figure 8.2: Representation of a binary search tree

The applications of binary search tree are as follows:

- To implement a dictionary.
- To implement multilevel indexing in a database.
- To implement a searching algorithm.

Exercise 32: Creating a Binary Search Tree in Java

In this exercise, we will create a binary search tree and implement left and right traversal.

1. Create a **BinarySearchTree** class with a **Node** class in it. The **Node** class should have two elements pointing to its left and right node.

```
//Public class holding the functions of Entire Binary Tree structure
public class BinarySearchTree
{
    private Node parent;
    private int  data;
    private int  size = 0;
    public BinarySearchTree() {
        parent = new Node(data);
    }
}
```

```
private class Node {
        Node left; //points to left node
        Node right; //points to right node
        int  data;

        //constructor of Node
        public Node(int data) {
            this.data = data;
        }
}
```

2. We will create a **add(int data)** function, which will check whether the parent node is empty. If it is empty, it will add the value to the parent node. If the parent node has data, we need to create a new **Node(data)** and find the right node (according to the BST rule) to attach this new node.

To help find the right node, a method, **add(Node root, Node newNode)**, has been implemented to use the recursive logic to go deeper and find the actual node to which this new node should belong.

As per BST rules, if the root data is greater than the **newNode** data, then **newNode** has to be added to the left Node. Again, recursively check whether it has child nodes, and the same logic of BST applies until it reaches the leaf node to add a value. If the root data is less than the **newNode** data, **newNode** has to be added to the right node. Again, recursively check whether it has child nodes, and the same logic of BST applies until it reaches the leaf node to add a value:

```
/**
 * This is the method exposed as public for adding elements into the Tree.
     * it checks if the size == 0 and then adds the element into parent
node. if
     * parent is already filled, creates a New Node with data and calls the
     * add(parent, newNode) to find the right root and add it to it.
     * @param data
     */
  public void add(int data) {
    if (size == 0) {
      parent.data = data;
      size++;
    } else {
      add(parent, new Node(data));
    }
  }
/**
```

```
 * Takes two params, root node and newNode. As per BST, check if the root
 * data is > newNode data if true: newNode has to be added in left Node
 * (again recursively check if it has child nodes and the same logic of
BST
 * until it reaches the leaf node to add value) else: newNode has to be
 * added in right (again recursively check if it has child nodes and the
 * same logic of BST until it reaches the leaf node to add value)
 *
 * @param root
 * @param newNode
 */
 private void add(Node root, Node newNode) {
    if (root == null) {
       return;
    }
  if (newNode.data < root.data) {
       if (root.left == null) {
          root.left = newNode;
          size++;
       } else {
          add(root.left, newNode);
       }
    }
    if ((newNode.data > root.data)) {
       if (root.right == null) {
          root.right = newNode;
          size++;
       } else {
          add(root.right, newNode);
       }
    }
 }
```

3. Create a **traverseLeft()** function to traverse and print all the values of the BST in the left-hand side of the root node:

```
public void traverseLeft() {
Node current = parent;
System.out.print("Traverse the BST From Left : ");
      while (current.left != null && current.right != null) {
         System.out.print(current.data + "->[" + current.left.data + "
" + current.right.data + "] ");
         current = current.left;
```

```java
    }
    System.out.println("Done");
}
```

4. Create a **traverseRight()** function to traverse and print all the values of the BST on the right-hand side of the root node:

```java
public void traverseRight() {
    Node current = parent;
    System.out.print("Traverse the BST From Right");
    while (current.left != null && current.right != null) {
        System.out.print(current.data + "->[" + current.left.data + "
" + current.right.data + "] ");
        current = current.right;
    }
    System.out.println("Done");
}
```

5. Let's create an example program to test the functionality of the BST:

```java
/**
 * Main program to demonstrate the BST functionality.
 * - Adding nodes
 * - finding High and low
 * - Traversing left and right
 * @param args
 */
public static void main(String args[]) {

    BinarySearchTree bst = new BinarySearchTree();

    // adding nodes into the BST
    bst.add(32);
    bst.add(50);
    bst.add(93);
    bst.add(3);
    bst.add(40);
    bst.add(17);
    bst.add(30);
    bst.add(38);
    bst.add(25);
    bst.add(78);
    bst.add(10);
    bst.traverseLeft();
```

```
                bst.traverseRight();
    }
        }
```

The output is as follows:

```
Traverse the BST From Left : 32->[3 50] Done
Traverse the BST From Right32->[3 50] 50->[40 93] Done
```

Activity 33: Implementing the Methods in the BinarySearchTree Class to Find the Highest and Lowest Value in the BST

1. Create a method, **getLow()**, that implements a **while** loop to iteratively check whether the parent node has any left children, and returns the node with no left child in the left BST as the lowest value.

2. Create a method, **getHigh()**, that implements a **while** loop to iteratively check if the parent node has any right children, and returns the node with no right child in the right BST as the highest value.

3. In the **main** method, add elements to the binary search tree, using the **add** method implemented earlier and call the **getLow()** and the **getHigh()** methods to identify the highest and the lowest values.

The output will be as follows:

```
Lowest value in BST :3
Highest value in BST :93
```

> **Note**
>
> The solution for this activity can be found on page 360.

Enumerations

Enumeration in Java (or enum) is a special type in Java whose fields consist of constants. It is used to impose compile-time safety.

For example, consider the days of the week, they are a set of fixed constants, therefore we can have an enum defined:

```
public enum DayofWeek {


 SUNDAY, MONDAY, TUESDAY, WEDNESDAY, THURSDAY, FRIDAY, SATURDAY


}
```

Now we can simply check if a variable that stores a day is part of the declared enum. We can also declare enums for non-universal constants, such as:

```
public enum Jobs {


 DEVELOPER, TESTER, TEAM LEAD, PROJECT MANAGER


}
```

This will enforce the job-type to be the constants declared in the **Jobs** enum. Here's an example enum holding currencies:

```
public enum Currency {
    USD, INR, DIRHAM, DINAR, RIYAL, ASD
}
```

Exercise 33: Using Enum to Store Directions

We will create an enum and will find values and compare enums.

1. Create a class **EnumExample** and in the **main** method. Get and print the enum using the value as enum. Get and print enum using the values as String:

```
public class EnumExample
{
    public static void main(String[] args)
    {
        Direction north = Direction.NORTH;
        System.out.println(north + " : " + north.no);
        Direction south = Direction.valueOf("SOUTH");
        System.out.println(south + " : " + south.no);


    }
}
```

2. Let's create a enum holding directions with an integer value representing the directions:

```
public enum Direction
    {
                    EAST(45), WEST(90), NORTH(180), SOUTH(360);
            int no;

    Direction(int i){
                no =i;
            }
    }
```

The output is as follows:

```
NORTH : 180
SOUTH : 360
```

Activity 34: Using an Enum to Hold College Department Details

Let's build a full-fledged enum to hold college departments and their numbers (BE ("Bachelor of Engineering", 100)).

Perform the following steps:

1. Create a **DeptEnum** enum using the **enum** keyword. Add two private attributes (String **deptName** and int **deptNo**) to hold the values to be kept in the enum.

2. . Override a constructor to take an acronym and **deptNo** and place it in the member variables. Add enum constants adhering to the constructor.

3. Add getter methods for **deptName** and **deptNo**.

4. Let's write a **main** method and sample program to demonstrate the use of enums:

Output will be as follows:

```
BACHELOR OF ENGINEERING : 1
BACHELOR OF ENGINEERING : 1
BACHELOR OF COMMERCE : 2
BACHELOR OF SCIENCE : 3
BACHELOR OF ARCHITECTURE : 4
BACHELOR : 0
true
```

> **Note**
>
> The solution for this activity can be found on page 362.

Activity 35: Implementing Reverse Lookup

Write an application that takes in a value of

1. Create an enum **App**, that declares constants BE, BCOM, BSC and BARC, along with their full forms and department numbers.

2. Also declare two private variables **accronym** and **deptNo**.

3. Create a parameterized constructor and assign the variables **accronym** and **deptNo** with values passed as arguments.

4. Declare a public method **getAccronym()** that returns the variable **accronym** and a public method **getDeptNo()** that returns the variable **deptNo**.

5. Implement reverse look up that takes in the course name, and searches the corresponding acronym in the **App** enum.

6. Implement the main method, and run the program.

Your output should be similar to:

```
BACHELOR OF SCIENCE : 3
BSC
```

> **Note**
>
> The solution for this activity can be found on page 363.

Set and Uniqueness in Set

In this topic, we are going to learn the logic behind a set that finds the uniqueness of an object being added and understand the importance of two object-level methods.

The magic lies in two methods of the **Object** class

- **hashCode()**
- **equals()**

Basic Rules for the equals() and hashCode() Methods

- Two objects can be identical only when the value returned using the **hashcode()** method is identical and the **equal()** method returns true.

- If the two objects return the same **hashCode()** value, it doesn't necessarily mean both objects are the same (as hash values may collide with other objects as well). In that case, it's necessary to find the equality by calling **equals()** and verifying the identity.

- We can't use **hashCode()** alone to find out the equality; we need to use **equals()** as well to do this. However, **hashCode()** alone is enough to find the inequality. If the **hashCode()** returns different values, it's safe to consider the objects different.

Adding an Object to a Set

Though many things happen when we add an object into a set, we will just look at details related to our subject of study:

- The method first calls the **hashCode()** method on that object and gets the **hashCode**, then **Set** compares it to the **hashCode** of other objects and checks whether any object matches that **hashCode**.

- If none of the objects in the set match the **hashCode** of the added object, then we can be 100% confident that no other object is available with the same identity. A newly added object will be added safely to the set (without needing to check **equals()**).

- If any of the objects match the **hashCode** of the object added, it means it might be an identical object added (as **hashCode** may be the same for two different objects). In this case, to confirm the suspicion, it will use the **equals()** method to see if the objects are really equal. If equal, the newly added object will not be rejected, else newly added objected will be rejected.

Exercise 34: Understanding the Behavior of equals() and hashCode()

Let's create a new class and walk through the behavior of **Set** before implementing **equals()** and **hashCode()**:

1. Create a Student class with three attributes: **Name (String)**, **Age (int)**, and **Year of passing (int)**. Also create getters and setters for these private members:

```
/**
 * Sample Class student containing attributes name, age and yearOfPassing
 *
 */
import java.util.HashSet;
class Student {
    private String name;
    private Integer age;
    private Integer yearOfPassing;
    public String getName() {
        return name;
    }
    public void setName(String name) {
        this.name = name;
    }
    public int getAge() {
        return age;
    }
    public void setAge(int age) {
        this.age = age;
    }
    public int getYearOfPassing() {
        return yearOfPassing;
    }
}
```

```java
        public void setYearOfPassing(int releaseYr) {
            this.yearOfPassing = releaseYr;
        }
    }
```

2. Write a sample class, **HashCodeExample**, to demonstrate the set behavior. In the main method, create three objects of **Students** with different names and other details (Raymonds, Allen, and Maggy):

```java
/**
 * Example class demonstrating the set behavior
 * We will create 3 objects and add into the Set
 * Later will create a new object resembling same as one of the 3 objects
 created and added into the set
 */
public class HashCodeExample {
    public static void main(String[] args) {
        Student m = new Student();
        m.setName("RAYMONDS");
        m.setAge(20);
        m.setYearOfPassing(2011);

        Student m1 = new Student();
        m1.setName("ALLEN");
        m1.setAge(19);
        m1.setYearOfPassing(2010);

        Student m2 = new Student();
        m2.setName("MAGGY");
        m2.setAge(18);
        m2.setYearOfPassing(2012);
    }
}
```

3. Create a **HashSet** to hold these students' objects (**set**). Add the three objects, one after the other, to the **HashSet**. Then, print the values in the **HashSet**:

```java
HashSet<Student> set = new HashSet<Student>();
    set.add(m);
    set.add(m1);
    set.add(m2);
    //printing all the elements of Set
System.out.println("Before Adding ALLEN for second time : ");
    for (Student mm : set) {
```

```
            System.out.println(mm.getName() + " " + mm.getAge());
        }
```

4. In the **main** method, create another **Student** object resembling one of the three objects created (for example: let's create a student, similar to Allen). Add this newly created **Student** object to the **HashSet** in which three students have already been **added(set)**. Then, print the values in the **HashSet**. You will notice that Allen has been added into the set twice (which means duplicates were not handled in the Set):

```
    //creating a student similar to m1 (name:ALLEN, age:19,
  yearOfPassing:2010)
        Student m3 = new Student();
        m3.setName("ALLEN");
        m3.setAge(19);
        m3.setYearOfPassing(2010);

  //this Student will be added as hashCode() and equals() are not
  implemented
        set.add(m3);
        // 2 students with same details (ALLEN 19 will be noticed twice)
  System.out.println("After Adding ALLEN for second time: ");
        for (Student mm : set) {
            System.out.println(mm.getName() + " " + mm.getAge());
        }
```

The output is as follows:

```
Before Adding ALLEN for second time :
RAYMONDS 20
MAGGY 18
ALLEN 19

After Adding ALLEN for second time:
RAYMONDS 20
ALLEN 19
MAGGY 18
ALLEN 19
```

Allen has indeed been added to the set twice (which means duplicates have not been handled in the Set yet). It needs to be handled in **Student** class.

Exercise 35: Overriding equals() and hashCode()

Let's override **equals()** and **hashCode()** for **Student** and see how the behavior of Set changes after this:

1. In the **Students** class, let's override the **equals()** method by checking each attribute of the **Student** object (**name**, **age**, and **yearOfPassing** are of equal importance to verify the identity). The **equals()** method in the **Object** level takes **Object** as an argument. To override the method, we need to provide logic with which we compare the self-attribute (**this**) to the **object o** argument. The logic of equality here is that two students are said be identical if, and only if, their **name**, **age**, and **yearOfPassing** is the same:

```java
@Override
public boolean equals(Object o) {
    Student m = (Student) o;
    return m.name.equals(this.name) &&
            m.age.equals(this.age) &&
            m.yearOfPassing.equals(this.yearOfPassing);
}
```

2. In the **Student** class, let's override the **hashCode()** method. The basic requirement is it should return the same integer for identical objects. One simple way to implement **hashCode** is taking the **hashCode** of each attribute in the object and summing it up. The rationale behind this is, if the **name**, **age**, or **yearOfPassing** is different, then **hashCode** will return different values, and it will be evident that no two objects are the same:

```java
@Override
public int hashCode() {
    return this.name.hashCode() +
            this.age.hashCode() +
            this.yearOfPassing.hashCode();
}
```

3. Let's run the main method of **HashCodeExample** to demonstrate the behavior of the set after overriding **equals()** and **hashCode()** in the Student object.

```java
public class HashCodeExample {

    public static void main(String[] args) {

        Student m = new Student();
        m.setName("RAYMONDS");
        m.setAge(20);
```

```java
        m.setYearOfPassing(2011);

        Student m1 = new Student();
        m1.setName("ALLEN");
        m1.setAge(19);
        m1.setYearOfPassing(2010);

        Student m2 = new Student();
        m2.setName("MAGGY");
        m2.setAge(18);
        m2.setYearOfPassing(2012);

        Set<Student> set = new HashSet<Student>();
        set.add(m);
        set.add(m1);
        set.add(m2);

        //printing all the elements of Set
System.out.println("Before Adding ALLEN for second time : ");
        for (Student mm : set) {
            System.out.println(mm.getName() + " " + mm.getAge());
        }
    //creating a student similar to m1 (name:ALLEN, age:19,
yearOfPassing:2010)
        Student m3 = new Student();
        m3.setName("ALLEN");
        m3.setAge(19);
        m3.setYearOfPassing(2010);

//this element will not be added if hashCode and equals methods are
implemented
        set.add(m3);
System.out.println("After Adding ALLEN for second time: ");
        for (Student mm : set) {
            System.out.println(mm.getName() + " " + mm.getAge());
        }

    }
}
```

The output is as follows:

```
Before Adding ALLEN for second time:
ALLEN 19
RAYMONDS 20
MAGGY 18

After Adding ALLEN for second time:
ALLEN 19
RAYMONDS 20
MAGGY 18
```

After adding **hashCode()** and **equals()**, our **HashSet** has the intelligence to identify and remove duplicates.

If we don't override **equals()** and **hashCode()**, JVM assigns a unique hash code value to each object when they are created in memory, and if developers don't override the **hashcode** method, then there is no guarantee that the two objects return the same hash code value.

Summary

In this lesson, we learned what a BST is and the steps to implement the basic functionalities of a BST in Java. We also learned a technique to traverse a BST to the right and left. We looked at the use of enums over constants and gained an understanding of the types of problems they solve. We also built our own enums and wrote code to fetch and compare the values of enums.

We also learned how **HashSet** is able to identify duplicates and looked at the significance of overriding **equals()** and **hashCode()**. Also, we learned how to correctly implement **equals()** and **hashCode()**.

Exception Handling

Learning Objectives

By the end of this lesson, you will be able to:

- Use exception-throwing libraries

- Use exception handling effectively

- Acquire and release resources in a way that respects exceptions without creating leaks

- Implement best practices to incorporate exceptions in Java

Introduction

Exception handling is a powerful mechanism for handling erroneous cases that occur while our code is running. It enables us to focus on the main execution of the program and separate the error-handling code from the expected execution path. The Java language forces programmers to write exception-handling code for library methods, and IDEs such as IntelliJ, Eclipse, and so on help us generate the boilerplate code necessary. However, without proper guidance and understanding, standard exception codes may result in more harm than good. This lesson is a practical introduction to exceptions that will push you to contemplate various aspects of exception handling, and will provide a number of rules of thumb that may be helpful when you are dealing with exceptions in your programming life.

Motivation behind Exceptions

When we are creating programs, we usually focus on expected scenarios. For example, we will get the data from somewhere, we will extract certain information from the data that we assume to be there, we will send it to somewhere else, and so on. We would like our code to be readable, so that members of our team can clearly understand the business logic and can spot mistakes that we may make. However, in practice, our assumptions may not hold and there can be deviations from expected scenarios. For example, we may not be able to get data because of a problem with the network or the disk. We may receive data that does not fit our assumptions. Or, we may not be able to send data because of similar problems. We have to create programs that behave gracefully in unexpected situations. For example: we should enable the user to retry on a broken network connection. Exceptions are the way we handle such situations in Java without making our code too complex.

As programmers, we have to write code that will run well in various unexpected situations. However, we also want our code to be clean and understandable. These two goals can often compete with each other.

We would like to write code that reads clearly, as follows:

```
Do step 1
Do step 2
Do step 3
Done
```

This reflects an optimistic scenario, in which nothing unexpected occurs. However, it is often the case that unexpected situations occur. The user's internet connection may be down, a web resource may be down, the client may run out of memory, a disk error may occur, and so on. Unless we write code that anticipates these problems, our programs may crash when such problems arise. It would be quite difficult to anticipate every kind of problem that may happen. Even if we simplify things and treat most errors the same way, we still may have to carry out many checks on our code. For example: we may have to write code that looks more like this:

```
Do step 1
If there was a problem with step 1,
     Handle the error, stop
Else
     Do step 2
     If there was a problem with step 2,
          Handle the error, stop
     Else
          Do step 3
          If there was a problem with step 3
               Handle the error, stop
          Else
Done
```

You can come up with alternative code structures, but once you incorporate the extra code to handle errors at every step, your code becomes less readable, less understandable, and less maintainable. If you do not include such error-handling code, your programs may result in unwanted situations such as crashes.

Here is a function in C that handles errors similar to our preceding pseudo code.

```
int other_idea()
{
    int err = minor_func1();
    if (!err)
        err = minor_func2();
    if (!err)
        err = minor_func3();
    return err;
}
```

When you code using primitive languages such as C, you inevitably feel strong tension between readability and completeness. Luckily, in most modern programming languages, we have exception handling capabilities that reduce this tension. Your code can both be readable and can handle errors at the same time.

The main language construct behind exception handling is the **try-catch** block. The code you put after the try is executed line by line. If any of the lines result in an error, the rest of the lines in the try block are not executed and the execution goes to the catch block, giving you a chance to handle the error gracefully. Here, you receive an exception object that contains detailed information about the problem. However, if no error happens in the try block, the catch block is never executed.

Here, we modify our initial example to handle errors using the try-catch block instead of many **if** statements:

```
Try
Do step 1
Do step 2
Do step 3
Catch error
    Handle error appropriately
Done
```

In this version, our code is placed between the try and catch keywords. Our code is free from error-handling code that would otherwise prevent readability. The default expected path of the code is quite clear: step 1, step 2, and step 3. However, if an error happens, the execution moves to the catch block immediately. There, we receive information about what the problem was in the form of an exception object and we are given a chance to handle the error gracefully.

Most of the time, you will have code pieces that depend on one another. So, if an error happens in one of the steps, you usually do not want to execute the rest of the steps, since they depend on the success of that earlier step. You can use **try-catch** blocks creatively to denote code dependencies. For example: in the following pseudo code, there are errors in steps 2 and step 5. The steps that successfully get executed are steps 1 and 4. Since step 4 and later steps are independent of the success of the first three steps, we were able to denote their dependencies with two separate **try - catch** blocks. The error in step 2 prevented the execution of step 3, but not step 4:

```
Try

Do step 1

Do step 2 - ERROR

Do step 3

Catch error

    Handle error appropriately

Done


Try

Do step 4

Do step 5 - ERROR

Do step 6

Catch error

    Handle error appropriately

Done
```

If there is an exception and you do not catch it, the error will be propagated to the caller. If this is your application, you should never let errors propagate out of your code, to prevent your app from crashing. However, if you are developing a library that is called by other code, letting errors propagate to the caller is sometimes a good idea. We will discuss this in more detail later.

Exercise 36: Introducing Exceptions

Now let's actually see exceptions in action. One of the canonical exceptions is to try to divide a number by zero. Here, we will use it to create exceptions and verify our pseudo code from earlier:

1. Create a new **Main** class and add the main method as follows:

```
public class Main {
    public static void main(String[] args) {
```

2. Write code to print the result of the division of two numbers. Add the **try** – **catch** block to handle the exceptions:

```
try {
System.out.println("result 1: " + (2 / 2));
System.out.println("result 2: " + (4 / 0));
System.out.println("result 3: " + (6 / 2));
    } catch (ArithmeticException e) {
System.out.println("---- An exception in first block");
}
try {
System.out.println("result 4: " + (8 / 2));
System.out.println("result 5: " + (10 / 0));
System.out.println("result 6: " + (12 / 2));
} catch (ArithmeticException e) {
System.out.println("---- An exception in second block");
}
}
}
```

Run the code and verify that the output looks like the following:

```
result 1: 1
---- An exception in block 1
result 4: 4
---- An exception in block 2
```

Note that results 2 and 5 contain division operations in which we divide a number by zero, which results in an exception. This way, we are intentionally creating exceptions in these two lines to see how execution progresses in the case of exceptions. Here is a breakdown of the expected execution:

- Result 1 should print well.

- During result 2's execution we should get an exception, which should prevent result 2 from printing.

- Because of the exception, execution should jump to the catch block, which should prevent result 3 from printing.

- Result 4 should print well.

- Just like result 2, during result 5's execution we should get an exception, which should prevent result 5 from printing.

- Similarly, because of the exception, the execution should jump to the catch block, which should prevent result 6 from printing.

With the help of the two **try-catch** blocks, we should skip results 3 and 6 because of the exceptions on results 2 and 5. This should leave only results 1 and 4, which will be executed successfully.

This shows that our preceding discussion was correct. Also, to verify the execution order, place a breakpoint in the result 1 line and click step over to watch how execution progresses step by step with the **try - catch** block.

With the help of exceptions and the **try-catch** block, we are able to write code that focuses more on the expected default execution path, while ensuring that we handle unexpected error cases and can recover or fail gracefully, depending on the severity of the error.

An Inevitable Introduction to Exceptions

Practically, most newbie Java developers meet with exceptions when they call an exception-throwing method from a library. Such a method can specify that it throws an exception using the throws statement. When you call this kind of method, your code will not compile unless you write code that does something about the exception that the method may throw.

So, as a newbie Java developer, all you wanted was to call a method and now you are forced to do something about an exception that it may throw. Your IDE can generate code that takes care of the exception. However, default generated code is usually not the best. A newbie with no guidance and the powers of IDE code generation can create code that is quite bad. In this section, you will be guided on how best to use IDE-generated exception-handling code.

Let's say you wrote the following code to open and read a file:

```java
import java.io.File;

import java.io.FileInputStream;


public class Main {
    public static void main(String[] args) {
        File file = new File("./tmp.txt");
        FileInputStream inputStream = new FileInputStream(file);
    }
}
```

Currently, your code will not compile and your IDE underlined the **FileInputStream** constructor in red. This is because it may throw an exception, as specified in its source code:

```java
public FileInputStream(File file) throws FileNotFoundException {
```

At this point, your IDE usually tries to be helpful. When you move the caret on to **FileInputStream** and hit *Alt + Enter* in IntelliJ, for example, you will see two quick-fix options: **Add exception to method signature** and **Surround with try/catch**. These correspond to the two options you have when dealing with specified exceptions, which we will learn about later in more depth. Here's what the first option converts your code into:

```java
import java.io.File;
import java.io.FileInputStream;
import java.io.FileNotFoundException;


public class Main {
    public static void main(String[] args) throws FileNotFoundException {
        File file = new File("input.txt");
        FileInputStream inputStream = new FileInputStream(file);
```

```
        }
    }
```

Now your main function also specifies that it can throw an exception. Such an exception causes the program to exit immediately, which may or may not be what you want. If this was a function that you give others as a library, this change would prevent their code from compiling, unless they, in turn, did something about the specified exception, just like you. Again, this may or may not be what you want to do.

If you selected "**Surround with try/catch**", which was the second option that IntelliJ provided, here is what your code would become:

```java
import java.io.File;

import java.io.FileInputStream;

import java.io.FileNotFoundException;


public class Main {
    public static void main(String[] args) {
        File file = new File("input.txt");
        try {
            FileInputStream inputStream = new FileInputStream(file);
        } catch (FileNotFoundException e) {
            e.printStackTrace();
        }
    }
}
```

In this example, we are writing code to handle the exception ourselves. This feels more appropriate; we are taking responsibility and writing code to do something about the exception. However, the code in its current form does more harm than good. First of all, it does not actually do anything useful with the exception; it just catches it, prints information about it to **stdout**, and continues the execution as if nothing happened. Especially in a project that is not a console application (like most Java programs), printing to the logs is hardly useful.

If we cannot find this file to open, we should think cleverly about what we can do. Should we ask the user to look for the file? Should we download it from the internet? Whatever we do, taking a note in an obscure log file and sweeping the problem under the rug is probably one of the worst ways to handle the problem. If we cannot do anything useful, maybe not handling the exception and letting our caller deal with it would be a more honest way of dealing with the problem.

Notice that there is no silver bullet, or one-size-fits-all suggestion here. Every exceptional case, every application, every context, and every user base is different, and we should come up with an exception handling strategy that fits the current situation best. However, if all you are doing is **e.printStackTrace()**, you are probably doing something wrong.

Exercise 37: Using an IDE to Generate Exception-Handling Code

In this exercise, we will have a look at generating exception handling code using an IDE:

1. Create a new Java console project in IntelliJ. Import **File** and the **FileInputStream** class:

    ```
    import java.io.File;
    import java.io.FileInputStream;
    ```

2. Create a class called **Main** and add the **main()** method:

    ```
    public class Main {
        public static void main(String[] args) {
    ```

3. Open the file as follows:

    ```
    File file = new File("input.txt");
    FileInputStream fileInputStream = new FileInputStream(file);
    ```

4. Read the file as follows:

    ```
    int data = 0;
    while(data != -1) {
    data = fileInputStream.read();
    System.out.println(data);
        }
        fileInputStream.close();
        }
    }
    ```

    Note that, in four places, IntelliJ underlines our code in red. These are functions that specify throwing an exception. This prevents your code from executing.

5. Go to the first issue (**FileInputStream**), press *Alt + Enter*, and select "**Add exception to method signature**". This is how your code should look now:

```java
import java.io.File;
import java.io.FileInputStream;
import java.io.FileNotFoundException;

public class Main {
    public static void main(String[] args) throws FileNotFoundException {
        File file = new File("input.txt");
        FileInputStream fileInputStream = new FileInputStream(file);

        int data = 0;
        while(data != -1) {
            data = fileInputStream.read();
            System.out.println(data);
        }
        fileInputStream.close();
    }
}
```

We specified that our **main** function can throw **FileNotFoundException**, but this was not enough as this is not the exception type that the other functions throw. Now go to the first remaining issue (**read**), press *Alt + Enter*, and select "**Add exception to method signature**" once again. This is how your code should look now:

```java
import java.io.File;
import java.io.FileInputStream;
import java.io.FileNotFoundException;
import java.io.IOException;

public class Main {
    public static void main(String[] args) throws IOException {
        File file = new File("input.txt");
        FileInputStream fileInputStream = new FileInputStream(file);

        int data = 0;
        while(data != -1) {
            data = fileInputStream.read();
            System.out.println(data);
        }

        fileInputStream.close();
```

```
        }
    }
```

Now let's run our code. Unless you created an **input.txt** in the meantime, this is what you should see as an output:

```
Exception in thread "main" java.io.FileNotFoundException: input.txt (The
system cannot find the file specified)
at java.io.FileInputStream.open0(Native Method)
at java.io.FileInputStream.open(FileInputStream.java:195)
at java.io.FileInputStream.<init>(FileInputStream.java:138)
at Main.main(Main.java:9)
```

The exception propagated out of our main function and the JVM caught it and logged into the console.

Two things happened here. First, fixing the problem for **read()** was enough to eliminate all problems from the code, since both **read** and **close** throw the same exception: **IOException**, which is listed in the throws statement in the main function's declaration. However, the **FileNotFoundException** exception that we had listed there disappeared. Why?

This is because exception classes are in a hierarchy and **IOException** is an ancestor class of **FileNotFoundException**. Since every **FileNotFoundException** is also an **IOException**, specifying **IOException** was enough. If these two classes were not related in that way, IntelliJ would list the possible thrown exceptions as a comma-separated list.

6. Now let's provide the **input.txt** to our program. You can create the **input.txt** anywhere in your hard drive and provide a full path in the code; however, we will use a simple approach: IntelliJ runs your program inside the main project folder. Right-click on your project's **src** folder and click **Show in Explorer**. Now you should see the contents of the folder that contains the **src** folder; this is the root of your project folder. Create an **input.txt** file here and write the text "**abc**" in it. If you run your program again, you should see an output similar to this:

```
97
98
99
-1
```

7. Specifying the exceptions was one way to make our program work. Another would be to catch them. Let's try that now. Go back to the following version of your file; you can use undo repeatedly to do that:

```java
import java.io.File;
import java.io.FileInputStream;

public class Main {
    public static void main(String[] args) {
        File file = new File("input.txt");
        FileInputStream fileInputStream = new FileInputStream(file);

        int data = 0;
        while(data != -1) {
            data = fileInputStream.read();
            System.out.println(data);
        }
        fileInputStream.close();
    }
}
```

8. Now move the caret on to **FileInputStream**, hit *Alt* + *Enter*, and select "**Surround with try/catch**". Here is how your code should look:

```java
import java.io.File;
import java.io.FileInputStream;
import java.io.FileNotFoundException;

public class Main {
    public static void main(String[] args) {
        File file = new File("input.txt");
        FileInputStream fileInputStream = null;
        try {
            fileInputStream = new FileInputStream(file);
        } catch (FileNotFoundException e) {
            e.printStackTrace();
        }
```

```
        int data = 0;
        while(data != -1) {
            data = fileInputStream.read();
            System.out.println(data);
        }
        fileInputStream.close();
    }
}
```

Notice what happened here. Instead of simply wrapping the line with a **try/catch** block, it actually separated the creation of the reference variable from the exception-generating constructor call. This is mainly because **fileInputStream** is used later in the code and moving it inside the **try/catch** block would prevent it from being visible to those usages. This is actually a common pattern; you declare the variable before the **try/catch** block, handle any issues with its creation, and make it available for later, if necessary.

9. The current code has a problem: if the **FileInputStream** inside the **try/catch** block fails, the **fileInputStream** will continue to be null. After the **try/catch** block, it will be dereferenced and you will get a null reference exception. You have two options: either you place all usages of the object in the **try/catch** block, or you check the reference for null. Here is the first of the two options:

```java
import java.io.File;
import java.io.FileInputStream;
import java.io.FileNotFoundException;

public class Main {
    public static void main(String[] args) {
        File file = new File("input.txt");
        FileInputStream fileInputStream = null;
        try {
            fileInputStream = new FileInputStream(file);

            int data = 0;
            while(data != -1) {
                data = fileInputStream.read();
                System.out.println(data);
            }
            fileInputStream.close();
        } catch (FileNotFoundException e) {
            e.printStackTrace();
        }
```

```
        }
    }
```

10. We moved the code inside the **try/ catch** block to make sure we don't dereference **fileInputStream** while null. However, we still have red underlines under **read()** and **close()**. *Alt + Enter* on **read()** gives you a couple of options, the first of which is to add a **catch** clause:

```java
import java.io.File;
import java.io.FileInputStream;
import java.io.FileNotFoundException;
import java.io.IOException;

public class Main {
    public static void main(String[] args) {
        File file = new File("input.txt");
        FileInputStream fileInputStream = null;
        try {
            fileInputStream = new FileInputStream(file);
            int data = 0;
            while(data != -1) {
                data = fileInputStream.read();
                System.out.println(data);
            }
            fileInputStream.close();
        } catch (FileNotFoundException e) {
            e.printStackTrace();
        } catch (IOException e) {
            e.printStackTrace();
        }
    }
}
```

Now we have fixed all of the issues with our code and we can actually run it. Notice that the second catch clause is placed after the first, because **IOException** is a parent class of **FileNotFoundException**. If their order was the other way around, exceptions of type **FileNotFoundException** would actually be caught by the **IOException** catch block instead.

11. Here is the second of the two options, not placing all the code inside the first try:

```java
import java.io.File;
import java.io.FileInputStream;
import java.io.FileNotFoundException;

public class Main {
    public static void main(String[] args) {
        File file = new File("input.txt");
        FileInputStream fileInputStream = null;
        try {
            fileInputStream = new FileInputStream(file);
        } catch (FileNotFoundException e) {
            e.printStackTrace();
        }
        if (fileInputStream != null) {
            int data = 0;
            while(data != -1) {
                data = fileInputStream.read();
                System.out.println(data);
            }
            fileInputStream.close();
        }
    }
}
```

We run the second part of the code if the **fileInputStream** is not null. This way, we prevent the second part from running if creating the **FileInputStream** was not successful. It does not make a lot of sense to write it separately like this, but it would make sense if there was other code in between that is unrelated. You cannot put everything in the same **try** block, and in a later code, you may have to depend on that **try** block's success. A simple null check such as this is useful in that sense.

12. Our code still has issues, though. Let's *Alt + Enter* on the **read()** and **close()**, and select **Surround with try/catch**:

```java
import java.io.File;
import java.io.FileInputStream;
import java.io.FileNotFoundException;
import java.io.IOException;

public class Main {
    public static void main(String[] args) {
```

```java
File file = new File("input.txt");
FileInputStream fileInputStream = null;
try {
    fileInputStream = new FileInputStream(file);
} catch (FileNotFoundException e) {
    e.printStackTrace();
}

if (fileInputStream != null) {
    int data = 0;
    while(data != -1) {
        try {
            data = fileInputStream.read();
        } catch (IOException e) {
            e.printStackTrace();
        }
        System.out.println(data);
    }
    try {
        fileInputStream.close();
    } catch (IOException e) {
        e.printStackTrace();
    }
}
```

It is not good practice to use code like this. Although the quick fixes with *Alt +
Enter* usually serve us quite well, in this example, they resulted in horrible code.
This code here implies that your stream may sometimes fail. In that case, those
failures should be ignored and we should keep trying to read from the stream.
Also, the stream may fail to close, which we should also ignore. This would be a
very rare scenario and this code is not good. It's not readable at all either, with
many **try/catch** blocks.

13. A better way would be to place the whole block in a **try/catch**. In this case, we
are giving up after the first error, which is a simpler and usually more correct
approach:

```java
import java.io.File;
import java.io.FileInputStream;
import java.io.FileNotFoundException;
import java.io.IOException;
```

```java
public class Main {
    public static void main(String[] args) {
        File file = new File("input.txt");
        FileInputStream fileInputStream = null;
        try {
            fileInputStream = new FileInputStream(file);
        } catch (FileNotFoundException e) {
            e.printStackTrace();
        }

        if (fileInputStream != null) {
            try {
                int data = 0;
                while(data != -1) {
                    data = fileInputStream.read();
                    System.out.println(data);
                }
                fileInputStream.close();
            } catch (IOException e) {
                e.printStackTrace();
            }
        }
    }
}
```

To create this code, we did not rely on IntelliJ's quick fix with *Alt + Enter*. Since it's quite good usually, you may think that the code it creates is correct. However, you have to use your judgement, and sometimes correct the code it creates, as in this example.

Now you have experienced the quick and dirty handling of exceptions using the help of an IDE. The skills you gained in this section should guide you when you are on a deadline and help you avoid pitfalls when using autogenerated exception code using an IDE.

Exceptions versus Error Codes

Recall the C code example that we gave earlier:

```c
int other_idea()
{
    int err = minor_func1();
    if (!err)
        err = minor_func2();
    if (!err)
        err = minor_func3();
    return err;
}
```

There are a number of drawbacks to the method of handling errors used here. In this code, all we are trying to do is call three functions. However, for each function call, we are passing around values to track error states and using **if** statements for each function call if there was an error. Furthermore, the return value of the function is the error state—you are not allowed to return a value of your choosing. All this extra work dilutes the original code and makes it difficult to understand and maintain.

Another limitation of this approach is that a single integer value may not represent the error sufficiently. Instead, we may want to have more details about the error, when it happened, about which resource, and so on.

Before exception handling, this was how programmers had to code to ensure the completeness of their programs. Exception handling brings a number of benefits. Consider this alternate Java code:

```java
int otherIdea() {
    try {
        minorFunc1();
        minorFunc2();
        minorFunc3();
    } catch (IOException e) {
        // handle IOException
```

```
    } catch (NullPointerException e) {
        // handle NullPointerException
    }
}
```

Here, we have the three function calls without any error-related code polluting them. These are placed in a **try/catch** block and error handling is done separately from the original code in the **catch** blocks. This is more desirable for the following reasons:

- We do not have to have an **if** statement for each function call. We can group the exception handling in one place. It does not matter which function raised the exception; we catch all of them in one single place.

- There is not only one kind of problem that can happen in a function. Each function can raise more than one kind of exception. These can be handled in separate catch blocks, whereas, without exception handling, this would have required multiple if statements per function.

- The exception is represented by an object, not a single integer value. While an integer can tell us which kind of problem it was, an object can tell us much more: the call stack at the time of exception, the related resource, the user-readable explanation about the problem, and so on, can all be provided along with the exception object. This makes it much easier to act appropriately to exceptions compared to a single integer value.

Exercise 38: Exceptions Versus Error Codes

To complete the discussion about exceptions versus error codes, let's experience both and see which one is simpler to deal with. In this exercise, we have a class with two different kinds of functions, with two functions in each kind. The **thFunction1()** and **thFunction2()** are functions that can throw exceptions upon errors. **ecFunction1()** and **ecFunction2()** are functions that return a value that indicates whether there was an error. We are using random numbers to simulate that errors occur sometimes:

1. Import the **IOException** and **Random** classes as follows:

   ```
   import java.io.IOException;
   import java.util.Random;
   ```

2. Create a class called **Main** with an instance of the **Random** class:

   ```
   public class Main {
       Random rand = new Random();
   ```

3. Create the **thFunction1()** and **thFunction2()** functions, which throw an **IOException** as follows:

```java
void thFunction1() throws IOException {
        System.out.println("thFunction1 start");
        if (rand.nextInt(10) < 2) {
            throw new IOException("An I/O exception occurred in
thFunction1");
        }
        System.out.println("thFunction1 done");
    }

    void thFunction2() throws IOException, InterruptedException {
        System.out.println("thFunction2 start");
        int r = rand.nextInt(10);
        if (r < 2) {
            throw new IOException("An I/O exception occurred in
thFunction2");
        }
        if (r > 8) {
            throw new InterruptedException("An interruption occurred in
thFunction2");
        }
        System.out.println("thFunction2 done");
    }
```

4. Declare three variables with final values as follows:

```java
private static final int EC_NONE = 0;
private static final int EC_IO = 1;
private static final int EC_INTERRUPTION = 2;
```

5. Create two functions, **ecFunction1()** and **ecFunction2()**, as follows:

```java
int ecFunction1() {
System.out.println("ecFunction1 start");
if (rand.nextInt(10) < 2) {
return EC_IO;
}
System.out.println("thFunction1 done");
return EC_NONE;
}
int ecFunction2() {
System.out.println("ecFunction2 start");
```

```
int r = rand.nextInt(10);
if (r < 2) {
return EC_IO;
}
if (r > 8) {
return EC_INTERRUPTION;
}
System.out.println("ecFunction2 done");
        return EC_NONE;
}
```

6. Create **callThrowingFunctions()** as follows:

```
private void callThrowingFunctions() {
try {
thFunction1();
thFunction2();
} catch (IOException e) {
System.out.println(e.getLocalizedMessage());
e.printStackTrace();
} catch (InterruptedException e) {
System.out.println(e.getLocalizedMessage());
e.printStackTrace();
}
}
```

7. Create a method called **callErrorCodeFunctions()** as follows:

```
private void callErrorCodeFunctions() {
int err = ecFunction1();
if (err != EC_NONE) {
if (err == EC_IO) {
System.out.println("An I/O exception occurred in ecFunction1.");
}
}
err = ecFunction2();
switch (err) {
case EC_IO:
System.out.println("An I/O exception occurred in ecFunction2.");
break;
case EC_INTERRUPTION:
```

```
    System.out.println("An interruption occurred in ecFunction2.");
    break;
    }
  }
```

8. Add the **main** method as follows:

```
public static void main(String[] args) {
    Main main = new Main();
    main.callThrowingFunctions();
    main.callErrorCodeFunctions();
}
}
```

In our **main** function, we are first calling the throwing functions, followed by the error code functions.

Run this program a couple of times to observe how errors are handled in each case. Here is an example of an error caught using exception handling:

```
thFunction1 start
thFunction1 done
thFunction2 start
An interruption occurred in thFunction2
java.lang.InterruptedException: An interruption occurred in thFunction2
    at Main.thFunction2(Main.java:24)
    at Main.callThrowingFunctions(Main.java:58)
    at Main.main(Main.java:88)
ecFunction1 start
thFunction1 done
ecFunction2 start
thFunction2 done
```

Note that **thFunction2** was started, but not completed. The exception that it threw contained information about **thFunction2**. The shared **catch** block did not have to know where this exception was coming from; it simply caught the exception. This way, a single exception-catching block was able to handle multiple function calls. The exception object that was thrown by **thFunction2** and was caught by the catch block is able to transfer detailed information about the problem (for example, the stack trace). This leaves the default expected execution path clean, and the exception-catching block can deal with the problem in a meticulous way.

On the other hand, take a look at this sample execution output:

```
thFunction1 start
thFunction1 done
thFunction2 start
thFunction2 done
ecFunction1 start
An I/O exception occurred in ecFunction1.
ecFunction2 start
ecFunction2 done
```

In **ecFunction1**, an unexpected error occurred. This was signaled simply by an error code value that was returned from this function. Note that this function could not have returned any other value; employee number, whether something is active, and so on, are some examples of things that a function might return. Using error codes returned from functions in this way prohibits passing such information in the return value.

Furthermore, since the error is represented simply by a number, we are not able to get detailed information in the error-handling code. We also have to have error-handling code for each function call, as we would not have a way of differentiating between error locations otherwise. This creates code that is much more complicated and verbose than it should be.

Play with the code further, run it many times, and observe its behavior. This should give you a better understanding of exceptions versus error codes and why exceptions are superior.

Activity 36: Handling Mistakes in Numeric User Input

Now we will make use of exception handling in a real-world scenario. We will create a console application in which we ask for three whole numbers from the user, add them together, and print the result. If the user does not enter non-numeric text or a fractional number, we will ask the user to provide a whole number instead. We will do this for each number separately—a mistake in the third number will only require us to re-enter the third number and our program will remember the first two numbers just fine.

These steps will help you complete this activity:

1. Start with an empty Java console project. Place the following code in it, which reads input from the keyboard and prints it back after the user hits the *Enter* key.

2. Use this as a starting point and convert the input to a number using the **Integer. parseInt()** function.

3. Notice that the IDE did not warn us about a possible exception, unlike what we had in the earlier examples. This is because there are two types of exceptions, which we will learn about in an upcoming topic. For now, be aware that **Integer.parseInt()** can raise **java.lang.NumberFormatException**. Using the things we learned before wrap this line with a **try/catch** block that expects **NumberFormatException**.

4. Now place this in a **while** loop. It should loop while we do not have a valid whole number (integer) input from the user. Once we have such a value, the **while** loop should not loop anymore. If the user does not enter a valid whole number, print out an appropriate message to the user. Do not print out a raw exception message or a stack trace. This way, we insist that we get a whole number from the user and will not give up until we get a whole number.

5. Using this strategy, get three whole numbers in and sum them up. The program should ask again and again if you do not provide a valid whole number for any of the inputs. Print the result to the console.

> **Note**
>
> The solution for this activity can be found on page 365.

Exception Sources

When an exceptional case occurs in code, an exception object is thrown by the source of the problem, which is in turn caught by one of the callers in the call stack. The exception object is an instance of one of the exception classes. There are many such classes, which represent various types of problems. In this topic, we will take a look at different types of exceptions, get to know some of the exception classes from Java libraries, learn how to create our own exceptions, and see how to throw them.

In the previous topic, we first played with **IOException**. Then, in the activity, we played with **NumberFormatException**. There was a difference between these two exceptions. The IDE would force us to handle **IOException** and would not compile our code otherwise. However, it did not care whether we caught **NumberFormatException** or not, it would still compile and run our code. The difference was in the class hierarchy. While both of them are descendants of the **Exception** class, **NumberFormatException** is a descendant of **RuntimeException**, a subclass of **Exception**:

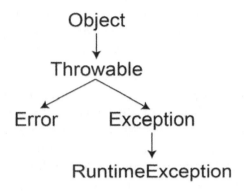

Figure 9.1: Hierarchy of the RuntimeException class

The preceding figure shows a simple class hierarchy. Any class that is a descendant of **Throwable** can be thrown and caught as an exception. However, Java provides a special treatment for the descendants of **Error** and **RuntimeException** classes. We'll explore these further in the upcoming sections.

Checked Exceptions

Any descendant of **Throwable** that is not a descendant of **Error** or **RuntimeException** falls in the category of checked exceptions. For example: **IOException**, which we used in the previous topic, is a checked exception. The IDE forced us to either catch it or to specify that we throw it in our function.

To be able to throw a caught exception, your function has to specify that it throws the exception.

Throwing a Checked Exception

Create a new project and paste the following code:

```java
import java.io.IOException;

public class Main {

    private static void myFunction() {
        throw new IOException("hello");
    }

    public static void main(String[] args) {
        myFunction();
    }
}
```

Here, we created a function and wanted it to throw an **IOException**. However, our IDE will not let us do that because this is a checked exception. Here is the type hierarchy of it:

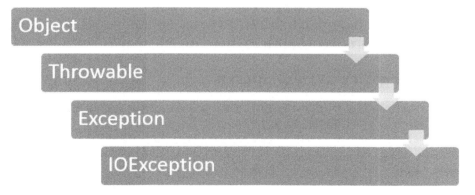

Figure 9.2: Hierarchy of the IOException class

Since **IOException** is a descendant of **Exception**, it is a checked exception and every function that throws a checked exception has to specify it. Move the caret to the error line, hit *Alt + Enter*, and select "**Add exception to method signature**". Here's how the code will look:

```
import java.io.IOException;


public class Main {

    private static void myFunction() throws IOException {
        throw new IOException("hello");
    }


    public static void main(String[] args) {
        myFunction();
    }
}
```

Notice that our code still has a problem. We will continue dealing with it in the next exercise.

Another requirement of checked exceptions is that if you call a method that specifies a checked exception, you have to either catch the exception or specify that you also throw that exception. This is also known as "the catch or specify rule."

Exercise 39: Working with catch or Specify

Let's have a look at throwing checked exceptions and calling methods that throw them. You should have the project already open:

1. If you do not have the preceding example in your IDE, create a project and add the following code:

```
import java.io.IOException;
public class Main {

    private static void myFunction() throws IOException {
        throw new IOException("hello");
    }
```

```
    public static void main(String[] args) {
        myFunction();
    }
}
```

Notice that the line with **myFunction()** is underlined in red, because this line is calling a checked exception and we are not doing anything about that potential exception. We either need to specify that we also throw it, or we need to catch and handle it. IntelliJ can help us do either of these. Move the caret over the **myFunction1()** line and hit *Alt + Enter*.

2. Select **Add exception to method signature**, to successfully specify that we throw the exception. Here is the code that this generates:

```
import java.io.IOException;
public class Main {

    private static void myFunction() throws IOException {
        throw new IOException("hello");
    }

    public static void main(String[] args) throws IOException {
        myFunction();
    }
}
```

As you can see, this compiles and runs just fine. Now undo (*Ctrl + Z*) and hit *Alt+ Enter* again to get the options back.

3. Alternatively, if we select **Surround with try/catch**, we'll successfully catch the exception. Here is the code that it generates:

```
import java.io.IOException;
public class Main {
    private static void myFunction() throws IOException {
        throw new IOException("hello");
    }

    public static void main(String[] args) {
        try {
            myFunction();
        } catch (IOException e) {
```

```
                    e.printStackTrace();
            }
        }
    }
```

While this compiles and runs, remember that simply printing information about it is not the greatest way to handle an exception.

In these exercises, we saw how to throw checked exceptions and how to call methods that throw them.

Unchecked Exceptions

Recall the top of the exception class hierarchy:

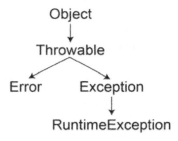

Figure 9.3: Hierarchy of the RuntimeException class

Here, the exception classes that are descendants of **RuntimeException** are called runtime exceptions. The descendants of **Error** are called errors. Both of these are called unchecked exceptions. They do not need to be specified, and if they are specified, they do not need to be caught.

Unchecked exceptions represent things that may happen more unexpectedly compared to checked exceptions. The assumption is that you have the option to ensure that they will not be thrown; therefore, they do not have to be expected. However, you should do your best to handle them if you have a suspicion that they may be thrown.

Here is the hierarchy of NumberFormatException:

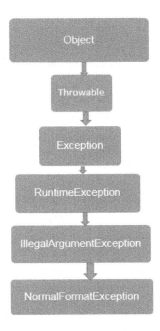

Figure 9.4: Hierarchy of the NormalFormatException class

Since it is a descendant of **RuntimeException**, it is a runtime exception, therefore an unchecked exception.

Exercise 40: Using Methods That Throw Unchecked Exceptions

In this exercise, we will write some code that throws a runtime exception:

1. Create a project in IntelliJ and paste in the following code:

```
public class Main {
public static void main(String[] args) {
int i = Integer.parseInt("this is not a number");
}
}
```

Note that this code is trying to parse a string as an integer, but the string clearly does not contain an integer. As a result, a **NumberFormatException** will be thrown. However, since this is an unchecked exception, we do not have to catch or specify it. This is what we see when we run the code:

```
Exception in thread "main" java.lang.NumberFormatException: For input
string: "this is not a number"
    at java.lang.NumberFormatException.
forInputString(NumberFormatException.java:65)
        at java.lang.Integer.parseInt(Integer.java:580)
        at java.lang.Integer.parseInt(Integer.java:615)
        at Main.main(Main.java:6)
```

2. Since we did not catch it, the **NumberFormatException** got thrown from the **main** function and crashed the application. Instead, we could catch it and print a message about it as follows:

```
public class Main {
public static void main(String[] args) {
try {
int i = Integer.parseInt("this is not a number");
} catch (NumberFormatException e) {
System.out.println("Sorry, the string does not contain an integer.");
}
}
}
```

Now, when we run the code, we get an output that shows that we are aware of the situation:

```
Sorry, the string does not contain an integer.
```

Although catching unchecked exceptions is optional, you should make sure you catch them in order to create code that is complete.

It's practically the same case for errors, which are descendants of the **Error** class. In the following section, we talk about the semantic differences between runtime exceptions and errors.

Exception Class Hierarchy

Any object that can be thrown as an exception is an instance of a class that is derived from the **Throwable** class. Any class that derives from **Error** or **RuntimeException** is treated as an unchecked exception, while any other class that derives from **Throwable** is a checked exception. Therefore, which exception class you use determines the mechanics (checked versus unchecked) of exception handling.

Beyond the mechanics of exception handling, the choice of exception class also carries semantic information. For example: if a library method encounters a case in which a file that was supposed to be in the hard drive is missing, it would throw an instance of **FileNotFoundException**. If there was a problem in a string that was supposed to contain a numeric value, the method that you give that string to would throw a **NumberFormatException**. The Java class library contains a number of exception classes that fit most unexpected situations. The following is a subset of classes in this hierarchy:

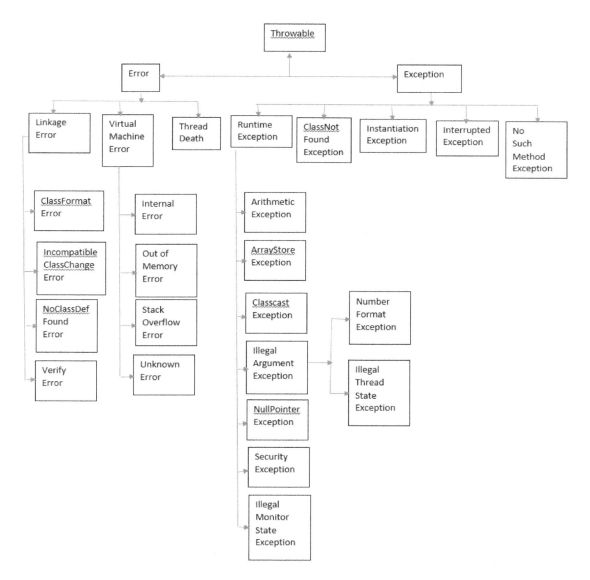

Figure 9.5: Subset of classes in hierarchy

If you read through this list, you will notice that there are a lot of exception types for various occasions.

Browsing the Exception Hierarchy

In IntelliJ, open any Java project or create a new one. Anywhere in your code, create a **Throwable** reference variable as follows:

```
Throwable t;
```

Now move the caret over **Throwable** and press **Ctrl** + **H**. The hierarchy window should open with the **Throwable** class in focus. It should look like this:

Figure 9.6: Hierarchy of Throwable class

Now expand **Error** and **Exception**, and read through the list of classes. These are various throwable classes defined in various libraries that your code has access to. As you can see, there is quite a broad list of exceptions to choose from. Next to each exception class, there is the package that it belongs to in parentheses. As a rule of thumb, if you are going to throw an exception yourself, you should try to use exceptions that are in the libraries that you are also using. For example: importing **com.sun.jmx.snmp.IPAcl** just so that you can use the **ParseException** defined in it is not a good thing to do.

Now you have a better idea about the existing exception classes that are in the Java Class Library and what your choice of exception class communicates to the users of your code.

Throwing Exceptions and Custom Exceptions

As a programmer, you will write methods that you or others will call. Inevitably, there will be things that go wrong in your code in undesirable situations. You should throw exceptions in those cases that are instances of appropriate exception classes.

To throw an exception, first, you need to create an instance of a class that is an ancestor of **Throwable**. Then, you populate that instance and use the **throw** keyword to throw it. Then, the throwable instance will travel up the call stack and pop entries until it meets a **try/catch** block with a catch statement that matches the type of this **Throwable** or is a subclass of it. The throwable is given to that catch block as the caught exception, and the execution continues from there.

Exercise 41: Throwing an Exception

In this exercise, we will use existing exception classes for our exceptions:

1. Create a new Java project and add the following code, which has a function that expects a string of length one that contains a single digit and prints it. If the string is empty, it will throw an **IllegalArgumentException**. If the string contains anything other than a single digit, it will throw a **NumberFormatException**. Since these are unchecked exceptions, we did not have to specify them:

```
public class Main {
public static void useDigitString(String digitString) {
if (digitString.isEmpty()) {
throw new IllegalArgumentException("An empty string was given instead of a
digit");
}
if (digitString.length() > 1) {
throw new NumberFormatException("Please supply a string with a single
digit");
}
}
}
```

2. Now we will call this function and handle the exceptions that it throws. We will intentionally call another function that calls this, and will have catch blocks in two different places to demonstrate exception propagation. The full code will look as follows:

```
public class Main {
    public static void useDigitString(String digitString) {
        if (digitString.isEmpty()) {
            throw new IllegalArgumentException("An empty string was given
instead of a digit");
        }

        if (digitString.length() > 1) {
            throw new NumberFormatException("Please supply a string with a
```

```
single digit");
        }

        System.out.println(digitString);
    }

    private static void runDigits() {
        try {
            useDigitString("1");
            useDigitString("23");
            useDigitString("4");
        } catch (NumberFormatException e) {
            System.out.println("A number format problem occurred: " +
e.getMessage());
        }

        try {
            useDigitString("5");
            useDigitString("");
            useDigitString("7");
        } catch (NumberFormatException e) {
            System.out.println("A number format problem occured: " +
e.getMessage());
        }
    }
```

3. Add the **main()** method as follows:

```
    public static void main(String[] args) {
        try {
            runDigits();
        } catch (IllegalArgumentException e) {
            System.out.println("An illegal argument was provided: " +
e.getMessage());
        }
    }

}
```

Notice that, from **main**, we call **runDigits**, which in turn calls **useDigitString**. The main function catches **IllegalArgumentException** and **runDigits** catches **NumberFormatException**. Although we throw all the exceptions in **useDigitString**, they are caught in different places.

Exercise 42: Creating Custom Exception Classes

In the previous exercise, we used existing exception classes for our exceptions. **NumberFormatException** sounded appropriate but **IllegalArgumentException** was a bit of an odd choice. Also, they are both unchecked exceptions; perhaps we would like to have checked ones instead. Therefore, existing exception classes are not suitable for our needs. We can create our own exception classes in this situation. Let's continue on the same course as the previous exercise:

1. Let's say that we are happy with **NumberFormatException**, but we want an **EmptyInputException** that is a checked exception. We can extend **Exception** to do that:

   ```
   class EmptyInputException extends Exception {
   }
   ```

2. If we had extra information to place in this exception, we could have added fields and a constructor for that purpose. However, in our case, we just want to signal that the input was empty; no other information is necessary for the caller. Now let's fix our code so that our function throws **EmptyInputException** instead of **IllegalArgumentException**:

   ```
   class EmptyInputException extends Exception {
   }
   public class Main {

       public static void useDigitString(String digitString) throws
   EmptyInputException {
           if (digitString.isEmpty()) {
               throw new EmptyInputException();
           }

           if (digitString.length() > 1) {
               throw new NumberFormatException("Please supply a string with a
   single digit");
           }
   ```

```
            System.out.println(digitString);
        }

    private static void runDigits() throws EmptyInputException {
        try {
            useDigitString("1");
            useDigitString("23");
            useDigitString("4");
        } catch (NumberFormatException e) {
            System.out.println("A number format problem occured: " +
    e.getMessage());
        }

        try {
            useDigitString("5");
            useDigitString("");
            useDigitString("7");
        } catch (NumberFormatException e) {
            System.out.println("A number format problem occured: " +
    e.getMessage());
        }
    }
```

3. Add the **main()** method as follows:

```
    public static void main(String[] args) {
        try {
            runDigits();
        } catch (EmptyInputException e) {
            System.out.println("An empty string was provided");
        }
    }

}
```

Notice that this made our code much simpler—we did not even have to write a message, as the name of the exception clearly communicates the problem. Here is the output:

```
1
A number format problem occured: Please supply a string with a single
digit
5
An empty string was provided
```

Now you know how to throw exceptions and create your own exception class if existing exception classes are insufficient.

Activity 37: Writing Custom Exceptions in Java.

We will write a program for an admission system for a roller coaster ride. For each visitor, we will get their name and age from the keyboard. Then, we will print out the name of the visitor and that they are riding the roller coaster.

Since roller coasters are only for adults, we will reject visitors that are younger than 15 years old. We will handle the rejection using a custom exception: **TooYoungException**. This exception object will contain the name and the age of the visitor. When we catch the exception, we will print an appropriate message that explains why they were rejected.

We will continue to accept visitors until the name is empty.

To achieve this, perform the following steps:

1. Create a new class and enter **RollerCoasterWithAge** as the class name.

2. Also create an exception class, **TooYoungException**.

3. Import the **java.util.Scanner** package.

4. In **main()**, create an infinite loop.

5. Get the user's name. If it is an empty string, break out of the loop.

6. Get the user's age. If it is lower than 15, throw a **TooYoungException** with this name and age.

7. Print the name as "John is riding the roller coaster".

8. Catch the exception and print an appropriate message for it.

9. Run the main program.

   The output should be similar to the following:

   ```
   Enter name of visitor: John
   Enter John's age: 20
   John is riding the roller coaster.
   Enter name of visitor: Jack
   Enter Jack's age: 13
   Jack is 13 years old, which is too young to ride.
   Enter name of visitor:
   ```

   Note

   The solution for this activity can be found on page 366.

Exception Mechanics

In the previous topics, we threw and caught exceptions and got a feel for how exceptions work. Now let's revisit the mechanics to make sure we got everything right.

How try/catch Works

The **try/catch** statement has two blocks: the **try** block and the **catch** block, as shown here:

```
try {
    // the try block
} catch (Exception e) {
    // the catch block, can be multiple
}
```

The **try** block is where your main execution path code goes. You optimistically write your program here. If an exception happens in any of the lines in the **try** block, the execution stops at that line and jumps to the **catch** block:

```
try {
    // line1, fine
    // line2, fine
    // line3, EXCEPTION!
    // line4, skipped
```

```
    // line5, skipped
} catch (Exception e) {
    // comes here after line3

}
```

The **catch** block catches throwables if they can be assigned to the exception reference it contains (**Exception e**, in this case). So, if you have an exception class here that is high up in the exception hierarchy (such as **Exception**), it will catch all exceptions. This will not catch errors, which is usually what you want.

If you want to be more specific about the types of exceptions that you catch, you can provide an exception class that is lower in the hierarchy.

Exercise 43: Exception Not Caught Because It Cannot Be Assigned to a Parameter in the catch Block

1. Create a new project and add the following code:

```java
public class Main {

    public static void main(String[] args) {
        try {
            for (int i = 0; i < 5; i++) {
                System.out.println("line " + i);
                if (i == 3) throw new Exception("EXCEPTION!");
            }
        } catch (InstantiationException e) {
            System.out.println("Caught an InstantiationException");
        }
    }

}
```

Note that this code will not even compile. The code throws an exception, but the catch clause expects an **InstantiationException**, which is a descendant of **Exception**, to which exception instances cannot be assigned. Therefore, the exception is neither caught, nor thrown.

2. Specify an exception so that the code can compile as follows:

```java
public class Main {
    public static void main(String[] args) throws Exception {
        try {
            for (int i = 0; i < 5; i++) {
                System.out.println("line " + i);
                if (i == 3) throw new Exception("EXCEPTION!");
            }
        } catch (InstantiationException e) {
            System.out.println("Caught an InstantiationException");
        }
    }

}
```

When we run the code, we see that we are not able to catch the exception that we threw:

```
line 0
line 1
line 2
line 3
Exception in thread "main" java.lang.Exception: EXCEPTION!
    at Main.main(Main.java:8)
```

Sometimes, you catch one type of a specific exception, but your code can throw other types of exceptions as well. You can provide multiple catch blocks in this case. The exception types being caught can be in different places in the class hierarchy. The first catch block of whose parameter the thrown exception can be assigned to is executed. So, if two exception classes have an ancestor relationship, the descendant's catch clause has to go before the ancestor's catch clause; otherwise, the ancestor would catch the descendant's exceptions as well.

Exercise 44: Multiple catch Blocks and Their Order

In this exercise, we will have a look at multiple catch blocks in a program and their order of execution. Let's continue with the previous exercise:

1. Go back to the initial form of the code:

```java
public class Main {
    public static void main(String[] args) {
        try {
            for (int i = 0; i < 5; i++) {
```

```
                System.out.println("line " + i);
                if (i == 3) throw new Exception("EXCEPTION!");
            }
        } catch (InstantiationException e) {
            System.out.println("Caught an InstantiationException");
        }
    }
}
```

2. When we hit *Alt + Enter* on **Exception** to add a catch clause for it, it is added after the existing one, which is correct:

```
public class Main {
    public static void main(String[] args) {
        try {
            for (int i = 0; i < 5; i++) {
                System.out.println("line " + i);
                if (i == 3) throw new Exception("EXCEPTION!");
            }
        } catch (InstantiationException e) {
            System.out.println("Caught an InstantiationException");
        } catch (Exception e) {
            e.printStackTrace();
        }
    }
}
```

3. If the thrown exception is an **InstantiationException**, it will be caught by the first catch. Otherwise, if it is any other exception, it will be caught by the second. Let's try reordering the catch blocks:

```
public class Main {
    public static void main(String[] args) {
        try {
            for (int i = 0; i < 5; i++) {
                System.out.println("line " + i);
                if (i == 3) throw new Exception("EXCEPTION!");
            }
        } catch (Exception e) {
            e.printStackTrace();
        } catch (InstantiationException e) {
            System.out.println("Caught an InstantiationException");
        }
```

```
        }

    }
```

Now our code will not even compile because instances of **InstantiationException** can be assigned to **Exception e**, and they will be caught by the first catch block. The second block will never be called—ever. The IDE is smart to catch this problem for us.

Another property of exceptions is that they travel up the call stack. Every function that is called essentially returns the execution to its caller, until one of them is able to catch the exception.

Exercise 45: Exception Propagation

In this exercise, we will go through an example in which we have multiple functions calling one another:

1. We throw the exception from the deepest method, which is caught by one of the methods higher in the call stack:

```java
public class Main {
    private static void method3() throws Exception {
        System.out.println("Begin method 3");
        try {
            for (int i = 0; i < 5; i++) {
                System.out.println("line " + i);
                if (i == 3) throw new Exception("EXCEPTION!");
            }
        } catch (InstantiationException e) {
            System.out.println("Caught an InstantiationException");
        }
        System.out.println("End method 3");
    }

    private static void method2() throws Exception {
        System.out.println("Begin method 2");
        method3();
        System.out.println("End method 2");
    }

    private static void method1() {
        System.out.println("Begin method 1");
        try {
```

```
        method2();
    } catch (Exception e) {
        System.out.println("method1 caught an Exception!: " +
e.getMessage());
        System.out.println("Also, below is the stack trace:");
        e.printStackTrace();
    }
    System.out.println("End method 1");
}
```

2. Add the **main()** method as follows:

```
public static void main(String[] args) {
    System.out.println("Begin main");
    method1();
    System.out.println("End main");
}

}
```

When we run the code, we get this output:

```
Begin main
Begin method 1
Begin method 2
Begin method 3
line 0
line 1
line 2
line 3
method1 caught an Exception!: EXCEPTION!
Also, below is the stack trace:
java.lang.Exception: EXCEPTION!
    at Main.method3(Main.java:8)
    at Main.method2(Main.java:18)
    at Main.method1(Main.java:25)
    at Main.main(Main.java:36)
End method 1
End main
```

Notice that method 2 and method 3 do not run to completion, while method 1 and **main** do. Method 2 throws the exception; method 3 does not catch it and lets it propagate up. Finally, method 1 catches it. Method 2 and method 3 abruptly return the execution to the method higher in the call stack. Since method 1 and main do not let an exception propagate up, they are able to run to completion.

There is one more feature of the catch block that we should talk about. Let's say we would like to catch two specific exceptions but not others, but we will do the exact same thing in their catch blocks. In this case, we are able to combine the catch blocks of these exceptions with a pipe character. This feature was introduced in Java 7 and will not work in Java 6 and below.

Multiple Exception Types in One Block

We have dealt with a single type of exception in one block of code. Now we will have a look at multiple exception types in one block.

Consider the following code:

```java
import java.io.IOException;
public class Main {
public static void method1() throws IOException {
System.out.println(4/0);
}
public static void main(String[] args) {
try {
System.out.println("line 1");
method1();
System.out.println("line 2");
} catch (IOException|ArithmeticException e) {
System.out.println("An IOException or a ArithmeticException was thrown.
Details below.");
e.printStackTrace();
}
}
}
```

Here, we have a catch block that can catch either an **IOException** or an **ArithmeticException** using the catch block with multiple exception types. When we run the code, we see that the **ArithmeticException** that we caused is successfully caught:

```
line 1

An IOException or a ArithmeticException was thrown. Details below.

java.lang.ArithmeticException: / by zero
    at Main.method1(Main.java:6)
    at Main.main(Main.java:12)
```

If the exception was an **IOException**, it would be caught the same way.

Now you know more about the mechanics of a **try/catch** block, exception propagation, multiple catch blocks, and multiple exceptions in a block.

Activity 38: Dealing with Multiple Exceptions in a Block

Remember that we wrote a program for an admission system for a roller coaster ride earlier? This time, we will also take the visitor's height into account. For each visitor, we will get their name, age, and height from the keyboard. Then, we will print out the name of the visitor and that they are riding the roller coaster.

Since roller coasters are only for adults of a certain height, we will reject visitors that are younger than 15 years old or shorter than 130 cm. We will handle the rejection using custom exceptions: **TooYoungException** and **TooShortException**. These exception objects will contain the name and the relevant property of the person (age or height). When we catch the exception, we will print an appropriate message that explains why they were rejected.

We will continue to accept visitors until the name is empty.

To achieve this, perform the following steps:

1. Create a new class and enter **RollerCoasterWithAgeAndHeight** as the class name.

2. Also create two exception classes, **TooYoungException** and **TooShortException**.

3. Import the **java.util.Scanner** package.

4. In **main()**, create an infinite loop.

5. Get the user's name. If it is an empty string, break out of the loop.

6. Get the user's age. If it is lower than 15, throw a **TooYoungException** with this name and age.

7. Get the user's height. If it is lower than 130, throw a **TooShortException** with this name and age.

8. Print the name as "John is riding the roller coaster."

9. Catch the two types of exceptions separately. Print appropriate messages for each.

10. Run the main program.

The output should be similar to the following:

```
Enter name of visitor: John
Enter John's age: 20
Enter John's height: 180
John is riding the roller coaster.
Enter name of visitor: Jack
Enter Jack's age: 13
Jack is 13 years old, which is too young to ride.
Enter name of visitor: Jill
Enter Jill's age: 16
Enter Jill's height: 120
Jill is 120 cm tall, which is too short to ride.
Enter name of visitor:
```

> **Note**
>
> The solution for this activity can be found on page 368.

What Are We Supposed to Do in a Catch Block?

When you catch an exception, you are supposed to do something about it. The ideal case is that you can find a strategy that recovers from the error and can resume the execution. However, sometimes you cannot do this and may choose to specify in your function that you let this exception propagate using a throws statement. We saw these in the previous topic.

However, in some cases, you may be in a position to add more information to the exception that you will propagate to your caller. For example: let's say that you called a method to parse the user's age and it threw a **NumberFormatException**. If you simply let it propagate to your caller, your caller will not know that this was related to the user's age. Perhaps adding this information to the exception before propagating it up would be beneficial. You can do this by catching the exception, wrapping it in another exception as the cause, and throwing that exception to your caller. This is also called "**chaining exceptions**."

Exercise 46: Chained Exceptions

In this exercise, we will have a look at the workings of chained exceptions:

1. Create a new project and add this code:

```java
public class Main {
public static int parseUsersAge(String ageString) {
return Integer.parseInt(ageString);
}
public static void readUserInfo()  {
int age = parseUsersAge("fifty five");
}
public static void main(String[] args) {
readUserInfo();
}
}
```

Notice that trying to parse "fifty five" as an integer will result in a **NumberFormatException**. We are not catching it and letting it propagate. Here is the output we get as a result:

```
Exception in thread "main" java.lang.NumberFormatException: For input
string: "fifty five"
    at java.lang.NumberFormatException.
forInputString(NumberFormatException.java:65)
    at java.lang.Integer.parseInt(Integer.java:580)
    at java.lang.Integer.parseInt(Integer.java:615)
    at Main.parseUsersAge(Main.java:4)
    at Main.readUserInfo(Main.java:8)
    at Main.main(Main.java:12)
```

Note that the exception's output does not give any indication that this problem was related to the user's age.

2. Catch the exception and chain it to add this information about age:

```java
public class Main {
public static int parseUsersAge(String ageString) {
return Integer.parseInt(ageString);
}
public static void readUserInfo() throws Exception {
try {
```

```
    int age = parseUsersAge("fifty five");
    } catch (NumberFormatException e) {
    throw new Exception("Problem while parsing user's age", e);
    }
    }
```

3. Add the **main()** method as follows:

```
    public static void main(String[] args) throws Exception {
    readUserInfo();
    }
    }
```

In this case, here is the output that we get:

```
Exception in thread "main" java.lang.Exception: Problem while parsing
user's age
    at Main.readUserInfo(Main.java:11)
    at Main.main(Main.java:16)
Caused by: java.lang.NumberFormatException: For input string: "fifty five"
    at java.lang.NumberFormatException.
forInputString(NumberFormatException.java:65)
    at java.lang.Integer.parseInt(Integer.java:580)
    at java.lang.Integer.parseInt(Integer.java:615)
    at Main.parseUsersAge(Main.java:4)
    at Main.readUserInfo(Main.java:9)
    ... 1 more
```

Note that this contains information about the age. This is an exception that has another exception as the cause. If you want, you can get it using the **e.getCause()** method and act accordingly. When simply logged, it prints the exception details in order.

finally Block and Their Mechanics

The **try/catch** block is very useful in catching exceptions. However, here is a common scenario in which it may have some shortcomings. In our code, we would like to acquire some resources. We are responsible for releasing the resources when we are done with them. However, a naive implementation may result in a file being left open when an exception happens.

Exercise 47: Leaving a File Open as a Result of an Exception

In this exercise, we will deal with the **finally** block:

1. Let's say we will read the first line of a file and print it. We can code this as follows:

```java
import java.io.BufferedReader;
import java.io.FileReader;
import java.io.IOException;
public class Main {
private static void useTheFile(String s) {
System.out.println(s);
throw new RuntimeException("oops");
}
```

2. Add the **main()** method as follows:

```java
public static void main(String[] args) throws Exception {
try {
BufferedReader br = new BufferedReader(new FileReader("input.txt"));
System.out.println("opened the file");
useTheFile(br.readLine());
br.close();
System.out.println("closed the file");
} catch (Exception e) {
System.out.println("caught an exception while reading the file");
}
}
}
```

Note that the **useTheFile** function raises an exception before we had a chance to close the file. When we run it, we get this result:

```
opened the file
line 1 from the file
caught an exception while reading the file
```

Note that we do not see a "closed the file" output because the execution could never get past the **useTheFile()** call. After catching the exception, even though we do not have access to the **BufferedReader** reference, the operating system is still holding the file resources. We just leaked a resource. If we do this many times in a loop, our application may crash.

3. You may try to devise various solutions to this resource-leaking problem. For example: you may duplicate the file-closing code and paste it to the catch block. Now you have it both in the **try** and in the **catch** blocks. If you have multiple **catch** blocks, all of them should have it as follows:

```java
import java.io.BufferedReader;
import java.io.FileReader;
import java.io.IOException;
public class Main {
private static void useTheFile(String s) {
System.out.println(s);
throw new RuntimeException("oops");
}
public static void main(String[] args) throws Exception {
BufferedReader br = null;
try {
br = new BufferedReader(new FileReader("input.txt"));
System.out.println("opened the file");
useTheFile(br.readLine());
br.close();
System.out.println("closed the file");
} catch (IOException e) {
System.out.println("caught an I/O exception while reading the file");
br.close();
System.out.println("closed the file");
} catch (Exception e) {
System.out.println("caught an exception while reading the file");
br.close();
System.out.println("closed the file");
}
}
}
```

4. The preceding code is correct, but it has code duplication, which makes it hard to maintain. Instead, you may think that you can close the file after the **catch** block in one single place:

```java
import java.io.BufferedReader;
import java.io.FileReader;
import java.io.IOException;
public class Main {
private static void useTheFile(String s) {
System.out.println(s);
```

```
throw new RuntimeException("oops");
}
public static void main(String[] args) throws Exception {
BufferedReader br = null;
try {
br = new BufferedReader(new FileReader("input.txt"));
System.out.println("opened the file");
useTheFile(br.readLine());
} catch (IOException e) {
System.out.println("caught an I/O exception while reading the file");
throw new Exception("something is wrong with I/O", e);
} catch (Exception e) {
System.out.println("caught an exception while reading the file");
}
br.close();
System.out.println("closed the file");
}
}
```

While this is almost correct, it is missing one possibility. Note that we are throwing an exception in the first **catch** block now. That will bypass the code after the catch blocks and the file will still be left open.

5. Therefore, what we need to do is to ensure that the file closing code will run no matter what happens. The **try / catch/ finally** block is the solution to this problem. It is like the **try/ catch** block, with an extra finally block that executes after we are done with the block, no matter what happens. Here is the solution with the **finally** block:

```
import java.io.BufferedReader;
import java.io.FileReader;
import java.io.IOException;
public class Main {
private static void useTheFile(String s) {
System.out.println(s);
throw new RuntimeException("oops");
}
public static void main(String[] args) throws Exception {
BufferedReader br = null;
try {
br = new BufferedReader(new FileReader("input.txt"));
System.out.println("opened the file");
useTheFile(br.readLine());
```

```
    } catch (IOException e) {
    System.out.println("caught an I/O exception while reading the file");
    throw new Exception("something is wrong with I/O", e);
    } catch (Exception e) {
    System.out.println("caught an exception while reading the file");
    } finally {
    br.close();
    System.out.println("closed the file");
    }
    }
    }
```

This new version closes the file whether there was an exception raised or not, or if another exception was raised after an exception was originally caught. In each case, the file-closing code in the finally block is executed and the file resource is released by the operating system appropriately.

There is still one problem with this code. The problem is, an exception might be raised while we are opening the file in the **BufferedReader** constructor, and the **br** variable may remain null. Then, when we try to close the file, we will dereference a null variable, which will create an exception.

6. To avoid this problem, we need to ignore **br** if it is null. The following is the complete code:

```
import java.io.BufferedReader;
import java.io.FileReader;
import java.io.IOException;

public class Main {

    private static void useTheFile(String s) {
        System.out.println(s);
        throw new RuntimeException("oops");
    }

    public static void main(String[] args) throws Exception {

        BufferedReader br = null;
        try {
            br = new BufferedReader(new FileReader("input.txt"));
            System.out.println("opened the file");
            useTheFile(br.readLine());
        } catch (IOException e) {
```

```
                System.out.println("caught an I/O exception while reading the
        file");
                throw new Exception("something is wrong with I/O", e);
            } catch (Exception e) {
                System.out.println("caught an exception while reading the
        file");
            } finally {
                if (br != null) {
                    br.close();
                    System.out.println("closed the file");
                }
            }
        }

    }
```

Activity 39: Working with Multiple Custom Exceptions

Remember that we wrote a program for an admission system for a roller coaster ride that verified the visitors' age and heights. This time, we will assume that we have to escort every applicant outside of the roller-coaster area afterward, whether they ride the roller coaster or not.

We will admit visitors one by one. For each visitor, we will get their name, age, and height from the keyboard. Then, we will print out the name of the visitor and that they are riding the roller coaster.

Since roller coasters are only for adults with a certain height, we will reject visitors who are younger than 15 years old or shorter than 130 cm. We will handle the rejection using custom exceptions: **TooYoungException** and **TooShortException**. These exception objects will contain the name and the relevant property of the person (age or height). When we catch the exception, we will print an appropriate message that explains why they were rejected.

Once we have finished with a visitor, whether they ride the roller coaster or not, we will print that we are escorting the visitor outside the roller-coaster area.

We will continue to accept visitors until the name is empty.

To achieve this, perform the following steps:

1. Create a new class and enter **RollerCoasterWithEscorting** as the class name.

2. Also create two exception classes, **TooYoungException** and **TooShortException**.

3. Import the **java.util.Scanner** package.

4. In **main()**, create an infinite loop.

5. Get the user's name. If it is an empty string, break out of the loop.

6. Get the user's age. If it is lower than 15, throw a **TooYoungException** with this name and age.

7. Get the user's height. If it is lower than 130, throw a **TooShortException** with this name and age.

8. Print name as "John is riding the roller coaster."

9. Catch the two types of exceptions separately. Print appropriate messages for each.

10. Print that you are escorting the user off the premises. You have to be careful about the scope of the name variable.

11. Run the main program.

    The output should be similar to the following:

    ```
    Enter name of visitor: John
    Enter John's age: 20
    Enter John's height: 180
    John is riding the roller coaster.
    Escorting John outside the premises.
    Enter name of visitor: Jack
    Enter Jack's age: 13
    Jack is 13 years old, which is too young to ride.
    Escorting Jack outside the premises.
    Enter name of visitor: Jill
    Enter Jill's age: 16
    Enter Jill's height: 120
    ```

```
Jill is 120 cm tall, which is too short to ride.
Escorting Jill outside the premises.
Enter name of visitor:
```

Note

The solution for this activity can be found on page 370.

The try with resource Block

The **try/ catch/ finally** block is a great way to handle resources that you have allocated. However, you will probably agree that it feels a bit like boilerplate. Allocating resources and releasing them in a finally block is a very common pattern. Java 7 introduced a new block that simplifies this common pattern—the **try with resource** block. In this new block, we place the resource allocations between parentheses right after the try block and forget about them. The system will automatically call their **.close()** methods:

```
try(Resource r1 = Resource(); OtherResource r2 = OtherResource()) {
    r1.useResource();
    r2.useOtherResource();
} // don't worry about closing the resources
```

For this to work, all of these resources have to implement the **AutoCloseable** interface.

Exercise 48: try with resources Block

In this exercise, we will have a look at the try with resource block:

1. Import the required classes as follows:

```
import java.io.BufferedReader;
import java.io.FileReader;
import java.io.IOException;
```

2. Create a **Main** class with the **useTheFile()** method, which takes a string parameter as follows:

```java
public class Main {

    private static void useTheFile(String s) {
        System.out.println(s);
        throw new RuntimeException("oops");
    }
```

3. Convert our earlier example to use the try with resources block as follows:

```java
public static void main(String[] args) throws Exception {

    try (BufferedReader br = new BufferedReader(new FileReader("input.txt"))) {
        System.out.println("opened the file, which will be closed automatically");
        useTheFile(br.readLine());
    } catch (IOException e) {
        System.out.println("caught an I/O exception while reading the file");
        throw new Exception("something is wrong with I/O", e);
    } catch (Exception e) {
        System.out.println("caught an exception while reading the file");
    }
}

}
```

Best Practices

While learning about exception handling and its statements, mechanics, and classes is required to use it, for most programmers this may not be enough. Usually, this set of theoretical information needs practical experience of various cases to get a better feel for exceptions. In this regard, some rules of thumb about the practical use of exceptions are worth mentioning:

- Do not suppress exceptions unless you really handled them.

- Inform the user and let them take responsibility unless you can fix things silently.

- Be aware of the caller's behavior and don't leak exceptions unless it is expected.

- Wrap and chain with more specific exceptions when possible.

Suppressing Exceptions

In your function, when you catch an exception and do no throw anything, you are signaling that you took care of the exceptional case and you fixed the situation so that it is as if that exceptional case had never happened. If you cannot make such a claim, then you should not have suppressed that exception.

Exercise 49: Suppressing Exceptions

For example: let's assume that we have a list of strings that we expect to contain integer numbers:

1. We will parse all of them and add them to a corresponding list of integers:

```java
import java.util.ArrayList;
import java.util.List;

public class Main {

    private static List<Integer> parseIntegers(List<String> inputList) {
        List<Integer> integers = new ArrayList<>();
        for(String s: inputList) {
            integers.add(Integer.parseInt(s));
        }
        return integers;
    }
```

2. Add a **main()** method as follows:

```java
    public static void main(String[] args) {
        List<String> inputList = new ArrayList<>();
        inputList.add("1");
        inputList.add("two");
        inputList.add("3");

        List<Integer> outputList = parseIntegers(inputList);

        int sum = 0;
        for(Integer i: outputList) {
            sum += i;
        }
        System.out.println("Sum is " + sum);
    }

}
```

When we run this, we get this output:

```
Exception in thread "main" java.lang.NumberFormatException: For input
string: "two"
    at java.lang.NumberFormatException.
forInputString(NumberFormatException.java:65)
        at java.lang.Integer.parseInt(Integer.java:580)
        at java.lang.Integer.parseInt(Integer.java:615)
        at Main.parseIntegers(Main.java:9)
        at Main.main(Main.java:20)
```

3. We should do something about this; at least, we should not let our code crash. What is the correct course of action? Should we catch the error inside the **parseIntegers** function, or should we catch it in main? Let's catch it in **parseIntegers** and see what happens:

```java
import java.util.ArrayList;
import java.util.List;

public class Main {

    private static List<Integer> parseIntegers(List<String> inputList) {
        List<Integer> integers = new ArrayList<>();
        for(String s: inputList) {
            try {
                integers.add(Integer.parseInt(s));
            } catch (NumberFormatException e) {
                System.out.println("could not parse an element: " + s);
            }
        }
        return integers;
    }
```

4. Add a **main()** method as follows:

```java
public static void main(String[] args) {
    List<String> inputList = new ArrayList<>();
    inputList.add("1");
    inputList.add("two");
    inputList.add("3");
```

```
        List<Integer> outputList = parseIntegers(inputList);

        int sum = 0;
        for(Integer i: outputList) {
            sum += i;
        }
        System.out.println("Sum is " + sum);
    }

}
```

Now here is our output:

```
could not parse an element: two
Sum is 4
```

It added 1 and 3 together, and ignored the "two." Is this what we wanted? We assumed that the "two" was the correct number and we expected it to be in the sum. However, at the moment, we are excluding it from the sum, and we are adding a note in the logs. If this was a real-life scenario, probably nobody would look at the logs and the result that we provide would be inaccurate. This is because we caught the error and did not do anything meaningful about it.

What would be a better approach? We have two possibilities here: we either can assume that every element in the list should actually be a number, or we can assume that there will be mistakes and we should do something about them.

The latter is a trickier approach. Perhaps we can collect the offending entries in another list and return it back to the caller, and then the caller would send it back to its origin for re-evaluation. For example, it could show them to the user and ask them to be corrected.

The former is an easier approach: we assume that the initial list contains number strings. If this assumption breaks, however, we have to let the caller know. So, we should throw an exception, rather than providing a half-correct sum.

What we should not do is take a third approach: hope that the list contains numbers, but ignore the ones that are not numbers. Note that this is a choice we made, but that's not what we thought of when we enumerated our two options above. This was convenient to program, but it created an assumption that was not there in the original business logic. Be very careful about situations like this. Make sure you write down your assumptions and be strict in enforcing them. Do not let the convenience of programming force you to accept weird assumptions.

If we take the assumption that the initial list contains number strings, here is how we should have coded it:

```java
import java.util.ArrayList;
import java.util.List;


public class Main {

    private static List<Integer> parseIntegers(List<String> inputList) {
        List<Integer> integers = new ArrayList<>();
        for(String s: inputList) {
            integers.add(Integer.parseInt(s));
        }
        return integers;
    }


    public static void main(String[] args) {
        List<String> inputList = new ArrayList<>();
        inputList.add("1");
        inputList.add("two");
        inputList.add("3");

        try {
            List<Integer> outputList = parseIntegers(inputList);

            int sum = 0;
            for(Integer i: outputList) {
                sum += i;
            }
            System.out.println("Sum is " + sum);
        } catch (NumberFormatException e) {
            System.out.println("There was a non-number element in the list.
Rejecting.");
```

```
        }
    }


}
```

And the output would simply be as follows:

```
There was a non-number element in the list. Rejecting.
```

Keeping the User in the Loop

The previous rule of thumb advised us not to provide half-correct results by sweeping problems under the rug. Now we'll extend it for cases when the program is an interactive one. Unless your program is a batch process, it usually has some interaction with a user. In that case, having the user be the arbiter of a problematic situation is usually the right approach.

In our example of a list of string numbers, obviously, one of the strings is not parsable as a number and there is not much the program can do. However, if the user saw the "two," they could replace it with a "2" to fix the situation. Therefore, rather than trying to silently fix things, we should find ways of involving the user in the decision-making process and get their help to resolve the problem.

Exercise 50: Asking the User for Help

We can extend our previous example so that we identify the offending entry in the list and ask the user to correct it:

1. Here is an approach for this:

    ```java
    import java.util.ArrayList;
    import java.util.List;
    import java.util.Scanner;

    class NonNumberInListException extends Exception {
        public int index;

        NonNumberInListException(int index, Throwable cause) {
            super(cause);
            this.index = index;
        }
    }
    ```

```java
public class Main {

    private static List<Integer> parseIntegers(List<String> inputList)
throws NonNumberInListException {
        List<Integer> integers = new ArrayList<>();
        int index = 0;
        for(String s: inputList) {
            try {
                integers.add(Integer.parseInt(s));
            } catch (NumberFormatException e) {
                throw new NonNumberInListException(index, e);
            }
            index++;
        }
        return integers;
    }
}
```

2. Add a **main()** method as follows:

```java
public static void main(String[] args) {
    List<String> inputList = new ArrayList<>();
    inputList.add("1");
    inputList.add("two");
    inputList.add("3");

    boolean done = false;
    while (!done) {
        try {
            List<Integer> outputList = parseIntegers(inputList);

            int sum = 0;
            for(Integer i: outputList) {
                sum += i;
            }
            System.out.println("Sum is " + sum);
            done = true;
        } catch (NonNumberInListException e) {
            System.out.println("This element does not seem to be a
number: " + inputList.get(e.index));
            System.out.print("Please provide a number instead: ");
            Scanner scanner = new Scanner(System.in);
            String newValue = scanner.nextLine();
            inputList.set(e.index, newValue);
```

```
                    }
                }
            }
        }
```

And here is a sample output:

```
This element does not seem to be a number: two
Please provide a number instead: 2
Sum is 6
```

Note that we identified the offending element and asked the user to fix it. This is a good way to keep the user in the loop and give them a chance to fix the problem.

Do Not Throw Unless It Is Expected

So far, we have been suggesting that throwing exceptions is a good thing and that we should not suppress them. However, in some cases, this may not be the case. This reminds us that everything about exceptions depends on the context and we should think about each situation rather than blindly following patterns.

Every now and then, you might use a third-party library and you might provide them with classes of yours so that they call your methods. For example: a game engine may get your object and call its **update()** method 60 times per second. In a case such as this, you should be careful about understanding what it may mean if you throw an exception. If it is the case that the exception that you throw exits the game, or shows a popup that an error happened, maybe you should not throw exceptions about things that are not showstoppers. Let's say that you are not able to calculate a required value in this frame, but maybe it will work in the next frame. Is it worth stopping the game for this? Perhaps not.

Especially when you are overriding classes/implementing interfaces and handing your object to another entity to manage, you should be mindful about what propagating an exception out of your methods entails. If the caller encourages exceptions, great. Otherwise you may have to wrap all your methods in a broad **try/catch** to ensure that you do not leak exceptions for things that are not showstoppers.

Consider Chaining and Being More Specific When You Let Exceptions Propagate

When you propagate an exception to your caller, you usually have a chance to add more information to that exception so that it will be more useful to the caller. For example: you may be parsing the user's age, phone number, height, and so on, from strings that they provided. Simply raising a `NumberFormatException`, without informing the caller about which value it was for is not a very helpful strategy. Instead, catching the `NumberFormatException` separately for each parse operation gives us the chance to identify the offending value. Then, we can create a new Exception object, provide more information in it, give the `NumberFormatException` as the initial cause, and throw that instead. Then, the caller can catch it and be informed about which entity was the offending one.

The earlier exercise, in which we used our custom `NonNumberInListException` to identify the index of the offending entry in the list, is a good example of this rule of thumb. Whenever possible, it is a better idea to throw a more informative exception that we create ourselves, rather than letting the internal exception propagate without much context.

Summary

In this lesson, we covered exceptions in Java from a practical point of view. First, we discussed the motivation behind exception handling and how it provides advantages over other ways of trying to handle erroneous cases. Then, we took the point of view of a newbie Java programmer with a powerful IDE and provided guidance on how to best handle and specify exceptions. Later, we dived deeper into causes of exceptions and various exception types, followed by the mechanics of exception handling using the try/catch, try/catch/finally, and try with resource blocks. We finish this discussion with a list of best practices to guide your decision process in various situations that involve exceptions.

Appendix

About

This section is included to assist the students to perform the activities in the book.

It includes detailed steps that are to be performed by the students to achieve the objectives of the activities.

Lesson 1: Introduction to Java

Activity 1: Printing the Results of Simple Arithmetic Operations

Solution:

1. Create a class named **Operations** as follows:

```
public class Operations
{
```

2. Within **main()**, print a sentence describing the operation on the values you will be performing along with the result:

```
public static void main(String[] args) {
    System.out.println("The sum of 3 + 4 is " + (3 + 4));
    System.out.println("The product of 3 + 4 is " + (3 * 4));
}
}
```

The output will be as follows:

```
The sum of 3 + 4 is 7
The product of 3 + 4 is 12
```

Activity 2: Reading Values from the User and Performing Operations Using the Scanner Class.

Solution:

1. Right-click the **src** folder and select **New | Class**.

2. Enter **ReadScanner** as the class name, and then click **OK**.

3. Import the **java.util.Scanner** package:

```
import java.util.Scanner;
```

4. In the **main()** enter the following:

```
public class ReadScanner
{
    static Scanner sc = new Scanner(System.in);
  public static void main(String[] args) {
    System.out.print("Enter a number: ");
    int a = sc.nextInt();
    System.out.print("Enter 2nd number: ");
    int b = sc.nextInt();
```

```
        System.out.println("The sum is " + (a + b) + ".");

    }
}
```

5. Run the main program.

    The output will be as follows:

    ```
    Enter a number: 12
    Enter 2nd number: 23
    The sum is 35.
    ```

Activity 3: Calculating the Percent Increase or Decrease of Financial Instruments

Solution:

1. Right-click the **src** folder and select **New | Class**.

2. Enter **StockChangeCalculator** as the class name, and then click **OK**.

3. Import the **java.util.Scanner** package:

    ```
    import java.util.Scanner;
    ```

4. In the **main()** enter the following:

    ```
    public class StockChangeCalculator{
    static Scanner sc = new Scanner(System.in);
    public static void main(String[] args) {
        System.out.print("Enter the stock symbol: ");
        String symbol = sc.nextLine();
        System.out.printf("Enter %s's day 1 value: ", symbol);
        double day1 = sc.nextDouble();
        System.out.printf("Enter %s's day 2 value: ", symbol);
        double day2 = sc.nextDouble();
        double percentChange = 100 * (day2 - day1) / day1;
        System.out.printf("%s has changed %.2f%% in one day.", symbol,
    percentChange);
    }
    }
    ```

5. Run the main program.

The output should be similar to:

```
Enter the stock symbol: AAPL
Enter AAPL's day 1 value: 100
Enter AAPL's day 2 value: 91.5
AAPL has changed -8.50% in one day.
```

Lesson 2: Variables, Data Types, and Operators

Activity 4: Inputting Student Information and Outputting an ID

Solution:

1. Import the **Scanner** package and create a new class

```
import java.util.Scanner;
{
public class Input{
static Scanner sc = new Scanner(System.in);
    public static void main(String[] args)
{
```

2. Take the student name as a string.

```
System.out.print("Enter student name: ");
String name = sc.nextLine();
```

3. Take the university name as a string.

```
System.out.print("Enter Name of the University: ");
String uni = sc.nextLine();
```

4. Take the student's age as an integer.

```
System.out.print("Enter Age: ");
int age = sc.nextInt();
```

5. Print out the student details.

```
System.out.println("Here is your ID");
System.out.println("********************************");
System.out.println("Name: " + name);
System.out.println("University: " + uni);
System.out.println("Age: " + age);
System.out.println("********************************");
    }
}
}
```

Activity 5: Calculating the Number of Full Fruit Boxes

Solution:

1. Right-click the **src** folder and select **New | Class**.

2. Enter **PeachCalculator** as the class name, and then click **OK**.

3. Import the **java.util.Scanner** package:

```
import java.util.Scanner;
```

4. In the **main()** enter the following:

```
public class PeachCalculator{
static Scanner sc = new Scanner(System.in);
public static void main(String[] args) {
    System.out.print("Enter the number of peaches picked: ");
    int numberOfPeaches = sc.nextInt();
    int numberOfFullBoxes = numberOfPeaches / 20;
    int numberOfPeachesLeft = numberOfPeaches - numberOfFullBoxes * 20;
    System.out.printf("We have %d full boxes and %d peaches left.",
numberOfFullBoxes, numberOfPeachesLeft);
    }
}
```

5. Run the main program.

    The output should be similar to:

```
Enter the number of peaches picked: 55
We have 2 full boxes and 15 peaches left.
```

Lesson 3: Control Flow

Activity 6: Controlling the Flow of Execution Using Conditionals

Solution:

1. Create a class named **Salary** and add **main()** method:

   ```
   public class Salary {
       public static void main(String args[]) {
   ```

2. Initialize two variables **workerhours** and **salary**.

   ```
   int workerhours = 10;
   double salary = 0;
   ```

3. In the **if** condition, check whether the working hours of the worker is below the required hours. If the condition holds **true**, then the salary should be (working hours * 10).

   ```
   if (workerhours <= 8 )
   salary = workerhours*10;
   ```

4. Use the **else if** statement to check if the working hours lies between 8 hours and 12 hours. If that is true, then the salary should be calculated at $10 per hour for the first eight hours and the remaining hours should be calculated at $12 per hour.

   ```
   else if((workerhours > 8) && (workerhours < 12))
   salary = 8*10 + (workerhours - 8) * 12;
   ```

5. Use the **else** block for the default of $160 (additional day's salary) per day.

   ```
   else
       salary = 160;
   System.out.println("The worker's salary is " + salary);
   }
   }
   ```

Activity 7: Developing a Temperature System

Solution:

1. Declare two strings, **temp** and **weatherWarning**, and then initialize **temp** with either **High**, **Low**, or **Humid**.

```
public class TempSystem
{
    public static void main(String[] args) {
        String temp = "Low";
        String weatherWarning;
```

2. Create a switch statement that checks the different cases of **temp**, and then initialize the variable **weatherWarning** to appropriate messages for each case of temp (**High**, **Low**, **Humid**).

```
switch (temp) {
        case "High":
            weatherWarning = "It's hot outside, do not forget sunblock.";
            break;
        case "Low":
            weatherWarning = "It's cold outside, do not forget your
coat.";
            break;
        case "Humid":
            weatherWarning = "The weather is humid, open your windows.";
            break;
```

3. In the default case, initialize **weatherWarning** to "The weather looks good. Take a walk outside".

```
default:
    weatherWarning = "The weather looks good. Take a walk outside";
    break;
```

4. After you complete the switch construct, print the value of **weatherWarning**.

```
    }
            System.out.println(weatherWarning);
        }
    }
```

5. Run the program to see the output, it should be similar to:

    ```
    It's cold outside, do not forget your coat.
    ```

    Full code is as follows:

    ```java
    public class TempSystem
    {
        public static void main(String[] args) {
            String temp = "Low";
            String weatherWarning;
                switch (temp) {
            case "High":
                weatherWarning = "It's hot outside, do not forget sunblock.";
                break;
            case "Low":
                weatherWarning = "It's cold outside, do not forget your
    coat.";
                break;
            case "Humid":
                weatherWarning = "The weather is humid, open your windows.";
                break;

            default:
                weatherWarning = "The weather looks good. Take a walk
    outside";
                break;
            }
            System.out.println(weatherWarning);
        }
    }
    ```

Activity 8: Implementing the for Loop

Solution:

1. Right-click the **src** folder and select **New | Class**.

2. Enter **PeachBoxCounter** as the class name, and then click **OK**.

3. Import the **java.util.Scanner** package:

    ```java
    import java.util.Scanner;
    ```

4. In the **main()** enter the following:

```
public class PeachBoxCounter
{
static Scanner sc = new Scanner(System.in);
public static void main(String[] args) {
System.out.print("Enter the number of peaches picked: ");
int numberOfPeaches = sc.nextInt();
for (int numShipped = 0; numShipped < numberOfPeaches; numShipped += 20)
{
System.out.printf("shipped %d peaches so far\n", numShipped);
}
}
}
```

Activity 9: Implementing the while Loop

Solution:

1. Right-click the **src** folder and select **New | Class**.

2. Enter **PeachBoxCounters** as the class name, and then click **OK**.

3. Import the **java.util.Scanner** package:

```
import java.util.Scanner;
```

4. In the **main()** enter the following:

```
public class PeachBoxCounters{
static Scanner sc = new Scanner(System.in);
public static void main(String[] args) {
    System.out.print("Enter the number of peaches picked: ");
    int numberOfPeaches = sc.nextInt();
    int numberOfBoxesShipped = 0;

    while (numberOfPeaches >= 20) {
        numberOfPeaches -= 20;
        numberOfBoxesShipped += 1;
        System.out.printf("%d boxes shipped, %d peaches remaining\n",
                numberOfBoxesShipped, numberOfPeaches);
    }
}
}
```

Activity 10: Implementing Looping Constructs

Solution:

1. Import the packages that are required to read data from the user.

    ```java
    import java.util.Scanner;
    public class Theater {
    public static void main(String[] args)
    ```

2. Declare the variables to store the total number of seats available, remaining seats, and tickets requested.

    ```java
    {
    int total = 10, request = 0, remaining = 10;
    ```

3. Within a **while** loop, implement the **if else** loop that checks whether the request is valid, which implies that the number of tickets requested is less than the number of seats remaining.

    ```java
    while (remaining>=0)
    {
    System.out.println("Enter the number of tickets");
    Scanner in = new Scanner(System.in);
    request = in.nextInt();
    ```

4. If the logic in the previous step is true, then print a message to denote that the ticket is processed, set the remaining seats to the appropriate value, and ask for the next set of tickets.

    ```java
    if(request <= remaining)
    {
    System.out.println("Your " + request +" tickets have been procced. Please
    pay and enjoy the show.");
    remaining = remaining - request;
    request = 0;
    }
    ```

5. If the logic in step 3 is false, then print an appropriate message and break out of the loop:

```
else
{
System.out.println("Sorry your request could not be processed");
break;
}
}
}
}
```

Activity 11: Continuous Peach Shipment with Nested Loops

Solution:

1. Right-click the **src** folder and select **New | Class**.

2. Enter **PeachBoxCounter** as the class name, and then click **OK**.

3. Import the **java.util.Scanner** package:

```
import java.util.Scanner;
```

4. In the **main()** enter the following:

```
public class PeachBoxCount{
static Scanner sc = new Scanner(System.in);
public static void main(String[] args) {
    int numberOfBoxesShipped = 0;
    int numberOfPeaches = 0;
    while (true) {
        System.out.print("Enter the number of peaches picked: ");
        int incomingNumberOfPeaches = sc.nextInt();
        if (incomingNumberOfPeaches == 0) {
            break;
        }
        numberOfPeaches += incomingNumberOfPeaches;
        while (numberOfPeaches >= 20) {
            numberOfPeaches -= 20;
```

```
                    numberOfBoxesShipped += 1;
                    System.out.printf("%d boxes shipped, %d peaches remaining\n",
                            numberOfBoxesShipped, numberOfPeaches);
                }
            }
        }
    }
```

Lesson 4: Object-Oriented Programming

Activity 12: Creating a Simple Class in Java

Solution:

1. Create a new project in the IDE named **Animals**.

2. In the project, create a new file named **Animal.java** under the **src/** folder.

3. Open **Animal.java** and paste in the following code:

   ```
   public class Animal {

   }
   ```

4. Inside the curly braces, create the following instance variables to hold our data, as shown here:

   ```
   public class Animal {
           int legs;
           int ears;
           int eyes;
           String family;
           String name;

       }
   ```

5. Below the instance variables, define two constructors. One will take no arguments and initialize legs to 4, ears to 2, and eyes to 2. The second constructor will take the value of legs, ears, and eyes as arguments and set those values:

   ```
   public class Animal {
           int legs;
           int ears;
           int eyes;
           String family;
   ```

```
        String name;

        public Animal(){
            this(4, 2,2);
        }
        public Animal(int legs, int ears, int eyes){
            this.legs = legs;
            this.ears = ears;
            this.eyes = ears;
        }
    }
```

6. Define four methods, two to set and get the family and two to set and get the name:

> **Note**
>
> The methods that set values in an object are called setters, while those that get those values are called getters.

```
public class Animal {
    int legs;
    int ears;
    int eyes;
    String family;
    String name;

    public Animal(){
        this(4, 2,2);
    }
    public Animal(int legs, int ears, int eyes){
        this.legs = legs;
        this.ears = ears;
        this.eyes = ears;

    }
    public String getFamily() {
        return family;
    }
```

```
        public void setFamily(String family) {
            this.family = family;
        }
        public String getName() {
            return name;
        }
        public void setName(String name) {
            this.name = name;
        }
    }
```

We have finished constructing our Animal class. Let's continue and create a few instances of this class.

7. Create a new file named **Animals.java** and copy the following code into it, as shown here:

```
public class Animals {

    public static void main(String[] args){

    }
}
```

8. Create two objects of the **Animal** class:

```
public class Animals {
        public static void main(String[] args){
            Animal cow = new Animal();
            Animal goat = new Animal();
        }
}
```

9. Let's create another animal with 2 legs, 2 ears and 2 eyes:

```
Animal duck = new Animal(2, 2, 2);
```

10. To set the animals' names and family, we will use the getters and setters we created in the class. Copy/write the following lines into the `Animals` class:

```
public class Animals {

    public static void main(String[] args){

        Animal cow = new Animal();
        Animal goat = new Animal();

        Animal duck = new Animal(2, 2, 2);

        cow.setName("Cow");
        cow.setFamily("Bovidae");

        goat.setName("Goat");
        goat.setFamily("Bovidae");

        duck.setName("Duck");
        duck.setFamily("Anatidae");

        System.out.println(cow.getName());
        System.out.println(goat.getName());
        System.out.println(duck.getFamily());

    }
}
```

The output of the preceding code is as follows:

```
Cow
Goat
Anatide
```

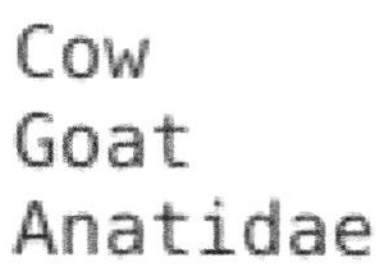

Cow
Goat
Anatidae

Figure 4.9: Output of the Animal class

Activity 13: Writing a Calculator Class

Solution:

1. Create a Calculator class as follows:

```
public class Calculator {
```

2. Create three fields **double operand1**, **double operand2**, and **String operator**. Add a constructor that sets all three fields.

```
private final double operand1;
private final double operand2;
private final String operator;

public Calculator(double operand1, double operand2, String operator){
this.operand1 = operand1;
this.operand2 = operand2;
this.operator = operator;
}
```

3. In this class, add an **operate** method that will check what operator is ("+", "-", "x" or "/") and executes the correct operation, returning the result:

```
public double operate() {
if (this.operator.equals("-")) {
return operand1 - operand2;
} else if (this.operator.equals("x")) {
return operand1 * operand2;
} else if (this.operator.equals("/")) {
return operand1 / operand2;
} else {
// If operator is sum or unknown, return sum
return operand1 + operand2;
}
}
```

4. Write a **main()** method as follows:

```
public static void main (String [] args) {
        System.out.println("1 + 1 = " + new Calculator(1, 1, "+").
operate());
        System.out.println("4 - 2 = " + new Calculator(4, 2, "-").
operate());
        System.out.println("1 x 2 = " + new Calculator(1, 2, "x").
operate());
```

```
        System.out.println("10 / 2 = " + new Calculator(10, 2, "/").
    operate());
        }
    }
```

Activity 14: Creating a Calculator Using Java

Solution:

1. Create a class **Operator** that has one String field initialized in the constructor that represents the operator. This class should have a default constructor that represents the default operator, which is sum. The **Operator** class should also have a method called **operate** that receives two doubles and return the result of the operator as a double. The default operation is **sum**:

```java
public class Operator {

    public final String operator;

    public Operator() {
        this("+");
    }

    public Operator(String operator) {
        this.operator = operator;
    }

    public boolean matches(String toCheckFor) {
        return this.operator.equals(toCheckFor);
    }

    public double operate(double operand1, double operand2) {
        return operand1 + operand2;
    }

}
```

2. Create another class named **Subtraction**. It extends from **Operator** and override the **operate** method with each operation that it represents. It also need a no-argument constructor that calls super passing the operator that it represents:

```java
public class Subtraction extends Operator {

    public Subtraction() {
        super("-");
    }

    @Override
    public double operate(double operand1, double operand2) {
        return operand1 - operand2;
    }

}
```

3. Create another class named **Multiplication**. It extends from Operator and override the **operate** method with each operation that it represents. It also need a no-argument constructor that calls super passing the operator that it represents:

```java
public class Multiplication extends Operator {

    public Multiplication() {
        super("x");
    }

    @Override
    public double operate(double operand1, double operand2) {
        return operand1 * operand2;
    }

}
```

4. Create another class named **Division**. It extends from Operator and override the **operate** method with each operation that it represents. It also need a no-argument constructor that calls super passing the operator that it represents:

```java
public class Division extends Operator {

    public Division() {
        super("/");
```

```
    }

    @Override
    public double operate(double operand1, double operand2) {
        return operand1 / operand2;
    }

}
```

5. As the previous **Calculator** class, this one will also have an **operate** method, but it will only delegate to the operator instance. Last, write a **main** method that calls the new calculator a few times, printing the results of the operation for each time:

```
public class CalculatorWithFixedOperators {
    public static void main (String [] args) {
        System.out.println("1 + 1 = " + new
CalculatorWithFixedOperators(1, 1, "+").operate());
        System.out.println("4 - 2 = " + new
CalculatorWithFixedOperators(4, 2, "-").operate());
        System.out.println("1 x 2 = " + new
CalculatorWithFixedOperators(1, 2, "x").operate());
        System.out.println("10 / 2 = " + new
CalculatorWithFixedOperators(10, 2, "/").operate());
    }

    private final double operand1;
    private final double operand2;

    // The current operator
    private final Operator operator;

    // All possible operations
    private final Division division = new Division();
    private final Multiplication multiplication = new Multiplication();
    private final Operator sum = new Operator();
    private final Subtraction subtraction = new Subtraction();
```

```java
    public CalculatorWithFixedOperators(double operand1, double operand2,
String operator) {
        this.operand1 = operand1;
        this.operand2 = operand2;

        if (subtraction.matches(operator)) {
            this.operator = subtraction;
        } else if (multiplication.matches(operator)) {
            this.operator = multiplication;
        } else if (division.matches(operator)) {
            this.operator = division;
        } else {
            this.operator = sum;
        }
    }

    public double operate() {
        return operator.operate(operand1, operand2);
    }

}
```

Activity 15: Understanding Inheritance and Polymorphism in Java

Solution:

1. Create a **Cat** class that inherits from **Animal**:

   ```java
   public class Cat extends Animal {
   ```

2. Create instance variables **owner**, **numberOfTeeth**, and **age** as follows:

   ```java
   //Fields specific to the Cat family
   String owner;
   int numberOfTeeth;
   int age;
   ```

3. Create **main()** method as follows:

   ```java
   public static void main(String[] args){
   Cat myCat = new Cat();
   //Since Cat inherits from Animal, we have access to it's methods and fields
   //We don't need to redefine these methods and fields
   myCat.setFamily("Cat");
   myCat.setName("Puppy");
   ```

```
myCat.ears = 2;
myCat.legs = 4;
myCat.eyes = 2;
System.out.println(myCat.getFamily());
System.out.println(myCat.getName());
System.out.println(myCat.ears);
System.out.println(myCat.legs);
System.out.println(myCat.eyes);
}
}
```

The output is as follows

```
Cat
Puppy
2
4
2
```

Lesson 5: OOP in Depth

Activity 16: Creating and Implementing Interfaces in Java

Solution:

1. Open our **Animals** project from the previous lesson.

2. Create a new interface called **AnimalBehavior**.

3. In this create two methods **void move()** and **void makeSound()**.

4. Create a new **public** class called **Cow** and implement the **AnimalBehavior** interface. Override the two methods, but leave them blank for now.

5. Inside the **Cow** class, create two fields, as follows:

```
public class Cow implements AnimalBehavior, AnimalListener {
String sound;
String movementType;
```

Edit the overridden methods to look like this:

```
@Override
public void move() {
    this.movementType = "Walking";
    this.onAnimalMoved();
}

@Override
public void makeSound() {
    this.sound = "Moo";
    this.onAnimalMadeSound();
}
```

6. Create another interface called **AnimalListener** with the following methods:

```
public interface AnimalListener {
    void onAnimalMoved();
    void onAnimalMadeSound();
}
```

7. Let the **Cow** class also implement this interface. Make sure that you override the two methods in the interface.

8. Edit the two methods to look like this:

```
@Override
    public void onAnimalMoved() {
        System.out.println("Animal moved: " + this.movementType);
    }

@Override
public void onAnimalMadeSound() {
    System.out.println("Sound made: " + this.sound);
}
```

9. Finally, create a **main** method to test your code:

```
public static void main(String[] args){
    Cow myCow = new Cow();
    myCow.move();
    myCow.makeSound();
}
}
```

10. Run the **Cow** class and view the output. It should look something like this:

```
Animal moved: Walking
Sound made: Moo
```

Activity 17: Using instanceof and Typecasting

Solution:

1. Import **Random** package to generate random employees:

    ```
    import java.util.Random;
    ```

2. Create an **EmployeeLoader** class that will serve as a datasource as follows:

    ```
    public class EmployeeLoader {
    ```

3. Declare a static pseudo-random generator as follows:

    ```
    private static Random random = new Random(15);
    ```

4. Generate a new randomly picked employee as follows:

    ```
    public static Employee getEmployee() {
            int nextNumber = random.nextInt(4);
            switch(nextNumber) {
                case 0:
                    // A sales person with total sales between 5000 and
    1550000
                    double grossSales = random.nextDouble() * 150000 + 5000;
                    return new SalesWithCommission(grossSales);
                case 1:
                    return new Manager();
                case 2:
                    return new Engineer();
                case 3:
                    return new Sales();
                default:
                    return new Manager();
            }
        }
    ```

5. Create another file with **SalesWithCommission** class that extends **Sales**. Add a constructor that receives the gross sales as double and store it as a field. Also add a method called **getCommission** which returns a double that is the gross sales times 15% (0.15):

```java
public class SalesWithCommission extends Sales implements Employee {

    private final double grossSales;

    public SalesWithCommission(double grossSales) {
        this.grossSales = grossSales;
    }
    public double getCommission() {
        return grossSales * 0.15;
    }

}
```

6. Write a class **ShowSalaryAndCommission** with **main()** method, that calls **getEmployee()** repeatedly inside a **for** loop and print the information about the Employee salary and tax. And if the employee is an instance of **SalesWithCommission**, also print his commission:

```java
public class ShowSalaryAndCommission {

    public static void main (String [] args) {
        for (int i = 0; i < 10; i++) {
            Employee employee = EmployeeLoader.getEmployee();
            System.out.println("--- " + employee.getClass().getName());

            System.out.println("Net Salary: " + employee.getNetSalary());
            System.out.println("Tax: " + employee.getTax());

            if (employee instanceof SalesWithCommission) {
                // Cast to sales with commission
                SalesWithCommission sales = (SalesWithCommission)
employee;
                System.out.println("Commission: " + sales.
getCommission());
            }
        }
    }
}
```

Activity 18: Understanding Typecasting in Java

Solution:

1. Open our **Animals** project.

2. Create a new class called **AnimalTest** and, inside it, create the main method:

```java
public class AnimalTest {

    public static void  main(String[] args){

    }
}
```

3. Inside the **main** method, create two variables:

```java
Cat cat = new Cat();
Cow cow = new Cow();
```

4. Print the owner of the **cat**:

```java
System.out.println(cat.owner);
```

5. Upcast the **cat** to **Animal** and try to print the owner once more. What error do you get? Why?

```java
Animal animal = (Animal)cat;
System.out.println(animal.owner);
```

The error message is as follows:

> Error:(9, 34) java: cannot find symbol
> symbol: variable owner
> location: variable animal of type Animal

Figure 5.7: Exception while accessing the variables of the subclass for upcasting

Reason: Since we did an upcast, we cannot access the variables of the subclass anymore.

6. Print the sound of the **cow**:

```java
System.out.println(cow.sound);
```

7. Try to upcast the **cow** to **Animal**. Why error do you get? Why?

```
Animal animal1 = (Animal)cow;
```

The error message is as follows:

> Error:(10, 34) java: incompatible types: Cow cannot be converted to Animal

Figure 5.8: Exception while upcasting cow to Animal

Reason: Cow does not inherit from the Animal class, so they don't share the same hierarchical tree.

8. Downcast the **animal** to **cat1** and print the owner again:

```
Cat cat1 = (Cat)animal;
System.out.println(cat1.owner);
```

9. The full **AnimalTest** class should look like this:

```
public class AnimalTest {

    public static void  main(String[] args){

        Cat cat = new Cat();
        Cow cow = new Cow();

        System.out.println(cat.owner);

        Animal animal = (Animal)cat;
        //System.out.println(animal.owner);
        System.out.println(cow.sound);

        //Animal animal1 = (Animal)cow;
        Cat cat1 = (Cat)animal;
        System.out.println(cat1.owner);
    }
}
```

The output is as follows:

Figure 5.9: Output of the AnimalTest class

Activity 19: Implementing Abstract Classes and Methods in Java

Solution:

1. Create a new project called **Hospital** and open it.

2. Inside the **src** folder, create an abstract class called **Person**:

   ```
   public abstract class Patient {


   }
   ```

3. Create an abstract method that returns the type of person in the hospital. Name this method String **getPersonType()**, returning a String:

   ```
   public abstract String getPersonType();
   ```

   We have finished our abstract class and method. Now, we will continue to inherit from it and implement this abstract method.

4. Create a new class called Doctor that inherits from the Person class:

   ```
   public class Doctor extends Patient {
   }
   ```

5. Override the **getPersonType** abstract method in our **Doctor** class. Return the string "**Arzt**". This is German for Doctor:

   ```
   @Override
   public String getPersonType() {
      return "Arzt";
   }
   ```

6. Create another class called **Patient** to represent the patients in the hospital. Similarly, make sure that the class inherits from **Person** and overrides the **getPersonType** method. Return **"Kranke"**. This is German for Patient:

```java
public class People extends Patient{
    @Override
    public String getPersonType() {
        return "Kranke";
    }
}
```

Now, we have the two classes. We will now test our code using a third test class.

7. Create a third class called **HospitalTest**. We will use this class to test the two classes we created previously.

8. Inside the **HospitalTest** class, create the **main** method:

```java
public class HospitalTest {
    public static void main(String[] args){

    }
}
```

9. Inside the **main** method, create an instance of **Doctor** and another instance of **Patient**:

```java
Doctor doctor = new Doctor();
People people = new People();
```

10. Try calling the **getPersonType** method for each of the objects and print it out to the console. What is the output?

```java
String str = doctor.getPersonType();
String str1 = patient.getPersonType();
System.out.println(str);
System.out.println(str1);
```

The output is as follows:

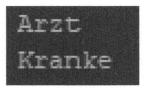

Figure 5.10: Output on calling getPersonType()

Activity 20: Use abstract class to Encapsulate Common Logic

Solution:

1. Create an abstract class **GenericEmployee** that has a constructor that receives the gross salary and stores that in a field. It should implement the Employee interface and have two methods: **getGrossSalary()** and **getNetSalary()**. The first will just return the value passed into the constructor. The latter will return the gross salary minus the result of calling **getTax()** method:

    ```java
    public abstract class GenericEmployee implements Employee {

        private final double grossSalary;

        public GenericEmployee(double grossSalary) {
            this.grossSalary = grossSalary;
        }

        public double getGrossSalary() {
            return grossSalary;
        }

        @Override
        public double getNetSalary() {
            return grossSalary - getTax();
        }

    }
    ```

2. Create a new generic version of each type of employee: **GenericEngineer**. It will need a constructor that receives gross salary and pass it to the super constructor. It also needs to implement the **getTax()** method, returning the correct tax value for each class:

    ```java
    public class GenericEngineer extends GenericEmployee {

        public GenericEngineer(double grossSalary) {
            super(grossSalary);
        }

        @Override
        public double getTax() {
    ```

```
            return (22.0/100) * getGrossSalary();
        }

    }
```

3. Create a new generic version of each type of employee: **GenericManager**. It will need a constructor that receives gross salary and pass it to the super constructor. It also needs to implement the **getTax()** method, returning the correct tax value for each class:

```
public class GenericManager extends GenericEmployee {

    public GenericManager(double grossSalary) {
        super(grossSalary);
    }

    @Override
    public double getTax() {
        return (28.0/100) * getGrossSalary();
    }

}
```

4. Create a new generic version of each type of employee: **GenericSales**. It will need a constructor that receives gross salary and pass it to the super constructor. It also needs to implement the **getTax()** method, returning the correct tax value for each class:

```
public class GenericSales extends GenericEmployee {

    public GenericSales(double grossSalary) {
        super(grossSalary);
    }

    @Override
    public double getTax() {
        return (19.0/100) * getGrossSalary();
    }

}
```

5. Create a new generic version of each type of employee: **GenericSalesWithCommission**. It will need a constructor that receives gross salary and pass it to the super constructor. It also needs to implement the **getTax()** method, returning the correct tax value for each class. Remember to also receive the gross sales on the **GenericSalesWithCommission** class, and add the method that calculates the commission:

```java
public class GenericSalesWithCommission extends GenericEmployee {
    private final double grossSales;

    public GenericSalesWithCommission(double grossSalary, double
grossSales) {
        super(grossSalary);
        this.grossSales = grossSales;
    }

    public double getCommission() {
        return grossSales * 0.15;
    }

    @Override
    public double getTax() {
        return (19.0/100) * getGrossSalary();
    }

}
```

6. Add a new method **getEmployeeWithSalary** to your **EmployeeLoader** class. This method will generate a random salary between 70,000 and 120,000 and assign to the newly created employee before returning it. Remember to also provide a gross sales when creating a **GenericSalesWithCommission** employee:

```java
public static Employee getEmployeeWithSalary() {
        int nextNumber = random.nextInt(4);

        // Random salary between 70,000 and 70,000 + 50,000
        double grossSalary = random.nextDouble() * 50000 + 70000;
        switch(nextNumber) {
            case 0:
                // A sales person with total sales between 5000 and
1550000
                double grossSales = random.nextDouble() * 150000 + 5000;
```

```
                        return new GenericSalesWithCommission(grossSalary,
        grossSales);
                    case 1:
                        return new GenericManager(grossSalary);
                    case 2:
                        return new GenericEngineer(grossSalary);
                    case 3:
                        return new GenericSales(grossSalary);
                    default:
                        return new GenericManager(grossSalary);
                }
            }


        }
```

7. Write an application that calls the **getEmployeeWithSalary** method multiple times from inside **for** loop. This method will work like the one in the previous activity: print the net salary and tax for all employees. If the employee is an instance of **GenericSalesWithCommission** also print his commission.

```java
public class UseAbstractClass {

    public static void main (String [] args) {
        for (int i = 0; i < 10; i++) {
            Employee employee = EmployeeLoader.getEmployeeWithSalary();
            System.out.println("--- " + employee.getClass().getName());

            System.out.println("Net Salary: " + employee.getNetSalary());
            System.out.println("Tax: " + employee.getTax());

            if (employee instanceof GenericSalesWithCommission) {
                // Cast to sales with commission
                GenericSalesWithCommission sales =
        (GenericSalesWithCommission) employee;
                System.out.println("Commission: " + sales.
        getCommission());
            }
        }
    }


}
```

Lesson 6: Data Structures, Arrays, and Strings

Activity 21: Finding the Smallest Number in an Array

Solution:

1. Set up the **main** method in a new class file known as **ExampleArray:**

```java
public class ExampleArray {
  public static void main(String[] args) {
  }
}
```

2. Create an array of 20 numbers:

```java
double[] array = {14.5, 28.3, 15.4, 89.0, 46.7, 25.1, 9.4, 33.12, 82,
11.3, 3.7, 59.99, 68.65, 27.78, 16.3, 45.45, 24.76, 33.23, 72.88, 51.23};
```

3. Set the minimum float as the first number

```java
double min = array[0];
```

4. Create a for loop to check all the numbers in the array

```java
for (doublefloat f : array) {
}
```

5. Use if to test each number against the minimum. If it is smaller than the minimum then make that number the new minimum:

```java
if (f < min)
min = f;
}
```

6. After the loop completes, print out the minimum number:

```java
System.out.println("The lowest number in the array is " + min);
}
}
```

The full code should look like this.

```java
public class ExampleArray {
        public static void main(String[] args) {
            double[] array = {14.5, 28.3, 15.4, 89.0, 46.7, 25.1, 9.4,
33.12, 82, 11.3, 3.7, 59.99, 68.65, 27.78, 16.3, 45.45, 24.76, 33.23,
72.88, 51.23};
            double min = array[0];
            for (double f : array) {
```

```
                    if (f < min)
                        min = f;
                }
                System.out.println("The lowest number in the array is " +
    min);
            }
        }
```

Activity 22: Calculator with Array of Operators

Solution:

1. Create a class **Operators** that will contain the logic of determining what operator to use based out of a String. In this class create a **public** constant field **default_ operator** that is going to be an instance of the **Operator** class. Then create another constant field called **operators** of type array of **Operator** and initialize it with an instance of each of the operators you have:

    ```
    public class Operators {

        public static final Operator DEFAULT_OPERATOR = new Operator();

        public static final Operator [] OPERATORS = {
            new Division(),
            new Multiplication(),
            DEFAULT_OPERATOR,
            new Subtraction(),
        };
    ```

2. In the **Operators** class, add a **public static** method called **findOperator** that receives the operator as a String and return an instance of **Operator**. Inside it iterate over the possible operators array and, using the **matches** method for each operator, return the selected operator, or the default one if it didn't match any of them:

    ```
    public static Operator findOperator(String operator) {
            for (Operator possible : OPERATORS) {
                if (possible.matches(operator)) {
                    return possible;
                }
            }
            return DEFAULT_OPERATOR;
    }
    ```

```
}
```

3. Create a new **CalculatorWithDynamicOperator** class with three fields: **operand1** and **operator2** as **double** and **operator** of type **Operator**:

```java
public class CalculatorWithDynamicOperator {

    private final double operand1;
    private final double operand2;

    // The current operator
    private final Operator operator;
```

4. Add a constructor that receives three parameters: **operand1** and **operand2** of type **double** and **operator** as a String. In the constructor, instead of having an if-else to select the operator, use the **Operators.findOperator** method to set the operator field:

```java
public CalculatorWithDynamicOperator(double operand1, double operand2,
String operator) {
        this.operand1 = operand1;
        this.operand2 = operand2;
        this.operator = Operators.findOperator(operator);
    }

    public double operate() {
        return operator.operate(operand1, operand2);
    }
```

5. Add a **main** method where you call the **Calculator** class multiple times and print the results:

```java
public static void main (String [] args) {
        System.out.println("1 + 1 = " + new
CalculatorWithDynamicOperator(1, 1, "+").operate());
        System.out.println("4 - 2 = " + new
CalculatorWithDynamicOperator(4, 2, "-").operate());
        System.out.println("1 x 2 = " + new
CalculatorWithDynamicOperator(1, 2, "x").operate());
        System.out.println("10 / 2 = " + new
CalculatorWithDynamicOperator(10, 2, "/").operate());
    }
}
```

Activity 23: Working with ArrayList

Solution:

1. Import **ArrayList** and **Iterator** from **java.util**:

   ```
   import java.util.ArrayList;
   import java.util.Iterator;
   ```

2. Create a new class called **StudentsArray**:

   ```
   public class StudentsArray extends Student{
   ```

3. In the **main** method define an **ArrayList** of **Student** objects. Insert 4 student instances, instantiated with different kinds of constructors we created earlier:

   ```
   public static void main(String[] args){
           ArrayList<Student> students = new ArrayList<>();
           Student james = new Student();
           james.setName("James");
           Student mary = new Student();
           mary.setName("Mary");
           Student jane = new Student();
           jane.setName("Jane");
           Student pete = new Student();
           pete.setName("Pete");
           students.add(james);
           students.add(mary);
           students.add(jane);
           students.add(pete);
   ```

4. Create an iterator for your list and print the name of each student:

   ```
           Iterator studentsIterator = students.iterator();
           while (studentsIterator.hasNext()){
               Student student = (Student) studentsIterator.next();
               String name = student.getName();
               System.out.println(name);
           }
   ```

5. Clear all the **students**:

   ```
           students.clear();
       }
   }
   ```

The final code should look like this:

```java
import java.util.ArrayList;
import java.util.Iterator;

public class StudentsArray extends Student{
    public static void main(String[] args){

        ArrayList<Student> students = new ArrayList<>();

        Student james = new Student();
        james.setName("James");

        Student mary = new Student();
        mary.setName("Mary");

        Student jane = new Student();
        jane.setName("Jane");

        students.add(james);
        students.add(mary);
        students.add(jane);
        Iterator studentsIterator = students.iterator();
        while (studentsIterator.hasNext()){
            Student student = (Student) studentsIterator.next();
            String name = student.getName();
            System.out.println(name);
        }

        students.clear();

    }

}
```

The output is as follows:

Figure 6.30: Output of the StudentsArray class

Activity 24: Input a String and Output Its Length and as an Array

Solution:

1. Import the **java.util.Scanner** package:

   ```
   import java.util.Scanner;
   ```

2. Create a public class called **NameTell** and a **main** method:

   ```
   public class NameTell
   {
       public static void main(String[] args)
       {
   ```

3. Use the **Scanner** and **nextLine** to input a string at the prompt "**Enter your name:**"

   ```
   System.out.print("Enter your name:");
   Scanner sc = new Scanner(System.in);
   String name = sc.nextLine();
   ```

4. Count the length of the string and find the first character:

   ```
   int num = name.length();
   char c = name.charAt(0);
   ```

5. Print an output:

   ```
   System.out.println("\n Your name has " + num + " letters including
   spaces.");
   System.out.println("\n The first letter is: " + c);
       }
   }
   ```

The output is as follows:

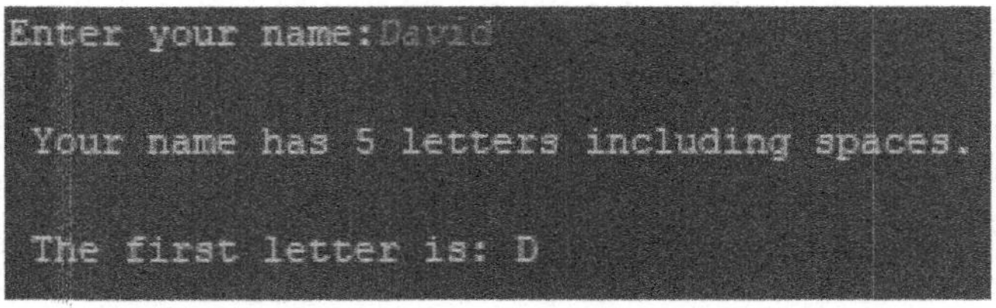

Enter your name:David

Your name has 5 letters including spaces.

The first letter is: D

Figure 6.31: Output of the NameTell class

Activity 25: Calculator Reads from Input

Solution:

1. Create a new class called **CommandLineCalculator** with a **main()** method in it:

```java
import java.util.Scanner;
public class CommandLineCalculator {
    public static void main (String [] args) throws Exception {
        Scanner scanner = new Scanner(System.in);
```

2. Use an infinite loop to keep the application running until the user asks to exit.

```java
while (true) {
            printOptions();
            String option = scanner.next();

            if (option.equalsIgnoreCase("Q")) {
                break;
            }
```

3. Collect the user input to decide which action to execute. If the action is **Q** or **q**, exit the loop:

```java
System.out.print("Type first operand: ");
            double operand1 = scanner.nextDouble();

            System.out.print("Type second operand: ");
            double operand2 = scanner.nextDouble();
            Operator operator = Operators.findOperator(option);
            double result = operator.operate(operand1, operand2);
            System.out.printf("%f %s %f = %f\n", operand1, operator.
operator, operand2, result);
            System.out.println();
        }
    }
```

4. If the action is anything else, find an operator and request two other inputs that will be the operands covering them to double:

```
private static void printOptions() {
        System.out.println("Q (or q) - To quit");
        System.out.println("An operator. If not supported, will use
sum.");
        System.out.print("Type your option: ");
    }
}
```

Call the **operate** method on the Operator found and print the result to the console.

Activity 26: Removing Duplicate Characters from a String

Solution:

1. Create a Unique class as follows:

    ```
    public class Unique {
    ```

2. Create a new method **removeDups** called that takes and returns a string. This is where our algorithm will go. This method should be **public** and **static**:

    ```
    public static String removeDups(String string){
    ```

3. Inside the method, check whether the string is null, empty, or has a length of 1. If any of these cases are true, then just return the original string since there checking is not needed:

    ```
    if (string == null)
                return string;
            if (string == "")
                return string;
            if (string.length() == 1)
                return string;
    ```

4. Create a string called **result** that is empty. This will be a unique string to be returned:

    ```
    String result = "";
    ```

5. Create for loop from **0** to the length of the string passed into the method. Inside the **for** loop, get the character at the current index of the string. Name the variable **c**. Also create a **boolean** called **isDuplicate** and initialize it to **false**. When we encounter a duplicate, we will change it to **true**.

```java
for (int i = 0; i < string.length() ; i++){
        char c = string.charAt(i);
        boolean isDuplicate = false;
```

6. Create another nested **for** loop from **0** to the **length()** of result. Inside the **for** loop, also get the character at the current index of result. Name it **d**. Compare **c** and d. If they are equal, then set **isDuplicate** to **true** and **break**. Close the inner **for** loop and go inside the first **for** loop. Check if **isDuplicate** is false. If it is, then append **c** to result. Go outside the first **for** loop and return the result. That concludes our algorithm:

```java
for (int j = 0; j < result.length(); j++){
            char d = result.charAt(j);
            if (c  == d){ //duplicate found
                isDuplicate = true;
                break;
            }
        }
        if (!isDuplicate)
            result += ""+c;
    }
    return result;
}
```

7. Create a **main()** method as follows:

```java
public static void main(String[] args){
        String a = "aaaaaaa";
        String b = "aaabbbbb";
        String c = "abcdefgh";
        String d = "Ju780iu6G768";
        System.out.println(removeDups(a));
        System.out.println(removeDups(b));
        System.out.println(removeDups(c));
        System.out.println(removeDups(d));
    }

}
```

The output is as follows:

Figure 6.32: Output of Unique class

The full code is as follows:

```java
public class Unique {
    public static String removeDups(String string){
        if (string == null)
            return string;
        if (string == "")
            return string;
        if (string.length() == 1)
            return string;
        String result = "";
        for (int i = 0; i < string.length() ; i++){
            char c = string.charAt(i);
            boolean isDuplicate = false;
            for (int j = 0; j < result.length(); j++){
                char d = result.charAt(j);
                if (c  == d){ //duplicate found
                    isDuplicate = true;
                    break;
                }
            }
            if (!isDuplicate)
                result += ""+c;
        }
        return result;
    }
    public static void main(String[] args){
        String a = "aaaaaaa";
        String b = "aaabbbbb";
        String c = "abcdefgh";
        String d = "Ju780iu6G768";
        System.out.println(removeDups(a));
```

```
        System.out.println(removeDups(b));
        System.out.println(removeDups(c));
        System.out.println(removeDups(d));
    }

}
```

The output is as follows:

Figure 6.33: Output of Unique class

Lesson 7: The Java Collections Framework and Generics

Activity 27: Read Users from CSV Using Array with Initial Capacity

Solution:

1. Create a class called **UseInitialCapacity** with a **main()** method

```
public class UseInitialCapacity {
    public static final void main (String [] args) throws Exception {
    }
}
```

2. Add a constant field that will be the initial capacity of the array. It will also be used when the array needs to grow:

```
private static final int INITIAL_CAPACITY = 5;
```

3. Add a **static** method that will resize arrays. It receives two parameters: an array of Users and an **int** that represents the new size for the array. It should also return an array of Users. Implement the resize algorithm using **System.arraycopy** like you did in the previous exercise. Be mindful that the new size might be smaller than the current size of the passed in array:

```
private static User[] resizeArray(User[] users, int newCapacity) {
    User[] newUsers = new User[newCapacity];
    int lengthToCopy = newCapacity > users.length ? users.length :
newCapacity;
```

```
        System.arraycopy(users, 0, newUsers, 0, lengthToCopy);
        return newUsers;
    }
```

4. Write another **static** method that will load the users from a CSV file into an array. It needs to ensure that the array has the capacity to receive the users as they are loaded from the file. You'll also need to ensure that after finishing loading the users, the array do not contain extra slots at the end:

```
public static User[] loadUsers(String pathToFile) throws Exception {
    User[] users = new User[INITIAL_CAPACITY];

    BufferedReader lineReader = new BufferedReader(new
FileReader(pathToFile));
    try (CSVReader reader = new CSVReader(lineReader)) {
        String [] row = null;
        while ( (row = reader.readRow()) != null) {
            // Reached end of the array
            if (users.length == reader.getLineCount()) {
                // Increase the array by INITIAL_CAPACITY
                users = resizeArray(users, users.length + INITIAL_CAPACITY);
            }

            users[users.length - 1] = User.fromValues(row);
        } // end of while

        // If read less rows than array capacity, trim it
        if (reader.getLineCount() < users.length - 1) {
            users = resizeArray(users, reader.getLineCount());
        }
    } // end of try

    return users;
}
```

5. In the **main** method, call the load users method and print the total number of users loaded:

```
User[] users = loadUsers(args[0]);
System.out.println(users.length);
```

6. Add imports:

```
import java.io.BufferedReader;
import java.io.FileReader;
```

The output is as follows:

```
27
```

Activity 28: Reading a Real Dataset Using Vector

Solution:

1. Before starting, change your **CSVLoader** to support files without headers. To do that, add a new constructor that receives a **boolean** that tells if it should ignore the first line or not:

```
public CSVReader(BufferedReader reader, boolean ignoreFirstLine) throws
IOException {
  this.reader = reader;
  if (ignoreFirstLine) {
    reader.readLine();
  }
}
```

2. Change the old constructor to call this new one passing true to ignore the first line. This will avoid you to go back and change any existing code:

```
public CSVReader(BufferedReader reader) throws IOException {
  this(reader, true);
}
```

3. Create a class called **CalculateAverageSalary** with **main** method:

```
public class CalculateAverageSalary {
  public static void main (String [] args) throws Exception {
  }
}
```

4. Create another method that reads data from the CSV and load the wages into a Vector. The method should return the Vector at the end:

```java
private static Vector loadWages(String pathToFile) throws Exception {
  Vector result = new Vector();
  FileReader fileReader = new FileReader(pathToFile);
  BufferedReader bufferedReader = new BufferedReader(fileReader);
  try (CSVReader csvReader = new CSVReader(bufferedReader, false)) {
    String [] row = null;
    while ( (row = csvReader.readRow()) != null) {
      if (row.length == 15) { // ignores empty lines
        result.add(Integer.parseInt(row[2].trim()));
      }
    }
  }
  return result;
}
```

5. In the **main** method, call the **loadWages** method and store the loaded wages in a Vector. Also store the initial time that the application started:

```java
Vector wages = loadWages(args[0]);
long start = System.currentTimeMillis();
```

6. Initialize three variables to store the min, max and sum of all wages:

```java
int totalWage = 0;
int maxWage = 0;
int minWage = Integer.MAX_VALUE;
```

7. In a for-each loop, process all wages, storing the min, max and adding it to the sum:

```java
for (Object wageAsObject : wages) {
  int wage = (int) wageAsObject;
  totalWage += wage;
  if (wage > maxWage) {
    maxWage = wage;
  }
  if (wage < minWage) {
    minWage = wage;
  }
}
```

8. At the end print the number of wages loaded and total time it took to load and process them. Also print the average, min and max wages:

```
System.out.printf("Read %d rows in %dms\n", wages.size(), System.
currentTimeMillis() - start);
System.out.printf("Average, Min, Max: %d, %d, %d\n", totalWage / wages.
size(), minWage, maxWage);
```

9. Add imports:

```
import java.io.BufferedReader;
import java.io.FileReader;
import java.util.Vector;
```

The output is as follows:

```
Read 32561 rows in 198ms
Average, Min, Max: 57873, 12285, 1484705
```

Activity 29: Iterating on Vector of Users

Solution:

1. Create a new class called **IterateOnUsersVector** with **main** method:

```
public class IterateOnUsersVector {
    public static void main(String [] args) throws IOException {
    }
}
```

2. In the main method, call the **UsersLoader.loadUsersInVector** passing the first argument passed from the command line as the file to load from and store the data in a Vector:

```
Vector users = UsersLoader.loadUsersInVector(args[0]);
```

3. Iterate over the users Vector using a **for-each** loop and print the information about the users to the console:

```
for (Object userAsObject : users) {
    User user = (User) userAsObject;
    System.out.printf("%s - %s\n", user.name, user.email);
}
```

4. Add imports:

```
import java.io.IOException;
import java.util.Vector;
```

The output is as follows:

```
Bill Gates - william.gates@microsoft.com
Jeff Bezos - jeff.bezos@amazon.com
Marc Benioff - marc.benioff@salesforce.com
Bill Gates - william.gates@microsoft.com
Jeff Bezos - jeff.bezos@amazon.com
Sundar Pichai - sundar.pichai@google.com
Jeff Bezos - jeff.bezos@amazon.com
Larry Ellison - lawrence.ellison@oracle.com
Marc Benioff - marc.benioff@salesforce.com
Larry Ellison - lawrence.ellison@oracle.com
Jeff Bezos - jeff.bezos@amazon.com
Bill Gates - william.gates@microsoft.com
Sundar Pichai - sundar.pichai@google.com
Jeff Bezos - jeff.bezos@amazon.com
Sundar Pichai - sundar.pichai@google.com
Marc Benioff - marc.benioff@salesforce.com
Larry Ellison - lawrence.ellison@oracle.com
Marc Benioff - marc.benioff@salesforce.com
Jeff Bezos - jeff.bezos@amazon.com
Marc Benioff - marc.benioff@salesforce.com
Bill Gates - william.gates@microsoft.com
Sundar Pichai - sundar.pichai@google.com
Larry Ellison - lawrence.ellison@oracle.com
Bill Gates - william.gates@microsoft.com
Larry Ellison - lawrence.ellison@oracle.com
Jeff Bezos - jeff.bezos@amazon.com
Sundar Pichai - sundar.pichai@google.com
```

Activity 30: Using a Hashtable to Group Data

Solution:

1. Create a class called **GroupWageByEducation** with a **main** method:

   ```java
   public class GroupWageByEducation {
     public static void main (String [] args) throws Exception {
     }
   }
   ```

2. Create a **static** method that creates and returns a **Hashtable** with keys of type String and values of type Vector of Integers:

   ```java
   private static Hashtable<String, Vector<Integer>> loadWages(String
   pathToFile) throws Exception {
     Hashtable<String, Vector<Integer>> result = new Hashtable<>();
     return result;
   }
   ```

3. Between creating the **Hashtable** and returning it, load the rows from the CSV ensuring they have the correct format:

   ```java
   FileReader fileReader = new FileReader(pathToFile);
   BufferedReader bufferedReader = new BufferedReader(fileReader);
   try (CSVReader csvReader = new CSVReader(bufferedReader, false)) {
     String [] row = null;
     while ( (row = csvReader.readRow()) != null) {
       if (row.length == 15) {
       }
     }
   }
   ```

4. In the **if** inside the **while** loop, get the education level and wage for the record:

   ```java
   String education = row[3].trim();
   int wage = Integer.parseInt(row[2].trim());
   ```

5. Find the Vector in the **Hashtable** that corresponds to the current education level and add the new wage to it:

   ```java
   // Get or create the vector with the wages for the specified education
   Vector<Integer> wages = result.getOrDefault(education, new Vector<>());
   wages.add(wage);
   // Ensure the vector will be in the hashtable next time
   result.put(education, wages);
   ```

6. In the main method, call your **loadWages** method passing the first argument from the command line as the file to load the data from:

```
Hashtable<String,Vector<Integer>> wagesByEducation = loadWages(args[0]);
```

7. Iterate on the **Hashtable** entries using a **for-each** loop and for each entry, get the Vector of the corresponding wages and initialize min, max and sum variables for it:

```
for (Entry<String, Vector<Integer>> entry : wagesByEducation.entrySet()) {
    Vector<Integer> wages = entry.getValue();
    int totalWage = 0;
    int maxWage = 0;
    int minWage = Integer.MAX_VALUE;
}
```

8. After initializing the variables, iterate over all wages and store the min, max and sum values:

```
for (Integer wage : wages) {
    totalWage += wage;
    if (wage > maxWage) {
        maxWage = wage;
    }
    if (wage < minWage) {
        minWage = wage;
    }
}
```

9. Then, print the information found for the specified entry, which represents an education level:

```
System.out.printf("%d records found for education %s\n", wages.size(),
entry.getKey());
System.out.printf("\tAverage, Min, Max: %d, %d, %d\n", totalWage / wages.
size(), minWage, maxWage);
```

10. Add imports:

```
import java.io.BufferedReader;
import java.io.FileReader;
import java.util.Hashtable;
import java.util.Map.Entry;
import java.util.Vector;
```

The output is as follows:

```
1067 records found for education Assoc-acdm
        Average, Min, Max: 193424, 19302, 1455435
433 records found for education 12th
        Average, Min, Max: 199097, 23037, 917220
1382 records found for education Assoc-voc
        Average, Min, Max: 181936, 20098, 1366120
5355 records found for education Bachelors
        Average, Min, Max: 188055, 19302, 1226583
51 records found for education Preschool
        Average, Min, Max: 235889, 69911, 572751
10501 records found for education HS-grad
        Average, Min, Max: 189538, 19214, 1268339
168 records found for education 1st-4th
        Average, Min, Max: 239303, 34378, 795830
333 records found for education 5th-6th
        Average, Min, Max: 232448, 32896, 684015
576 records found for education Prof-school
        Average, Min, Max: 185663, 14878, 747719
514 records found for education 9th
        Average, Min, Max: 202485, 22418, 758700
1723 records found for education Masters
        Average, Min, Max: 179852, 20179, 704108
933 records found for education 10th
        Average, Min, Max: 196832, 21698, 766115
413 records found for education Doctorate
        Average, Min, Max: 186698, 19520, 606111
7291 records found for education Some-college
        Average, Min, Max: 188742, 12285, 1484705
646 records found for education 7th-8th
        Average, Min, Max: 188079, 20057, 750972
1175 records found for education 11th
        Average, Min, Max: 194928, 19752, 806316
```

Activity 31: Sorting Users

Solution:

1. Write a comparator class to compare Users by ID:

    ```java
    import java.util.Comparator;
    public class ByIdComparator implements Comparator<User> {
      public int compare(User first, User second) {
        if (first.id < second.id) {
          return -1;
        }
        if (first.id > second.id) {
          return 1;
        }
        return 0;
      }
    }
    ```

2. Write a comparator class to compare Users by email:

    ```java
    import java.util.Comparator;
    public class ByEmailComparator implements Comparator<User> {
      public int compare(User first, User second) {
        return first.email.toLowerCase().compareTo(second.email.toLowerCase());
      }
    }
    ```

3. Write a comparator class to compare Users by name:

    ```java
    import java.util.Comparator;
    public class ByNameComparator implements Comparator<User> {
      public int compare(User first, User second) {
        return first.name.toLowerCase().compareTo(second.name.toLowerCase());
      }
    }
    ```

4. Create a new class called **SortUsers** with a **main** method which loads the unique users keyed by email:

    ```java
    public class SortUsers {
      public static void main (String [] args) throws IOException {
        Hashtable<String, User> uniqueUsers = UsersLoader.
    loadUsersInHashtableByEmail(args[0]);
      }
    }
    ```

5. After loading the users, transfer the users into a Vector of Users to be able to preserve order since **Hashtable** doesn't do that:

```
Vector<User> users = new Vector<>(uniqueUsers.values());
```

6. Ask the user to pick what field he wants to sort the users by and collect the input from standard input:

```
Scanner reader = new Scanner(System.in);
System.out.print("What field you want to sort by: ");
String input = reader.nextLine();
```

7. Use the input in a **switch** statement to pick what comparator to use. If the input is not valid, print a friendly message and exit:

```
Comparator<User> comparator;
switch(input) {
  case "id":
    comparator = newByIdComparator();
    break;
  case "name":
    comparator = new ByNameComparator();
    break;
  case "email":
    comparator = new ByEmailComparator();
    break;
  default:
    System.out.printf("Sorry, invalid option: %s\n", input);
    return;
}
```

8. Tell the user what field you're going to sort by and sort the Vector of users:

```
System.out.printf("Sorting by %s\n", input);
Collections.sort(users, comparator);
```

9. Print the users using a **for-each** loop:

```
for (User user : users) {
  System.out.printf("%d - %s, %s\n", user.id, user.name, user.email);
}
```

10. Add imports:

```
import java.io.IOException;
import java.util.Collections;
import java.util.Comparator;
import java.util.Hashtable;
import java.util.Scanner;
import java.util.Vector;
```

The output is as follows:

```
5 unique users found.
What field you want to sort by: email
Sorting by email
30 - Jeff Bezos, jeff.bezos@amazon.com
50 - Larry Ellison, lawrence.ellison@oracle.com
20 - Marc Benioff, marc.benioff@salesforce.com
40 - Sundar Pichai, sundar.pichai@google.com
10 - Bill Gates, william.gates@microsoft.com
```

Lesson 8: Advanced Data Structures in Java

Activity 32: Creating a Custom Linked List in Java

Solution:

1. Create a class named, **SimpleObjLinkedList**.

    ```
    public class SimpleObjLinkedList {
    ```

2. Create a class named Node that represents each element in a Linked List. Each node will have an Object that it needs to hold, and it will have a reference to the next Node. The **LinkedList** class will have a reference to the head node and will be able to traverse to the next Node by using **Node.getNext()**. Head being the first element, we could traverse to the next element by moving **next** in the current Node. Like this, we could traverse till the last element of the list:

    ```
    static class Node {
    Object data;
    Node next;
    Node(Object d) {
    data = d;
    next = null;
    }
    ```

```
Node getNext() {
return next;
}
void setNext(Node node) {
next = node;
}
Object getData() {
return data;
}
}
```

3. Implement a **toString()** method to represent this object. Starting from the head Node, iterate all the nodes until the last node is found. On each iteration, construct a string representation of the object stored in each node:

```
public String toString() {
String delim = ",";
StringBuffer stringBuf = new StringBuffer();
if (head == null)
return "LINKED LIST is empty";
Node currentNode = head;
while (currentNode != null) {
stringBuf.append(currentNode.getData());
currentNode = currentNode.getNext();
if (currentNode != null)
stringBuf.append(delim);
}
return stringBuf.toString();
}
```

4. Implement the **add(Object item)** method so that any item/object can be added into this List. Construct a new Node object by passing the **newItem = new Node(item)** Item. Starting at the head node, crawl to the end of the list. In the last node, set the next node as our newly created node (**newItem**). Increment the index:

```
// appends the specified element to the end of this list.
public void add(Object element) {
// create a new node
Node newNode = new Node(element);
//if head node is empty, create a new node and assign it to Head
//increment index and return
if (head == null) {
head = newNode;
return;
```

```
}
Node currentNode = head;
// starting at the head node
// move to last node
while (currentNode.getNext() != null) {
currentNode = currentNode.getNext();
}
// set the new node as next node of current
currentNode.setNext(newNode);
}
```

5. Implement **get(Integer index)** method to retrieve the item from the list based on the index. Index must not be less than 0. Write a logic to crawl to the specified index, identify the node, and return the value from the node.

```
public Object get(int index) {
// Implement the logic returns the element
// at the specified position in this list.
if (head == null || index < 0)
return null;
if (index == 0){
return head.getData();
}
Node currentNode = head.getNext();
for (int pos = 0; pos < index; pos++) {
currentNode = currentNode.getNext();
if (currentNode == null)
return null;
}
return currentNode.getData();
}
```

6. Implement the **remove(Integer index)** method to remove the item from the list based on the index. Write logic to crawl to the node before the specified index and identify the node. In this node, set the **next** as **getNext()**. Return true if the element was found and deleted. If the element was not found, return false:

```
public boolean remove(int index) {
if (index < 0)
return false;
if (index == 0)
{
head = null;
return true;
```

```
        }

    Node currentNode = head;
    for (int pos = 0; pos < index-1; pos++) {
    if (currentNode.getNext() == null)
    return false;
    currentNode = currentNode.getNext();
    }
    currentNode.setNext(currentNode.getNext().getNext());
    return true;
    }
```

7. Create a member attribute of type Node (pointing to the head node). Write a **main** method, create an object of **SimpleObjLinkedList**, and add five strings, one after the other (**"INPUT-1", "INPUT-2", "INPUT-3", "INPUT-4","INPUT-5"**), to it respectively. Print the **SimpleObjLinkedList** object. In the **main** method, get the item from the list using **get(2)** and print the value of the item retrieved. Also, remove the item from list **remove(2)** and print the value of the list. One element should have been deleted from the list:

```
Node head;
    public static void main(String[] args) {
        SimpleObjLinkedList list = new SimpleObjLinkedList();
        list.add("INPUT-1");
        list.add("INPUT-2");
        list.add("INPUT-3");
        list.add("INPUT-4");
        list.add("INPUT-5");
        System.out.println(list);
        System.out.println(list.get(2));
        list.remove(3);
        System.out.println(list);
    }
    }
```

The output is as follows:

```
[INPUT-1 ,INPUT-2 ,INPUT-3 ,INPUT-4 ,INPUT-5 ]
INPUT-3
[INPUT-1 ,INPUT-2 ,INPUT-3 ,INPUT-5 ]
```

Activity 33: Implementing the Methods in the BinarySearchTree Class to Find the Highest and Lowest Value in the BST

Solution:

1. Take the same class we used in the previous exercise: **BinarySearchTree**. Add a new method, **int getLow()**, to find the lowest value in the BST and return it. As we learned about the BST, the leftmost node will be the lowest of all the values. Iterate all of the left nodes until we reach an empty left node and get the value of its root:

```
/**
 * As per BST, the left most node will be lowest of the all. iterate all the
 * left nodes until we reach empty left and get the value of it root.
 * @return int lowestValue
 */
public int getLow() {
    Node current = parent;
    while (current.left != null) {
        current = current.left;
    }
    return current.data;
}
```

2. Add a new method, **int getHigh()**, to find the highest value in the BST and return it. As we learned about the BST, the rightmost node will be the highest of all the values. Iterate all the right nodes until we reach an empty right node and get the value of its root:

```
/**
 * As per BST, the right most node will be highest of the all. iterate all
 * the right nodes until we reach empty right and get the value of it root.
 * @return int highestValue
 */
public int getHigh() {
    Node current = parent;
    while (current.right != null) {
        current = current.right;
    }
    return current.data;
}
```

3. In the **main** method, construct a BST, add values to it, and then print the highest and lowest values by calling **getLow()** and **getHigh()**:

```
/**
    * Main program to demonstrate the BST functionality.
    * - Adding nodes
    * - finding High and low
    * - Traversing left and right
    * @param args
    */
public static void main(String args[]) {
    BinarySearchTree bst = new BinarySearchTree();
    // adding nodes into the BST
    bst.add(32);
    bst.add(50);
    bst.add(93);
    bst.add(3);
    bst.add(40);
    bst.add(17);
    bst.add(30);
    bst.add(38);
    bst.add(25);
    bst.add(78);
    bst.add(10);
    //printing lowest and highest value in BST
    System.out.println("Lowest value in BST :" + bst.getLow());
    System.out.println("Highest value in BST :" + bst.getHigh());
}
```

The output is as follows:

```
Lowest value in BST :3
Highest value in BST :93
```

Activity 34: Using an Enum to Hold College Department Details

Solution:

1. Create a **DeptEnum** enum using the **enum** keyword. Add two private attributes (**String deptName** and **int deptNo**) to hold the values to be kept in the enum. Override a constructor to take an acronym and **deptNo** and place it in the member variables. Add enum constants adhering to the constructor:

```java
public enum DeptEnum {
    BE("BACHELOR OF ENGINEERING", 1), BCOM("BACHELOR OF COMMERCE", 2),
BSC("BACHELOR OF SCIENCE",
            3), BARCH("BACHELOR OF ARCHITECTURE", 4), DEFAULT("BACHELOR",
0);

    private String acronym;
    private int deptNo;

    DeptEnum(String accr, int deptNo) {
        this.accronym = acr;
        this.deptNo = deptNo;
    }
```

2. Add getter methods for **deptName** and **deptNo**:

```java
    public String getAcronym() {
        return acronym;
    }

    public int getDeptNo() {
        return deptNo;
    }
```

3. Let's write a **main** method and sample program to demonstrate the use of enums:

```java
public static void main(String[] args) {
// Fetching the Enum using Enum name as string
DeptEnum env = DeptEnum.valueOf("BE");
System.out.println(env.getAcronym() + " : " + env.getDeptNo());

// Printing all the values of Enum
for (DeptEnum e : DeptEnum.values()) {
System.out.println(e.getAcronym() + " : " + e.getDeptNo());     }
// Compare the two enums using the the equals() method or using //the ==
operator.
```

```
    System.out.println(DeptEnum.BE == DeptEnum.valueOf("BE"));
    }
}
```

4. Output:

```
BACHELOR OF ENGINEERING : 1
BACHELOR OF ENGINEERING : 1
BACHELOR OF COMMERCE : 2
BACHELOR OF SCIENCE : 3
BACHELOR OF ARCHITECTURE : 4
BACHELOR : 0
True
```

Activity 35: Implementing Reverse Lookup

Solution:

1. Create an enum **App**, that declares constants BE, BCOM, BSC and BARC, along with their full forms and department numbers.

```
public enum App {
    BE("BACHELOR OF ENGINEERING", 1), BCOM("BACHELOR OF COMMERCE", 2),
    BSC("BACHELOR OF SCIENCE", 3), BARCH("BACHELOR OF ARCHITECTURE", 4),
    DEFAULT("BACHELOR", 0);
```

2. Also declare two private variables **accronym** and **deptNo**.

```
    private String accronym;
    private int deptNo;
```

3. Create a parameterized constructor and assign the variables **accronym** and **deptNo** with values passed as arguments.

```
    App(String accr, int deptNo) {
        this.accronym = accr;
        this.deptNo = deptNo;
    }
```

4. Declare a public method **getAccronym()** that returns the variable **accronym** and a public method **getDeptNo()** that returns the variable **deptNo**.

```
public String getAccronym() {
    return accronym;
}
public int getDeptNo() {
    return deptNo;
}
```

5. Implement reverse look up that takes in the course name, and searches the corresponding acronym in the **App** enum.

```
//reverse lookup
public static App get(String accr) {
    for (App e : App.values()) {
        if (e.getAccronym().equals(accr))
            return e;
    }
    return App.DEFAULT;
}
```

6. Implement the main method, and run the program.

```
public static void main(String[] args) {

    // Fetching Enum with value of Enum (reverse lookup)
    App noEnum = App.get("BACHELOR OF SCIENCE");
    System.out.println(noEnum.accronym + " : " + noEnum.deptNo);
    // Fetching Enum with value of Enum (reverse lookup)

    System.out.println(App.get("BACHELOR OF SCIENCE").name());
}
}
```

Your Output should be similar to:

```
BACHELOR OF SCIENCE : 3
BSC
```

Lesson 9: Exception Handling

Activity 36: Handling Mistakes in Numeric User Input

Solution:

1. Right-click the **src** folder and select **New | Class**.

2. Create a class **Adder**, and then click **OK**.

3. Import the **java.util.Scanner** package:

   ```
   import java.util.Scanner;
   ```

4. Create a class named **Adder**:

   ```
   import java.util.Scanner;
   public class Adder {
   ```

5. In **main()** method, use the **for** loop to read values from the user:

   ```
   public static void main(String[] args) {
       Scanner input = new Scanner(System.in);
       int total = 0;
       for (int i = 0; i < 3; i++) {
           System.out.print("Enter a whole number: ");
   ```

6. In the same loop, check if the valid value is entered. If the value is valid, add a try block to calculate the sum of three numbers.

   ```
   boolean isValid = false;
   while (!isValid) {
       if (input.hasNext()) {
           String line = input.nextLine();
           try {
               int newVal = Integer.parseInt(line);
               isValid = true;
               total += newVal;
   ```

7. The catch block should prompt the user to input valid numbers.

   ```
   } catch (NumberFormatException e) {
                   System.out.println("Please provide a valid whole
   number");
               }
           }
       }
   }
   ```

8. Print the sum:

```
System.out.println("Total is " + total);
    }
}
```

Print the result to the console. Here is a sample output of a case with no errors:

```
Enter a whole number: 10
Enter a whole number: 11
Enter a whole number: 12
Total is 33
```

And here is a sample output of a run with errors:

```
Enter a whole number: 10
Enter a whole number: hello
Please provide a valid whole number
11.1
Please provide a valid whole number
11
Enter a whole number: 12
Total is 33
```

Activity 37: Writing Custom Exceptions in Java

Solution:

1. Right-click the **src** folder and select **New | Class**.

2. Enter **RollerCoasterWithAge** as the class name, and then click **OK**.

3. Import the **java.util.Scanner** package:

```
import java.util.Scanner;
```

4. Create an exception class, **TooYoungException**:

```
class TooYoungException extends Exception {
    int age;
    String name;
    TooYoungException(int age, String name) {
        this.age = age;
        this.name = name;
    }
}
```

5. In **main()**, create a loop that reads in the names of the visitors:

```java
public class RollerCoasterWithAge {
    public static void main(String[] args) {
        Scanner input = new Scanner(System.in);

        while (true) {
            System.out.print("Enter name of visitor: ");
            String name = input.nextLine().trim();
            if (name.length() == 0) {
                break;
            }
```

6. The **try** block, read the age of the visitors, throws **TooYoungException** if the age is below 15, prints the name of the visitor riding the Roller Coaster:

```java
        try {
            System.out.printf("Enter %s's age: ", name);
            int age = input.nextInt();
            input.nextLine();
            if (age < 15) {
                throw new TooYoungException(age, name);
            }

            System.out.printf("%s is riding the roller coaster.\n",
name);
```

7. The catch block will display the message that is to be displayed for visitors below the age of 15:

```java
        } catch (TooYoungException e) {
            System.out.printf("%s is %d years old, which is too young
to ride.\n", e.name, e.age);
            }
        }
    }
}
```

Activity 38: Dealing with Multiple Exceptions in a Block

Solution:

1. Right-click the **src** folder and select **New | Class**.

2. Enter **RollerCoasterWithAgeAndHeight** as the class name, and then click **OK**.

3. Import the **java.util.Scanner** package:

   ```
   import java.util.Scanner;
   ```

4. Create an exception class, **TooYoungException**:

   ```
   class TooYoungException extends Exception {
       int age;
       String name;
       TooYoungException(int age, String name) {
           this.age = age;
           this.name = name;
       }
   }
   ```

5. Create an exception class, **TooShortException**:

   ```
   class TooShortException extends Exception {
       int height;
       String name;
       TooShortException(int height, String name) {
           this.height = height;
           this.name = name;
       }
   }
   ```

6. In **main()**, create a loop that reads in the names of the visitors:

   ```
   public class RollerCoasterWithAgeAndHeight {
       public static void main(String[] args) {
           Scanner input = new Scanner(System.in);

           while (true) {
               System.out.print("Enter name of visitor: ");
               String name = input.nextLine().trim();
               if (name.length() == 0) {
                   break;
               }
   ```

7. The **try** block, read the age of the visitors, throws **TooYoungException** if the age is below 15, **TooShortException** if the height is below 130, and prints the name of the visitor riding the Roller Coaster:

```
try {
    System.out.printf("Enter %s's age: ", name);
    int age = input.nextInt();
    input.nextLine();
    if (age < 15) {
        throw new TooYoungException(age, name);
    }
    System.out.printf("Enter %s's height: ", name);
    int height = input.nextInt();
    input.nextLine();
    if (height < 130) {
        throw new TooShortException(height, name);
    }

    System.out.printf("%s is riding the roller coaster.\n",
name);
}
```

8. The catch block will display the message that is to be displayed for visitors below the age of 15 or height below 130:

```
catch (TooYoungException e) {
            System.out.printf("%s is %d years old, which is too young
to ride.\n", e.name, e.age);
        } catch (TooShortException e) {
            System.out.printf("%s is %d cm tall, which is too short to
ride.\n", e.name, e.height);
        }
    }
}
}
```

Activity 39: Working with Multiple Custom Exceptions

Solution:

1. Right-click the **src** folder and select **New | Class**.

2. Enter **RollerCoasterWithAgeAndHeight** as the class name, and then click **OK**.

3. Import the **java.util.Scanner** package:

   ```
   import java.util.Scanner;
   ```

4. Create an exception class, **TooYoungException**:

   ```
   class TooYoungException extends Exception {
       int age;
       String name;
       TooYoungException(int age, String name) {
           this.age = age;
           this.name = name;
       }
   }
   ```

5. Create an exception class, **TooShortException**

   ```
   class TooShortException extends Exception {
       int height;
       String name;
       TooShortException(int height, String name) {
           this.height = height;
           this.name = name;
       }
   }
   ```

6. In **main()**, create a loop that reads in the names of the visitors:

   ```
   public class Main {
       public static void main(String[] args) {
           Scanner input = new Scanner(System.in);

           while (true) {
               System.out.print("Enter name of visitor: ");
               String name = input.nextLine().trim();
               if (name.length() == 0) {
                   break;
               }
   ```

7. The **try** block, read the age of the visitors, throws **TooYoungException** if the age is below 15, **TooShortException** if the height is below 130, and prints the name of the visitor riding the Roller Coaster:

```java
try {
    System.out.printf("Enter %s's age: ", name);
    int age = input.nextInt();
    input.nextLine();
    if (age < 15) {
        throw new TooYoungException(age, name);
    }
    System.out.printf("Enter %s's height: ", name);
    int height = input.nextInt();
    input.nextLine();
    if (height < 130) {
        throw new TooShortException(height, name);
    }

    System.out.printf("%s is riding the roller coaster.\n",
name);
}
```

8. Create a catch block for **TooYoungException**:

```java
catch (TooYoungException e) {
    System.out.printf("%s is %d years old, which is too young
to ride.\n", e.name, e.age);
}
```

9. Create a catch block for **TooShortException**:

```java
catch (TooShortException e) {
    System.out.printf("%s is %d cm tall, which is too short to
ride.\n", e.name, e.height);
}
```

10. Create a finally block that prints a message for escorting visitors off the premises:

```java
finally {
    System.out.printf("Escorting %s outside the premises.\n",
name);
        }
    }
  }
}
```

Index

About

All major keywords used in this book are captured alphabetically in this section. Each one is accompanied by the page number of where they appear.

W